storytelling with **you**

storytelling

with **you**

plan, create, and deliver a stellar presentation

cole nussbaumer knaflic

illustrations by catherine madden

WILEY

Published by John Wiley & Sons, Inc., Hoboken, New Jersey.
Published simultaneously in Canada.

For general information on our other products and services or for technical support, please contact our Customer Care Department within the United States at (800) 762-2974, outside the United States at (317) 572-3993 or fax (317) 572-4002.

Wiley also publishes its books in a variety of electronic formats. Some content that appears in print may not be available in electronic formats. For more information about Wiley products, visit our web site at www.wiley.com.

Library of Congress Cataloging-in-Publication Data is Available:

ISBN 9781394160303 (Paperback)
ISBN 9781394160310 (ePub)
ISBN 9781394160327 (ePDF)

Cover Image: Catherine Madden
Cover Design: Flight Design Co.
SKY10035336_081022

To **you** and your next presentation

contents

acknowledgments

The **basic story** of this book

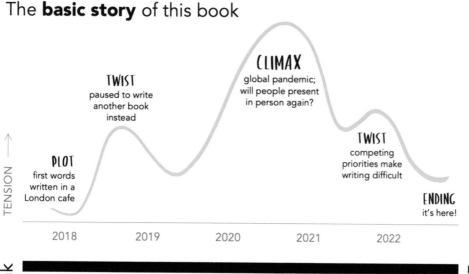

The **people** I'd like to thank

My family
Randy, Avery, Dorian, and Eloise: for inspiring me every day and your unwavering support; I love you

SWD team
Jody Riendeau, Elizabeth Ricks, Alex Velez, Mike Cisneros, Amy Esselman, Simon Rowe, and Katelyn Tans: for being fantastic individuals and an amazing team; I learn so much from you

My editor
Marika Rohn: for wielding commas wisely and being a great friend

Flight Design
Ariana Wolf, Matt Meikle, Catherine Madden, Eliza Ausiello: for your skills & patience

Thanks also to the individuals who helped this book in other ways and to those who support my business and family:
Kim Scheffler, Michelle Elsner, Bill Falloon, Purvi Patel, Samantha Enders, Samantha Wu, Jean-Karl Martin, Amy Laudicano, Bec Sandercock, Steven Kyritz, Heather Jones, Shannon Vargo, Michael Friedberg, Rhea Siegel, Martha Gallant, Missy Garnett, Steve Csipke, Colleen Kubiak, Jennifer Rash, Brandy Blake, Dipankar Pradhan, James Savage, Lee Prout, Yi Zheng, Theresa Enea, Diana Halenz, Boris Desancic, Maureen O'Leary, Betty Tapia, Yolimel Roa Cáceres, and Olesya Banakh

about the author

Cole Nussbaumer Knaflic tells stories that drive change. In her analytical roles in banking, private equity, and as a manager on the Google People Analytics team, she grew to appreciate the potent pairing of well-designed visuals with engaging delivery. Cole's desire to help others understand and develop these skills propelled this self-described introvert to step out from behind her computer and onto the stage. Today, she is a highly sought-after speaker, having honed her craft through more than a thousand workshops and as a keynote presenter at marquee conferences and Fortune 500 events.

Cole is founder and CEO of storytelling with data (SWD) and author of best-selling books *storytelling with data: let's practice!* and *storytelling with data: a data visualization guide for business professionals*, which has been translated into more than 20 languages, is used as a textbook by hundreds of universities, and serves as the course book for tens of thousands of SWD workshop participants. For more than a decade, Cole and her team have delivered interactive learning sessions to data-minded individuals, companies, and philanthropic organizations all over the world. They also help people create graphs that make sense and weave them into compelling stories through the popular SWD community, blog, podcast, and videos.

Cole has a BS in Applied Mathematics and an MBA from the University of Washington. When she isn't ridding the world of ineffective graphs or galvanizing others to present powerfully, Cole is undertaking the adventures of parenting three children with her husband at home in the Midwest and on travels abroad.

introduction

Let's begin with a story

When I was twelve years old, I ran for senator.

I was in junior high school, and this was my first time running for an elected position in student government. I recall spending many hours perfecting my campaign signs. I'd beg my mother to take me to our small town's general store, where I would pick out the perfect combination of colorful poster boards and paint. I was discerning about which friends I enlisted to help—was Lisa's penmanship up to par? Leading up to the election, my bedroom floor was littered with materials: rulers to ensure straight lines, stencils for precise lettering, and supplies for the button maker. A large piece of butcher paper taped to the wall registered contending ideas for my campaign slogan. Looking back, choosing "Be picky, vote for Nicky" was not one of my prouder moments.

I also spent a good amount of time on my speech. Introducing freshly baked cookies into the student store, having one school dance al fresco on the football field (instead of the malodorous gym), and building volunteer time into the school calendar were top priorities. I typed furiously on my family's electric typewriter, perfecting one line at a time as it appeared in the small display before moving onto the next. It was a great speech.

When election day came, I clearly remember the nerve-wracking walk across the gym to the podium to deliver those carefully crafted promises. Two hundred familiar faces looked at me expectantly from the bleachers. My hands trembled as I started to read what I had written. "Talk louder!" someone shouted from the crowd. I could hear my voice shaking, amplified through the speakers. It was difficult to breathe. It was *not* a good performance.

Despite all of that, I won the election. Apparently, the allure of cookies was enough to overcome my lack of confidence. I got one thing right: I knew my audience. This was an early presentation lesson that I didn't fully appreciate until later. Though baked goods aren't always an option, it is *always* about the cookie— identifying that idea, opportunity, potential reward, or vision of the future that your audience will find irresistible.

My journey to storyteller

I am not a naturally strong speaker nor an innate storyteller. I consider myself to be an introvert. The environment in which I feel most at ease is where I am sitting now, writing these words: alone, behind my laptop. You wouldn't guess any of this about me. That's because today I am comfortable and effective speaking in front of a packed room or standing on stage confidently delivering a presentation. This did not happen by chance; these are carefully practiced and honed skills. While the learning has absolutely been intentional, it's also been somewhat curious, since I didn't initially set out to do any of this.

My first job was in banking. I was fresh out of undergrad with an applied mathematics degree, working as an analyst in credit risk management. A hard worker and always looking for ways to make things efficient, I had a knack for analyzing data and graphing it effectively. I was promoted. Within a couple of years, I found myself managing a small team and was responsible for presenting monthly data to our Chief Risk Officer and his leadership group.

The challenge was that I still had the same shaky hands and quivering voice as I did in junior high. This audience of leaders—mostly men and at least a decade my senior—made me nervous. Over time, I learned to put my paper down so my trembling hands wouldn't be the first thing they noticed. Breathing more deeply helped to steady my voice. But I still had a big issue: filler words. I was uncomfortable with silence and as a result simply didn't ever pause. If I couldn't find the word I was looking for, I wouldn't stop to collect my thoughts. Instead, I would fill that space with "likes," "ahs," and "ums." I tried introducing disincentives to change my behavior. I had my team listen to my monthly meetings via teleconference and count my offenses. I'd owe a dime for each one. This paid for a number of team happy hours. However, I was no better off in my meetings with management.

Though my career was growing professionally and I could do great work behind the scenes, my lackluster live presentations weren't doing the material and findings justice.

When the credit risk crisis hit in 2007, I left banking to apply the analytical skills I'd developed to another area on the Google People Analytics team. Google was a fantastic environment in which to work, and I feel tremendously grateful for the advancement this role afforded me. One such opportunity was being able to create a class and teach others how to effectively communicate their data.

The course's focus on data visualization was something that had been an area of interest for me for some time. It turned out to be a popular topic and was rolled out as an offering across Google globally. This was amazing—and highly intimidating, given that I'd never formally taught anything! Fortunately, I was able to sign up for an internal series of courses to help *learn* how to *teach*. Two simple tips I picked up during that program greatly impacted me, forever changing the way I communicate: stand up and don't shift. You'll hear more about these later.

During my years at Google, in addition to my core role in People Analytics, I taught scores of classes on visualizing data. Participants came from all parts of the organization: Sales, Engineering, Product, Marketing, and People Operations. I started to recognize how different types of individuals communicate in distinct ways. I gained visibility to various scenarios, challenges, and opportunities for communicating—both through participants' stories and through the different situations in which I taught. I built experience guiding small teams through hands-on activities and large groups through structured content and facilitated discussions. I was invited to speak on stage at my first conference. Eventually, interest in my course outside of Google led me to teach at other companies.

By early 2012, it was becoming clear to me that the need for communicating effectively with data extended far beyond Google. I took a leap and decided to take my passion project—*storytelling with data*—to the next level, leaving my day job to concentrate on ridding the world of exploding 3D pie charts one workshop at a time. This started small, and admittedly, the stakes were relatively low (I was happy to have my travel expenses covered and a willing audience!). Those early workshops gave me an opportunity to gain traction and a good amount of practice. At first, I focused mainly on making sure my slides were superb, the lessons made sense, and the flow was smooth. It was only after I was comfortable with my content that I turned my attention to delivery. It was time to face my demons from that old gymnasium.

In the same way I had observed how graphing data differently changed the way people reacted, I started to notice how nuances in my delivery influenced others. Watching my audience for cues and feedback, I would see the impact of varying simple things, like my volume and speed. I could get someone to contribute to the discussion based on where I stood in the room and use my hands and body for emphasis. When a group became pensive, softening my voice could draw them into the present, their ears perking up in attention. Becoming animated would immediately shift the energy in the room. Every new audience meant a fresh opportunity to experiment, learn, and refine my storytelling and presentation skills.

Along with this, I had a growing—and revolutionary—realization. As a good presenter, I could get others to invest in what I care about. Conversely, if I can't present my ideas effectively, there's no way I can drive the change I seek.

Over time, justly serving *storytelling with data*'s mission to inspire positive change through the way people communicate with data meant I could use some help (it's a big job!). The company has grown to include a small group of talented individuals. Each member must be adept at communicating, able to present skillfully, and capable of speaking in a way that makes others want to listen and engage. Sharing what I've learned, I've guided my team to become powerful presenters and inspiring storytellers. By practicing and implementing the lessons outlined in this book, you will become one, too.

Why you should be a better storyteller

Have you ever lost control of your audience before you could get your point across? Or had someone steer you in an unexpected direction or ask an unanticipated question that threw you off track? Or started talking, only to realize you were lacking credibility in the eyes of those listening? Or finished giving a presentation and wondered whether you had changed minds or if anyone would take action based on the information you shared?

Being a better storyteller or a better presenter doesn't keep these challenges from arising, but it can drastically reduce their frequency. You likely spend a ton of time on activities that happen behind the scenes, doing your work. Yet the communication of your project is typically the only part that others see. *This* is where all of your efforts succeed or fail. There is a tremendous amount of value to be obtained from work you are already doing that simply isn't being communicated as effectively as it could be.

By applying the lessons in this book, your chances for success improve. When we are effective, we capture our audience's attention, engage them, and—ultimately—inspire action.

Who this book is for

This book is written for anyone who prepares or delivers presentations. This can take the form of business meetings, conference presentations, and keynote speeches.

Given the focus on planning and practicing, the comprehensive lessons in this book will be most appropriate for situations where the stakes are higher than a weekly status meeting or monthly review, though you'll encounter tips that will help you in these instances as well. Employ the strategies you learn here in scenarios where you need to encourage someone to see something in a different light, take an action, or make a change.

What you'll find in this book

This book is organized into three sections: *plan*, *create*, and *deliver*. In the *plan* chapters, you'll learn the importance of taking time to consider your audience, carefully craft your message, and set your content. As part of this, we'll dive deep into story and discuss applications for storytelling in business presentations, both as an illustrative device and as a strategy for organizing content. In the *create* section, we'll explore how to build effective materials that will ensure that story gets across and is remembered. The *deliver* chapters will help prepare and develop you as the presenter, both when it comes to getting to know your content thoroughly as well as readying you to feel and exude confidence. Together, these sections will equip you with strategies to plan, create, and deliver stellar presentations, whether in a meeting or formally on stage.

Specific chapter summaries follow.

Chapter 1: consider your audience

You are not communicating for yourself—first and foremost, you are communicating for your audience. In this opening chapter, we analyze audience: who they are, how you will connect with them, and the action they should take.

By reflecting on your audience before doing anything else, you put yourself in the optimal position to communicate successfully.

Chapter 2: craft your message

What exactly do you need to communicate? While it sounds straightforward, being clear and concise in response to this critically important question is a common challenge. I introduce strategies for crafting your key message. You'll learn to articulate your point of view and convey what's at stake in a single sentence.

Chapter 3: compile the pieces

Once you know your audience and message, you can begin to plan content. We do this through brainstorming and then editing and arranging ideas into a storyboard, your low-tech plan of attack. I discuss the importance of intentional discard, getting feedback, and tips for doing all of this both on your own and in a collaborative team environment.

Chapter 4: form a story

Stories resonate and stay with us in ways that facts do not. In this final chapter of the planning section, I introduce the narrative arc and the importance of tension in communication. We examine different shapes of stories and ways to think about these concepts while revisiting your storyboard from the prior chapter. You'll learn how to use story in a business setting to gain attention and drive action.

Chapter 5: set the style & structure

This chapter marks the transition from planning your content to creating it. We begin with an overview of general design considerations, then establish the framework for your presentation. This includes a pragmatic process for transforming your low-tech preparation into slides.

Chapter 6: say it with words

Text plays an important role in visual communications, and in this chapter we look at several strategies for using words wisely. I introduce the takeaway title and illustrate how it can be employed effectively. We also explore the power of words on their own as slide content.

Chapter 7: show data in graphs

When communicating data to support your message, it often means you should visualize it. The best practices for using graphs in presentations I share in this chapter include an overview of data visualization design principles that will help ensure your data is easily understood.

Chapter 8: illustrate with images

Is a picture worth a thousand words? Not exactly, but images used well have an important place in presentation design. In this final chapter within the create section, we delve into the use of photographs, illustrations, and diagrams, including common pitfalls to avoid.

Chapter 9: refine through practice

Now that your content is created, we turn our attention to you, the presenter. I discuss strategies for mastering your content and ways to rehearse to ensure a smooth delivery. We also cover how to get meaningful feedback to refine and improve.

Chapter 10: build your confidence

Mastering your content is one thing, but commanding the attention of a room is another. In this chapter, we examine the importance of exuding confidence through what you do and say, including the effective use of body and voice to establish presence.

Chapter 11: introduce yourself

Whether a formal introduction or some brief context about who you are and why you're the one presenting, how you introduce yourself matters. In the penultimate chapter, we dive deep into the art of the introduction, outlining a process you can use to craft the story of *you*.

Chapter 12: have a stellar session

You've planned, created, and practiced—it's time to deliver. There are things you can do before, during, and after your important meeting or presentation that will help ensure success: an engaged audience that is inspired to act!

plan

consider
your audience

Your audience: these are the people you are going to inform, inspire, and incite to act. Ultimately, *everything you do* when you plan, create, and deliver content is for them.

Yet, this is a dramatic shift from how we typically operate.

Take me, for instance. The most natural way for me to communicate is for myself, from my perspective, and with my preferences in mind. I live in my head, so I'm pretty familiar with what goes on in there. This means it's quite easy—I don't have to give it much thought—for me to communicate for myself.

Communicating to others is more complex. It's harder, because we have to actively work to understand them. What compels people to do the things they do? When we can identify our audience's motivations and appeal to them, we can gain their attention and drive the action we seek. In other words, it's by being thoughtful about those we are communicating to that we can get our own needs met.

In this chapter, we'll begin by prioritizing our target audience and then explore how we can better appreciate their needs. We'll also cover strategies for getting to know an unfamiliar audience. Once we have clarity on who they are, we can tailor a great number of aspects to our audience, setting the foundation to communicate effectively.

Prioritize your target audience

Who are you communicating to? When I pose this query to clients or workshop attendees, it's not uncommon for them to hold out their hands and begin counting on their fingers. They start listing groups generally: senior leadership, the board, peers, internal stakeholders, clients, customers, the public. If I allow this to go on for a bit, they get more specific: auditors, scientists, engineers, finance, store managers, regulators.

Consider your own list of audiences, the people you communicate to regularly. As you think about the various groups, note how they're each made up of different types of people who have varying requirements.

It's almost always the case—when you are communicating in the type of instances that we are focusing on here, a meeting or presentation—that you will have a number of individuals in your audience. But even given that, we often communicate too broadly and to more people than necessary. This is dangerous because it is harder to meet multiple different needs at the same time, and multiple people will almost always have different needs.

This doesn't mean that you can't communicate to more than one person at a time. It *does* highlight, however, the importance of actively prioritizing your target audience. Then you can think about them first and foremost when you craft your approach and content.

Let's explore this idea further, starting with the simplest situation. We'll ratchet up the sophistication and complexity of scenarios from there.

Clear single-person audience

Sometimes, there is an obvious individual audience for what you're doing. Take the instance where you've been asked to tackle a project or do an analysis. Your audience is likely the person who commissioned the work. In other cases, there may be a clear decision maker. When we identify a single-person audience, we can ask ourselves: what do they care about? What motivates them? What scares them? What will incite them to act? What makes them hesitant? How do they want to be communicated to? We can design the way we do everything with that person in mind, communicating *for* that individual.

Let's make this more concrete through an example. Imagine that your organization recently conducted an employee-wide survey to measure many different aspects of the work environment. You are part of the team that has analyzed the data and are now preparing to convey the results.

One unexpected finding your analysis revealed is related to communication. Employee sentiment is generally positive, with the exception of the Engineering team. So you dig deeper, further segmenting the data. You learn that the low scores are specific to one director within Engineering. This is surprising, because he's an action-oriented and tenured superstar who is highly respected by his peers. The comments from his team indicate they don't feel he communicates frequently enough or with sufficient transparency.

We can take this feedback into account when we set our communication plan. We need to relay that something isn't going well. But before simply jumping in with that, let's think about *him*—the director. There are a number of different ways we could position this finding. It might be framed as an opportunity to tackle or a blindspot to address. Perhaps he'd be best motivated by the positive impact he could have on his team's productivity by making changes to how he communicates. Or maybe the risk of losing credibility with his peer group would get his attention.

None of the ways I've outlined to potentially position the message are inherently right or wrong. They are different, and they are personal. Taking that a step further, while I wouldn't call them right or wrong, there are definitely better or worse approaches based on *who you are communicating to* in a given situation.

Use competition to drive action

I'll share another relevant lesson from my husband's experience. He was working for an organization leading HR and wanted to make changes to the paternity leave program. He recognized that he might face resistance; this wasn't necessarily high on the CEO's priority list. He also knew that this particular leader cared tremendously about offering benefits and a work environment that were at least as good as, if not better than, other organizations in the industry. Rather than lead with the idea to increase paternity leave, the HR team tried a different technique to get the CEO's support. They started by presenting the paternity leave offered by peer companies. Then they showed their own shorter leave program. They asked the CEO what he wanted to do: keep the status quo or make adjustments. With this positioning, they were able to motivate him to suggest the changes. They accomplished this by being thoughtful about how to best influence the individual.

When you have a clear single-person audience, you can address them directly. There are many aspects of how you communicate that you can tailor, which we'll discuss later in this chapter. Before we get there, let's examine the more common scenario: a mixed group.

Narrowing within a mixed audience

Mixed audiences—those consisting of people from different teams across an organization, having varying levels of seniority, or representing a multitude of companies—are challenging. The individuals who comprise them have distinct preferences and may not be aligned on the things they care about or upon which they are willing to act. It's hard to meet multiple priorities simultaneously or to encourage a group to act in a certain way when individuals are motivated by different factors. Yet, mixed audiences are a reality, and we can be smart about how we communicate to them.

When you find yourself facing a mixed group, the first thing to ask yourself is whether you can narrow it. Could you prioritize a person or smaller subset with shared interests and focus first and foremost on them?

The answer is often yes.

Let's explore this further. Imagine you work for a company that is getting ready to launch a new product. You're trying to determine how to price the product in the marketplace. The team you manage has undertaken an analysis of competitor pricing as one input into the decision-making process, and you are the one who will be communicating it.

Let's start by casting a broad net and list some prospective audiences. Who will care how we price our product? First, there are the internal stakeholders. The board will be interested in pricing. Senior management will care. Within that group, there are various people who will be involved (for different reasons): the CEO, the CFO, the Head of Product, and the Head of Sales, to name a few. Finance will want to be apprised because they'll have to factor price into their revenue models. The Sales team will be interested since they'll be the ones trying to sell the product in the marketplace. What about external stakeholders? Retailers will care how we're priced when determining whether to carry our product. Competitors will pay attention as a potential input into their own strategies. Consumers will want to know as they weigh their purchase decisions. The whole world may eventually care!

I'm being facetious to emphasize that there are a number of different potential audiences. How can we communicate successfully with so many disparate groups in mind? We can't! They care about different things. There are distinct actions we'd want each to take. We cannot communicate to all of them simultaneously. Or perhaps I should rephrase to say that, if we were to do so, we would not be successful.

We should narrow our audience for the purpose of our communication. There is a process, and more specifically, two steps we can take: narrow to now, and then identify the decision maker.

When it comes to **narrowing to now**, I mean contemplating who has to be communicated to at the current point in time. Eventually, all of the groups we listed could be interested in how we price our product, but they aren't necessarily each concerned at this moment. Let's think about our audience in the near term. The product isn't even in the marketplace, so we can strike external stakeholders from the list. We haven't yet priced it; that eliminates Finance and Sales from caring. That leaves the board and the leadership team. Narrowing to now helped us focus on a smaller group.

Next, let's **identify the decision maker** within our already reduced audience. Our goal is to price the product. The board won't be making that decision, so let's cross them off our list. That leaves us with the leadership team. Each individual may have a stake in the product price and provide input. However, they don't all have decision-making responsibility. The ultimate decision makers will be the Head of Product and the CEO. We've just successfully narrowed our audience from the whole world (or if not that, at least a lot of people) to two specific individuals. Success!

Adapting for the virtual setting

Virtual meetings are now the norm in many organizations. With this format comes some new and unique advantages—and challenges. What once might have been a small in-office meeting can expand greatly in number of attendees due to the ease with which virtual allows us to include more people. When the invite list grows, consider whether scaling back is possible or preferable. Just because you *can* invite everyone doesn't mean you should. When you don't have control over this aspect, take care to prioritize your target audience and apply select strategies outlined in the forthcoming section for communicating successfully to a mixed group.

Stepping back, not a great deal changes for the virtual environment when it comes to how we plan for our communication. There are distinct ways to optimize the materials we present for a virtual setting, which we'll discuss in the *create* chapters. Equipment and delivery differences also exist, which we'll explore in Chapters 9, 10, and 12.

This intentional process of narrowing our audience makes our jobs as communicators easier by reducing the variety of personalities and individual concerns we need to address. When getting this targeted is possible, do it. In other instances, you may face a true mixed group where you must communicate to multiple individuals simultaneously. Let's examine that now.

Facing a mixed audience

The leadership team, a steering committee, employees, customers, conference attendees: these are the kinds of groups I have in mind when someone says they have to communicate to a diverse audience. This is a tough scenario, for the reasons I've outlined. It's hard to meet varying demands equally and simultaneously. Still, there are absolutely things you can do to set yourself up for success. Let's discuss a few strategies.

Recognize—and call out—differences. One way is to start by acknowledging up front that people are coming from different viewpoints and have disparate needs. In a live meeting or presentation, articulate this challenge of mixed interests. Have a thoughtful plan on how you'll address those diverse preferences. For example, if I'm presenting a project proposal to a steering committee made up of individuals from various parts of the company, it could make sense to stick with the big picture and not get into the details. But if I know that some people are going to want more than that, I can explicitly call it out: "I'm going to stay high level today. Tom, I know you're going to want me to elaborate; I'm happy to sit down with you afterwards to walk through it." Even better—meet with Tom ahead of time to deliver his desired level of granularity so you are able to remain focused on the big picture when everyone is together.

On stage in a conference setting, you might set expectations by first explaining: "I appreciate that there are attendees with varying levels of knowledge on the topic about which I'll be speaking. I'm going to take a short amount of time up front to cover the basics, and then we'll quickly get more nuanced from there." This tells everyone in advance that their needs have been recognized and will be accounted for in some way before you're done.

Identify areas of overlap. Flipping the prior strategy around, rather than reflecting on how people or segments are different, look for similarities. Is there a common goal or pain point that will unite a group or anchor what you're going to discuss? The Big Idea worksheet is sometimes a useful tool at this juncture, which we will dive into deeply in Chapter 2. The most pertinent part to consider is *what is at stake* for your audience. In the case of a mixed group, thinking through this for each member or similar segment can be useful. Identify areas of overlap that may help you frame your approach. Recognize the consistent theme and use that to pique people's attention, get them on the same page, and motivate them to act.

Creating personas for different categories of people

When facing a large mixed audience, it is sometimes useful to create personas to segment the group and the differing perspectives you could face when presenting. These can be based on their desires or motivations and often means generalizing. I might craft Persona A, an individual with a certain type of role or personality (articulate it); who has a similar set of biases (list them); who typically cares about A, B, and C; and who is most likely to question X, Y, and Z. If you have 100 different people in your audience, it will be impossible to envisage these dimensions for each person. But if you group them into a handful of similar subgroups, it stops you from throwing your hands up in the air and simply saying, *I can't address them all.* By segmenting similar individuals in this way, you think about a number of different viewpoints and preferences, which better equips you to address them. Once you have a comprehensive mapping of the main personas, step back and strategize how to best inform them in light of their personalities and requirements.

Show something that relates to everyone. Building on the idea of looking for commonalities, one way to create areas of overlap is to show everyone something that is relevant to each person that can be compared across the broader group. Let's take the employee survey scenario that I mentioned earlier and put a twist on it. Suppose we must disseminate the results to the entire leadership team. I might include a table or graph that shows an interesting piece of the survey—for instance, the aggregate favorable score across themes broken down by the areas each individual on the leadership team oversees. This provides everyone with similar context: they see how their own function performed relative to the others and the overall company. There may also be consistent high points or low points that can be used to introduce the next level of detail or drive good discussion.

If you've ever been in a conference setting where the presenter shows a demographic breakdown of the audience or introduces real-time polling and shares the results, this is an attempt to do the same thing. They are showing something that relates to everyone and getting people involved so they are more willing to pay attention to what follows.

Verbalize to gain attention. When addressing a mixed group, you don't necessarily need everyone's attention equally all the time. Given this, when you want to make sure you have a specific person's or segment's focus (particularly where you may have lost attention by covering other content less relevant to this subset), call that out. For example, assume you are communicating to a steering committee made up of various individuals. I could say something like, "Jane, you're going to want to listen to this part because it involves your group." Or, taking the instance of a conference keynote address, I might announce, "Managers in the room, this upcoming strategy is one you'll want to bring to your teams." In this way, use vocal cues to ensure you have the right people's attention when you seek it.

Irrespective of which of these strategies you employ or combine, when you face a mixed group, ask yourself: what does success look like? Acknowledge what you can reasonably accomplish in the mixed group setting and which pieces should be broken out and shared separately in a more targeted way.

Whether dealing with a single person, communicating to a small group, or presenting to a large mixed audience, you'll have to take steps to get into their heads and understand them. Let's address that next.

Understand and assess your audience

You may know your audience. Perhaps you've communicated to them before. But have you ever paused and spent time critically assessing their priorities, preferences, and requirements? When the stakes are high, this is a task worth undertaking.

While there will be queries specific to your situation that are important to identify, this starter list of questions will help you better understand the people to whom you are speaking:

- What do they care about? What drives them?

- What scares them or keeps them up at night?

- What motivates them? What causes them to want to act?

- What prevents them from acting or makes them hesitate?

- What do they like? What makes them happy?

- What annoys or irritates them?

- To whom do they listen? What influences them?

- What is their opinion of you? Are you credible in their eyes?

- Why will they support you? (In a mixed group, *who* is likely to support you?)

- Why might they resist you? (In a mixed group, *who* will resist? Why?)

- What biases do they have?

- What constraints bind them?

- How do they measure success?

Draw and brainstorm to better understand your audience

Grab a blank piece of paper and a writing utensil for this quick exercise. Orient the paper in landscape fashion (where width is greater than height). Picture a person in your audience and then draw them in the middle of the paper, leaving blank space on either side. Your depiction will remind you that you are doing this all for someone else.

It's okay if you aren't an artist. The drawing can be a simple face or stick figure (though if you prefer to get more creative, go for it). Add a title for the person underneath your sketch. If it's a specific person, use their name or genericize with something like "supportive manager" or "hesitant client."

On the left-hand side, write words or phrases describing why the person is likely to support you. What's going to be easy? Where will they agree with you? On the right-hand side, list reasons the person might resist you. Where do they have biases or skepticism? What points will you make with which they may have contention? Try to get inside this person's head, and acknowledge or make assumptions about what drives them to feel the way you've outlined.

When you're done, read through it all and reflect: given the ways you expect support or are likely to meet resistance, how can you best set yourself up for success?

What if I don't know what my audience cares about?

Remember, the reason we are doing all of this is so we can be thoughtful about how we communicate to our audience, taking their needs into account. But what do we do if we *don't know* our audience? How do we tailor our approach to meet their preferences? Here are some tactics for getting to know an unfamiliar audience.

Talk to them. When you have direct access in advance to your audience and it makes sense to speak with them, do so. This isn't always feasible, but when it is, start here. Ask questions. Work to understand what we've discussed: what they care about, what motivates them, and what scares them. If you can't connect with your audience ahead of time, look for opportunities to understand their preferences directly before or during your presentation. Use the moments before you start to chat with people and ask questions to gain insight. Alternatively, at the beginning of your presentation, prompt discussion to uncover attendee expectations. Use that knowledge to resonate with them through your choice of words and how you navigate your materials.

Talk to someone who knows them. When you can't speak to your audience directly, consider whether there is someone who knows them with whom you could have a conversation. This could be someone who works with them or has previously communicated with them successfully—or unsuccessfully. Get insights from their work with your audience.

Talk to people who are similar to your audience. Determine what aspect of your stakeholders are least familiar to you. Are they in a role or job function that you haven't communicated to before or at a different skill level? Do they work in an industry with which you are less familiar? Find someone you can speak to who can lend a similar perspective or other helpful context.

Collect data. In some cases—for example, if you are communicating to potential consumers of your company's products or services—you may undertake market research to better understand your target audience. Other ways of collecting data include piloting or beta testing to learn how people are using your product and get feedback about their motivation. For a conference presentation, ask for information on attendees. Many conference organizers will share aggregated data about industries, companies, and roles so you can get a sense of who they are.

Read about them. If you'll be presenting to a prominent person, company, or organization, look for information online. Browse their website, look at current job postings, scan social media, and read related news. Even in the instance where it's an individual or group you're communicating to, this will give insight into the organizational culture, which can help your framing.

If you don't do any of these things—due to time constraints or other reasons—you are left to make assumptions about what matters to your audience and how best to convey information to them. When you do, think critically about how your audience is different from you. Often when we communicate, our default is to assume that everyone has the same priorities and preferences as we do. Be clear on where they are likely to deviate. This will help you to express your needs with *their* goals in mind.

Identify & pressure test your assumptions

Any time you make suppositions—whether about your audience or elsewhere as part of your project, analysis, or communication—discuss them with colleagues. Ask your peers to help you identify and pressure test any assumptions you're making by asking critical questions. If you've presumed something incorrectly, does that change things? How? In some cases, a wrong assumption won't have material impact, whereas in other situations it could change everything or call your credibility into question. Be aware of when you are making assumptions and make them as bulletproof as possible.

Working to better understand your audience and getting to know unfamiliar audiences takes time. But when the stakes are high, it's worth the effort because it means you can customize the way you communicate with their preferences in mind. Let's shift our attention to address that challenge.

Tailor for your audience

Your general approach, the materials you create, and the environment in which you meet are important aspects of the communication you can tailor specifically for your audience. Below, I've listed some questions that may help you identify specifics for each. They are primarily framed from the standpoint of having a single person or small group audience (rather than a conference session with many attendees, though you can consider variations for that scenario, too). This is not a comprehensive list but rather some ideas to get you started.

General approach

- **How do others want to be communicated to?** Will they favor an in-person meeting, a video conference, or phone call or email?

- **What's a good amount of time to plan for?** Should you keep things quick to respect their busy schedule, or do you expect they'll be generous with their time?

- **How can you best frame the general conversation?** Do they want you to build to your main point, taking them first through the relevant context, or lead by directly answering the question, "So what?"

Materials

- **How formal do you need to be?** Will your audience demand a polished slide deck or might a casual conversation better suit?

- **How do they want to receive information?** Would they prefer you send a pre-read ahead of time and meet to address questions or that you cover everything during the designated time?

- **How can you best share information?** Do they want to see slides presented on a screen or have a printed handout to flip through and use to record their notes?

- **What level of granularity do they care about?** Is it better to stick to the big picture, or will they want to go through the full details?

- **Will you incorporate data and graphs?** Does your audience value or expect data? Do they embrace or reject graphs? Should you stick to the basics, or is complex okay?

Environment

- **Where do you meet?** Do they want you to come to their office, meet in a conference room, or walk and talk? If it's a video conference, what is their preferred technology?

- **What time of day is best?** Are they energized in the morning, impatient before lunch, or typically frustrated after a specific regular meeting?

- **Should you involve others?** Will you be best off communicating on your own? Would it make sense to involve members of your team, a supporter from elsewhere in the organization, or an influencer whose involvement could help ensure success?

When you step back and think about it, you can customize numerous facets of how you plan material for your audience. You won't always be able to optimize for every element. But the more you *can* do, the better. As we discussed at the onset of this chapter, when you meet your audience's needs, you put yourself in a great position to get your own met as well.

Next, let's take a look at how to apply the ideas we've just framed.

Consider your audience: TRIX case study

I'll introduce a scenario that we will revisit throughout this book. This will allow you to see the progression through the various planning stages, the way they come together into presentation materials, and how you can prepare and deliver a stellar presentation using a real-world model. This situation is based on actual events, with details changed to preserve confidentiality.

Imagine that I work at a market research firm that gathers and analyzes information about consumer preferences. I've just led a pilot project with a new client, a prominent food manufacturing company called Nosh. If this trial run goes well, Nosh will enter into an ongoing partnership with my firm to conduct market research across all of their product lines. In other words, the stakes are high.

Nosh is interested in reworking the blend for their popular trail mix snack product, TRIX, to reduce the cost of production. Together with my research team, I've analyzed the competitive landscape and performed an in-depth study across a variety of dimensions of the current TRIX trail mix. This included the design, execution, and data analysis of a series of tests to understand consumer preference related to alternative recipes and packaging. With the help of my team, I am planning the communication—a slide deck—that I will present to Nosh outlining our findings and recommendations.

My overarching goal is to drive a discussion among the group I'll be presenting to and have them make a decision on what, if any, changes to make to the trail mix ingredients and packaging. Further, I'd like them to be sufficiently impressed with my team's work so that they recommend shifting Nosh's business in this area to our firm.

Let's start by prioritizing the target audience. Many people will be impacted by the outcome of whether to change the trail mix: individuals across numerous parts of Nosh and even outside of it if we include suppliers and customers. We don't, however, need to form our communication with all of these groups in mind. Many of them will be addressed through additional communications downstream.

If I narrow to now—the current point in time—and the decision makers, I should target the team that has been assembled from Nosh to interface with me on this project. It is a mixed group, each with unique personalities, perspectives, and interests. Let's examine the individuals who comprise it.

Vanessa is Head of Product for the product line that includes TRIX trail mix, our focus for the pilot project. She is the individual who commissioned the study with my firm and will be an advocate for ongoing work, assuming she's dazzled by what I demonstrate. On the one hand, she seems hesitant to change what time has proven is a strong product. However, she understands that the rising cost of a main ingredient is making the current mix untenable. She is highly concerned about the negative impact that modifying the product mix could have on consumer sentiment and the overall success of the TRIX brand.

Matt is Vanessa's chief of staff. He's been one of my primary points of contact throughout the project, helping to provide direction and in some cases insight into Vanessa's preferences and how to best work with her. Matt is relatively new to Nosh—he started only a few weeks prior to the beginning of this project—but he came up to speed quickly and has the benefit of having worked with Vanessa in a prior role as well as her trust. By keeping him apprised and on board with the direction I'm taking, he may be able to help influence Vanessa in useful ways.

Jack is the divisional CFO. He has a strong personality and looks closely at the numbers and cost—when he's present. Jack has a busy schedule and often misses or arrives late to project meetings. When he's unable to attend, he sends Shannon from his team to represent Finance. Shannon doesn't say much, but when Jack attends, he is extremely detail oriented and expects immediate and clear answers to his questions. Given all of this, it could make sense to meet with Jack and Shannon separately ahead of the final presentation to share full detail, get Jack's perspective, and fully answer any questions.

Jack's perception of the overall project will influence whether Nosh pursues ongoing work with my firm, so it is critical that it be a positive one.

Riley is the VP of Marketing for the TRIX brand. She's likely to be resistant to changes that will impact the marketing assets her team has already created. This includes packaging changes, which would render some marketing materials obsolete, resulting in more work for them to create new advertising collateral.

Charlie is the Customer Satisfaction Manager for the TRIX product line. He is concerned about changing what historically has been regarded as a magical mix of ingredients due to strong favorability in the market. Charlie seems to be the most risk-averse out of the group. I will need to get him comfortable with our procedures and be thoughtful about how I frame suggested changes, particularly if there's any uncertainty around consumer sentiment.

Abbey and Simon are two sensory scientists from Nosh's R&D team. It is the limited bandwidth of their team—who would normally do this type of work but is concentrating primarily on new products rather than changes to existing ones—that led Vanessa to contract my firm in the first place. Though I feared there might be some territorial issues, that hasn't materialized. Instead, Abbey and Simon have each contributed some helpful guidance that indicates support of our work. They are also meant to provide a review of our methodology to ensure consistency with the R&D team's internal processes, which my close communication throughout the project has hopefully helped safeguard.

Clearly, the people in this group have varying desires and objectives. Though they have disparate individual concerns, one care that unites them is the success of TRIX trail mix. Balancing customer sentiment and cost to manufacture will be of high interest to the group. I will use this common ground to set the stage, walk through options, and frame a hopefully fruitful discussion that leads to clear decisions.

I know our team has done amazing work here—all that's left is to convince the client group at Nosh. I've built some understanding of the various personalities

I'll be presenting to from the meetings we've had with them so far. Some of the clear allies within that group can provide insights to further inform how to best tailor my approach and materials. My final presentation to the full client group has been scheduled for three weeks from today.

We've done it: we've considered our audience. Let's turn attention to our message.

chapter 2

craft your message

You've identified your target audience and acknowledged their needs. Next comes what might seem like an obvious question: *what do you want to communicate?*

Too often, we don't pause to think about this. We finish our project or decide on a presentation topic and begin indiscriminately generating content, creating slides or directing others to do so on our behalf. But if we can't succinctly articulate our point, how do we pull together content that will get that message across? That's a tough feat.

Counter that with the scenario where you are able to simply state your key message in a sentence. This puts you in a much stronger position to intentionally plan your materials.

What should my audience do?

When you are getting ready to communicate, identify what you want others to do—a specific action they should follow. The action itself can take many different forms. It could be a discussion, options to weigh, an idea to respond to, or a decision to make. This is an area in which presentations often fall short. We spend a great deal of time putting together content and taking our audience through masses of information without ever thinking about what we want them to actually *do*. What specific activity will your hard work inform? If you can't clearly articulate the action, you should consider whether you need to communicate in the first place.

We'll touch upon the 3-minute story briefly and cover the Big Idea in depth as tools to empower you as you craft your communication. A clear message helps everything else in the process run smoother, from planning and preparing content to talking to others and getting the attention and action that you seek.

Let's discuss what these concepts are and how to use them, then I'll illustrate through example.

Form your 3-minute story

The 3-minute story is precisely what it sounds like. If you had only a few minutes to tell your audience what they need to know, what would you say? In this boiled-down version, it's essential to recognize the critical components that must be included. It's equally useful to have a good understanding of which details you can omit. The 3-minute story is useful in the event that you encounter a stakeholder (in the elevator or as the first other person on a video conference, for instance) and want to give a quick update or get some input. It's also helpful in the instance where your allotted time on the meeting agenda is reduced.

If you've already formulated a succinct version, it means you know your stuff. You understand your story. You can make it fit into the designated period. It also reduces reliance on your slides, which is a useful feat.

The 3-minute story has an important word in it—*story*. We'll delve into story in Chapter 4. At this point, let's use a simple definition: something that has a plot, a twist, and an ending. In your 3-minute story, the plot is the context to set for your audience so they are ready to take in what you're going to communicate. The twist encapsulates the interesting or unexpected part, or the new information that is critical to understand. The ending is the call to action: what you want your audience to do in light of the information you've shared. To recap, here's the 1-2-3 of the 3-minute story:

1. **Plot:** the context for your audience
2. **Twist:** the new information your audience needs to know
3. **Ending:** the action you want your audience to take

It is helpful to write out the 3-minute story that includes these components. Then read through it aloud and refine (we'll revisit this strategy of practicing out loud in greater detail in the context of refining our presentation in Chapter 9). We'll look at an example later in this chapter.

Once you've formulated your 3-minute story, it becomes an anchor from which you can either expand or condense—and there is value in realizing each of these additional forms. You may expound upon it when discussing your project with a colleague for feedback, in a preemptive conversation with a detail-oriented stakeholder, or when planning your approach to ultimately communicate your work. We'll explore the latter in Chapters 3 and 4 when we brainstorm potential content, organize it in a storyboard, and then arrange it into a robust narrative.

But before we expand on our story, let's practice condensing it. I introduce the 3-minute story concept first because it is difficult to go from the overall scenario down to a single sentence—which is where we're heading next.

Compose the Big Idea

Remember the idea I began with in this chapter? We often go straight to our tools and start building content without necessarily having a clear goal in mind. The Big Idea is that end goal—the key message you want to get across. Think of it as your guiding North Star, helping to direct you through the process of generating supporting content. Once you've formulated it, you have a built-in litmus test for the content that you contemplate including: will it help me get my Big Idea across?

I adapted the Big Idea—which I first read about in Nancy Duarte's *Resonate* (Wiley, 2010)—for use in workshops and have taught and practiced forming and using it with thousands of people over the years. It is one of the most important concepts that we teach.

The Big Idea should:

1. Articulate your point of view,

2. Convey what's at stake, and

3. Be a complete sentence.

Let's review each of these elements.

Articulate your point of view

The first component encourages you to be specific and frame what you think about the matter. One pitfall I sometimes see people stumble into as a result of the single-sentence restriction is that they are too general with the Big Idea. "Let's improve processes to make more money." While no one would argue with that statement, it also isn't meaningful since we've kept things at such a high level that it doesn't convey anything tangible or compelling. For success, you actually want to go the other direction—get specific. "By fixing this particular pain point in our sales process, we estimate we can keep an additional 10% of potential customers from falling out of the process, leading to increased revenue of $300K."

Depending on the scenario and the audience, we might make that even more explicit by rephrasing to recommend a definitive action: "Approve the spend required to fix this pain point in our sales process, allowing us to save potential customers who would have otherwise fallen out of the sales process and leading to increased revenue."

Convey what is at stake

In conveying what's at stake, this is not what is at stake *for you*, but rather what is at stake *for your audience*. This often means a paradigm shift because you are much more used to explaining why someone should care from your perspective than from theirs. Framing your Big Idea for your audience means focusing on what will be most compelling for them. It's the value proposition, the answer to the question of why they should listen to you. It brings the ideas that we discussed in Chapter 1 clearly through into our messaging.

You can articulate what is at stake with positive or negative framing. **Positive framing** means focusing on what the audience has to gain or the benefits if they act in the way you recommend. **Negative framing** is the opposite. What do they stand to lose or what are the risks associated with *not* acting accordingly? As a thought exercise to help figure out what is at stake, I'll often prompt people to start by imagining the absolute worst-case scenario: your audience doesn't follow what you recommend, which leads to X (that's not good), which leads to Y (that's even worse), which leads to Z (absolute disaster). Once you've hit rock bottom, figure out how much to back off from there to appropriately match the given circumstance. Do the same activity in the positive direction. Then decide which will better suit your audience and the situation.

Make it a complete sentence

This is not a bulleted list or a half-thought; the Big Idea is a complete sentence. Perhaps more challenging, though, is that it be a *single* sentence. While it sounds simple to write or say a sentence, when it's work that you're close to, this is often difficult. But it is also incredibly worthwhile.

The single-sentence constraint, while arbitrary, is an important one. First, when you're only allowed a sentence, it forces you to let go of the minutiae. You have to ruthlessly prioritize what you include because there is limited space. This effort will help you home in on your key message. Given the length limitation, every word is important. This means that when you write and rewrite and incorporate feedback (we'll talk more about all of this soon), you may find yourself repeatedly replacing words or changing the phrasing. While this wordsmithing doesn't always feel productive as you're working through it, there is important clarity of thought that arises along the way.

The beauty of constraints

Time constraints. Tool constraints. Space constraints. People often view these as negative forces imposed upon them. I encourage you to reframe. Constraints breed creativity. Self-imposed constraints—like the single-sentence restriction for the Big Idea or the beneficial space limitations of small sticky notes that we will soon discuss—can help you problem solve in new ways. To hear more on this idea, check out Episode 5 of the *storytelling with data* podcast, entitled "the beauty of constraints" (storytellingwithdata.com/podcast).

One tool that is helpful for crafting your single-sentence message is the Big Idea worksheet.

The Big Idea worksheet

When I first started teaching the Big Idea in workshops, I'd introduce it, give a couple examples, and then ask attendees to draft the Big Idea for a specific communication need. This worked reasonably well, but I found that participants sometimes struggled. So I developed a better method: the Big Idea worksheet. The worksheet breaks the Big Idea into its component pieces and poses targeted questions about each. Once you've answered the individual questions, you simply have to fit them together in a way that makes sense as you would the pieces of a puzzle.

Figure 2.1 shows the Big Idea worksheet.

the BIG IDEA worksheet

Identify a project you are working on where you need to communicate something to someone. Reflect upon and fill out the following.   PROJECT:_____

WHO IS YOUR AUDIENCE?

(1) List the primary groups or individuals to whom you'll be communicating.

(3) What does your audience care about?

(4) What action does your audience need to take?

(2) If you had to narrow that to a *single person*, who would that be?

WHAT IS AT STAKE?

What are the *benefits* if your audience acts in the way that you want them to?

What are the *risks* if they do not?

FORM YOUR BIG IDEA

It should:

(1) articulate your point of view,

(2) convey what is at stake, and

(3) be a complete (and single!) sentence.

FIGURE 2.1 The Big Idea worksheet

Using the Big Idea worksheet is simple. Identify a project you are working on where you need to communicate something to an audience. Then take about ten minutes to complete the worksheet. This culminates in you drafting a Big Idea. Building up to it in this piecewise manner helps you break free of the natural inclination to communicate first and foremost for yourself by forcing you to think critically about your audience. As discussed previously, this means centering your message around not why *you* think they must act in a certain way, but rather why *they* should want to.

We'll look at a specific example using the Big Idea worksheet momentarily. First, let's review some frequently asked questions.

Common questions related to the Big Idea

I have taught the concept of the Big Idea and asked participants to practice it in the majority of workshops I've led over the past decade. As part of this, I've fielded many questions related to it. I'll share the common ones along with my thoughts and some related illustrative anecdotes.

I can't get it all into a single sentence. What should I do? Keep trying. Seriously. You can do it, and there are big benefits when you do. I'll rephrase a concern I raised before: if you can't clearly articulate your idea in a single sentence, how in the world are you going to put together a presentation that gets your message across to someone else? The Big Idea won't be the only thing you communicate. You will have supporting material, which is where additional details will come into play. We'll turn our attention there in Chapter 3. By first getting clear and succinct on your primary message, you put yourself in a much better position to form supportive content that will effectively convey it to others.

If you're struggling—even with the inclusion of creative punctuation like commas and semicolons—to get your key message down to a sentence, there are a few things to try. One approach is to start with more. Write as many sentences as necessary, then cull from there. This is one of the reasons I start this chapter with the 3-minute story. It's hard to go from everything to a single sentence. Forming a highly condensed version that still preserves some context is a helpful interim step before you get fully succinct. Another strategy is to build the sentence piece by piece. Use the Big Idea worksheet to tackle a single component at a time, then pull it together. It's harder for extraneous information to sneak in following this method.

Won't negative framing for conveying what's at stake always be more effective? Focusing on the risks is certainly one way to light a fire, getting people to pay attention and promote action. But there are cases where negative framing may not be the best route. If it's already a highly emotionally charged situation, for example, tread lightly.

I recall a scenario when I worked at Google that illustrates such a case. Each year, we conducted an employee survey, where we asked questions about all sorts of dimensions related to the job and work environment, including a thorough section about managers.

I was tasked with walking a director, who had *awful* feedback from members of his team, through his survey results. The negative input didn't stop with low scores on the manager-related survey items but was supported by some scathing commentary. This is tough feedback to deliver and is definitely illustrative of a potentially emotionally charged situation. If I'd gone into this with negative framing ("You have a problem!"), I would have put the manager on the defensive, making it difficult to have a productive discussion. Instead, I highlighted the positive: how hard but extremely helpful it is to get candid feedback and the resources available to help him. This meant we could spend time reflecting and putting the initial building blocks of an action plan into place. It was a difficult conversation, but one that was made a little bit easier for both of us given the thought I'd put into framing ahead of time. I kept one thing top of mind above all else: my audience.

If you're ever unsure whether positive or negative framing will work best, think through both. Then reflect on which one will more likely achieve your desired results. If you are still uncertain, talk it over with someone else.

Be aware also that you may have a personal tendency for positive or negative framing. This is not related to being considered a positive or negative person but instead is driven by how you are best motivated. I tend to have an easier time with positive framing because I've always been motivated by pleasing others.

It isn't only personal proclivities that play into this, but organizational culture as well. I've had some interesting discussions about this idea with workshop attendees. The way organizations communicate in general influences which framing—positive (benefits) or negative (risks)—comes more naturally, as well as what is likely to be better accepted by others in the organization. In one workshop, a participant described the organizational culture as overwhelmingly supportive and collaborative. Those in the room could all succinctly describe the core company values. They were in general agreement that negatively framing the Big Idea would backfire in this environment. That might be true, but it may also be an opportunity to get attention by doing something out of the norm. There's no single right approach here. However, it is imperative that you are aware of the perspective you are taking and why.

What if my audience doesn't care about what's at stake? I've had numerous conversations with people crafting the Big Idea who have grappled with this question. In nearly every case, the challenge was that the person was focusing on what mattered to *them*, rather than what mattered *to their audience*. If you position things right, others will naturally care because you will have made it personal for them.

The tip I touched on earlier to play things out to extremes is sometimes helpful here and can be useful to do in both positive and negative directions. The positive direction would go something like this: if the action I want taken happens, this thing follows (that's good); then as a result, this other thing transpires (that's great). Continue with this until you get world peace, world domination, or whatever your ultimate goal might be. Doing this in the negative direction ends in the ultimate doomsday scenario. Are either of these conclusions likely to play out? No. The learning is in the exercise, then figuring out how to back up to a position that is appropriate framing for what is at stake in the given situation.

This final point is important. Thoughtfully assess what will be pertinent, but avoid going overly extreme with your audience. I once had a conversation with a workshop participant after doing the Big Idea activity where we both had an "aha" moment. Let's call her Kate. Kate worked on an audit team and had been trying to get her colleagues to prepare for blockchain (the digital ledger in which transactions made in bitcoin or another cryptocurrency are recorded publicly). Kate believed that the audit profession as a whole would be in danger unless they took actions to prepare for the future in regard to this. Her challenge was getting anyone to listen to her. She read her Big Idea to me, which basically said (I'm paraphrasing): "You are going to become obsolete, and the audit profession as a whole is destined to end as a result of blockchain; you must take action now to prepare for it!"

Let's think back to my worst-case scenario advice. Kate had done this. The challenge was that she hadn't backed up from there appropriately. The entire profession failing and everyone losing their job tomorrow was such an unlikely outcome that she was easy to ignore. As we talked about this, I witnessed Kate's pivotal moment when she understood why she wasn't getting a positive response.

The solution? We discussed reputational risk and perceptions in the organization, and Kate thought these would be better for conveying what was at stake for this group in a way that would cause them to want to listen to her and act in the near term.

Will my Big Idea have numbers in it? One reason the Big Idea is short is that it forces you to let go of many of the details, including numbers. Frequently, the Big Idea will not have a number in it. Unless there is a figure that's going to be particularly compelling or sticky (easy to remember), you'll typically want to concentrate on the words and ideas—*not* the numbers. Notice in my rewrite of the Big Idea I shared earlier, I removed the numbers altogether and instead highlighted the action I want my audience to take. This parlays nicely into the next common question.

Should my Big Idea have the action in it? If your audience walks out of the room at the end of your meeting or presentation—what is the thing they remember? This is one way to think about the Big Idea. If there is an action you want people to take (as we've discussed, there ought to be), then yes, it belongs in the Big Idea. Note that this won't always be as simple as, "We found X; therefore, you must do Y." The action can take countless forms: a discussion you'd like your stakeholders to have, a decision they should make, options to weigh, or an understanding you require from them. Be clear on the step you want your audience to take and thoughtfully integrate it into your Big Idea.

I don't simply have a single idea to get across. I have a number of things to convey. How do I do this? People are much more likely to remember one or two key points than a laundry list of items. If many actions are desired, one way to tackle it is to make the Big Idea something broader that connects them: *We need to prioritize and assign ownership of the 20 action items in order to...* or, *Without budget approval for our key initiatives, we run the risk of....*

Your audience may not be able to recall the key initiatives, and they definitely won't remember the 20 action items. They actually don't have to. They'll have supporting documentation to refer back to if necessary. But it is important for your audience to remember what you need most from them. In reframing, think about what they must remember and act upon, noting how to structure your Big Idea to best accomplish that.

I am facing a mixed audience—how do I deal with this? Mixed groups are a difficult challenge, as we discussed in Chapter 1. The individuals that comprise them often care about different things. This makes it hard to compose a single sentence that applies to everyone. Still, there are a few things you can do. Narrow by focusing on the decision makers. Group people according to what matters to them, look for areas of overlap, and communicate from those intersections. Formulate the Big Idea separately for your different audiences, then figure out whether there is a single Big Idea that can be formed from them.

What I've outlined are the most common questions raised in a workshop setting related to the Big Idea. One way to answer these questions as well as others that arise as you create your own Big Idea is to talk through it with someone else. Let's talk about the important role of feedback.

Seek feedback

Once you've taken the time to formulate the Big Idea—whether by writing and condensing or through use of the Big Idea worksheet—the subsequent critical step is to discuss with another person. When practicing the Big Idea in a live setting, I give the instruction: "Partners, your job is very important. Ask the person sharing their Big Idea a *ton* of questions. Help them get clear and concise on their message." People are always surprised at how helpful this short conversation is for helping clarify their thinking.

Seeking feedback from someone else is super important because it helps you to get out of your head. Over time, you develop a good deal of tacit knowledge about the area in which you work. It's hard to imagine that others aren't working from that same set of information and assumptions. This means it's relatively easy to formulate something that makes total sense to you but that sounds completely foreign to someone else. This is one reason getting feedback is important. The person you seek out to do this doesn't need to be familiar with your project. On the contrary, it is helpful to discuss with someone who does not have context given the queries they will pose. The basic questions of "Who?," How?," and "So what?" prompt you to express your logic and thought process. Doing this leads to productive conversations and gives you insights to further refine your Big Idea.

Generate the Big Idea in a team setting

The Big Idea is a fantastic exercise to do when you are working on something as part of a team. Have individuals first independently formulate their Big Idea. Then write each idea on a whiteboard or in a shared document (the latter works well for geographically dispersed teams). Simply seeing different approaches together can be a great way to know that people are in alignment or identify when they are not.

Take the time as a team to discuss and form a master Big Idea. This process is beneficial for a few reasons. First, the resulting Big Idea is likely superior to any individually crafted one. People invariably tackle the sentence differently; there's value in having multiple approaches, words, and phrases from which to pull. It helps create buy-in and ownership as individuals see pieces of their work being incorporated into the final version. The topics of discussion that arise out of this process also tend to be informative and establish that everyone is clear and consistent when it comes to overall message and goal.

Next, I'll illustrate these concepts through an example.

Craft your message: TRIX case study

Let's revisit the market research scenario introduced at the end of Chapter 1.

As a reminder, my team has been contracted by the prominent food manufacturer, Nosh, to conduct research and advise modifications to their popular TRIX trail mix to reduce cost without negatively impacting consumer sentiment. We've just wrapped up the project and are planning the communication that I will present to the client team at Nosh outlining our findings and recommendations. The desired outcome is a well-informed discussion and clear decision on what changes to make to trail mix ingredients and packaging, with the senior stakeholders in the group sufficiently impressed to advocate that Nosh shift future business to our firm.

I start by outlining the components of the overarching story for this situation—the plot, twist, and ending.

1. **Plot:** Given the rising cost of TRIX ingredients, the mix needs to be modified.

2. **Twist:** Neither alternative mix tested as well with consumers as the original mix.

3. **Ending:** There are still good options to consider; let's discuss and set next steps.

Given these components (plus some additional details that I'll impart to you now), I formulate the following 3-minute story:

The cost of macadamia nuts—a key ingredient in the popular TRIX trail mix—is on the rise. Nosh engaged us to advise changes to the product that will lower cost without sacrificing consumer preference. We've thoroughly analyzed the competitive market and performed research that included the design, execution, and analysis of a series of tests to understand consumer preference across a variety of dimensions of the current TRIX trail mix related to alternative recipes and packaging.

When it comes to ingredients, none of the alternative mixes scored as strongly with consumers as the original recipe; however, there are still good options to consider. We believe another mix that wasn't directly tested but incorporates learnings from those that were could be the winning combination when it comes to both reduced cost and high customer satisfaction. That said, your risk tolerance will play into the decision at hand.

There are a few options to weigh. If consumer sentiment can't be jeopardized, you can maintain it by sticking with the existing mix. To make that sustainable given current and expected ingredient costs, you'd have to raise consumer price to make it work, which we're not confident the market will support. You could go directly to market with the new alternative mix I mentioned, which would reduce macadamia nuts and introduce flaked coconut. This has some risk associated with it since it hasn't been explicitly tested. Another option is to run additional tests and analysis to fully vet this recommended mix or additional alternatives, though that has the drawback of both additional cost and time.

We also did research and testing with product packaging. A new option that incorporates a view window through which the product is directly visible was preferred. We understand there are marketing collateral concerns when it comes to changing the look of the product. However, intent to purchase is higher with the view window. Making a change to this has the potential to help the product appeal to a wider customer base at no long-term increase in cost to manufacture.

Given all of this, let's discuss and determine where you'd like to go from here.

I'll expand upon this 3-minute story in Chapter 3, when I brainstorm detailed content to support it. Before I do that, I'll condense it into a clear and concise single statement: the Big Idea.

When it comes to the key message, there is a decision to make regarding how forward to be with a given recommendation. This is something that is frequently worth weighing when determining how to message our communications, and it plays into how we frame our Big Idea. Do we simply suggest a menu of potential options without any stated preference, or push for the one we personally think is best?

Let's apply this question to the scenario we're working through here. One option would be to simply outline the various potential changes to TRIX trail mix for our client group to consider and let them discuss and decide—similar to how I framed the 3-minute story. As another approach, I could make a clear recommendation on what course of action *I believe they should take* based on my point of view. Both have their merits and downsides, and which makes the most sense will be highly situationally driven.

In this case—given the great stakes when it comes to potentially winning this client's future business—I want to be bold. I will present them with options but also a clear recommendation for a course of action based on my expertise in this space and informed by the robust research my team has conducted. It's a little risky, but I decide it is a worthwhile gamble given what I stand to gain if all goes well.

Before sharing my Big Idea, I encourage you to look back at the Big Idea worksheet (Figure 2.1) in light of all of this context and ponder how you'd respond to the individual questions. After you've given this some thought (and perhaps even made some notes!), check out Figure 2.2, which shows my completed Big Idea worksheet.

the BIG IDEA worksheet   storytelling ▮▮▮ data

Identify a project you are working on where you need to communicate in a data-driven way. Reflect upon and fill out the following.

PROJECT *TRIX Market Research*

WHO IS YOUR AUDIENCE?

(1) List the primary groups or individuals to whom you'll be communicating.

Stakeholders at Nosh:
- *Vanessa + Matt (product)*
- *Jack + Shannon (finance)*
- *Riley (marketing)*
- *Charlie (cust. satisfaction)*
- *Abbey + Simon (R+D)*

(2) If you had to narrow that to a *single person*, who would that be?

Vanessa (head of product)

(3) What does your audience care about?

- *Reducing cost to produce TRIX*
- *Keeping high customer satisfaction*
- *Unknown: Risk tolerance*

(4) What action does your audience need to take?

- *Consider an untested option that incorporates research learnings*
- *Determine changes to TRIX ingredients & packaging*

WHAT IS AT STAKE?

What are the *benefits* if your audience acts in the way that you want them to?

- *reduced cost to manufacture*
- *maintain beloved ingredient*
- *delight consumers with revamped mix, positive brand impact*

What are the *risks* if they do not?

- *Current mix too costly to produce, reduced profits, demise of products*
- *Additional testing will delay, cost $ and time*

FORM YOUR BIG IDEA

It should:

(1) articulate your point of view,
(2) convey what's at stake, and
(3) be a complete (and single!) sentence.

Change the TRIX mix: don't eliminate the beloved macadamia nuts, reduce them, and also introduce coconut & modify packaging to balance cost and consumer sentiment.

FIGURE 2.2 The Big Idea worksheet for TRIX market research project

I enlist four colleagues at my market research firm who have been involved in the project to each complete the Big Idea worksheet and craft their respective Big Ideas. I put them all into a shared document. Here they are (you'll recognize the final one from my worksheet):

1. Macadamia nuts have become too expensive; product success will decline if you don't modify the ingredient mix to reduce the cost to produce TRIX trail mix.

2. There are differences in both manufacturing cost and consumer preference across the options tested for TRIX; let's discuss the tradeoffs and set future strategy.

3. We can reduce cost to produce by refreshing the TRIX blend and packaging.

4. Decide what's more important, cost to produce or consumer response, to determine whether to keep the current mix and increase price or go with a new alternative blend.

5. Change the TRIX mix: don't eliminate the beloved macadamia nuts, reduce them, and also introduce coconut and modify packaging to balance cost and consumer sentiment.

I have a meeting with my colleagues to review, discuss, and form a single master Big Idea. There is some interesting discussion about positive versus negative framing, after which we decide that the positive framing—highlighting what our audience stands to gain rather than what they might lose—sets a better tone for fruitful conversation. We also note that while some individuals focused mainly on cost in their Big Idea, others also brought in consumer sentiment. There is consensus that our client group cares highly about both of these elements and that they each warrant mentioning in the ultimate Big Idea. We also decide conclusively (after some healthy debate) that we'd like to be direct about recommending a specific course of action. Our Big Idea will encapsulate this, while the content we use to support it will include a robust set of potential options with tradeoffs for our client to weigh as they decide which course of action to pursue.

Given all of this, my colleagues and I land on the following Big Idea after our thorough discussion and a good amount of patient wordsmithing:

Consider an alternative trail mix blend that balances consumer preference with the desire to lower cost by decreasing macadamia nuts, adding coconut, and modifying the packaging so potential buyers can see the product.

We agree that this is the main message we want to get across. We'll use the communication we eventually build with this in mind to facilitate a discussion around the specific tradeoffs with different courses of action and guide our stakeholders to make a decision regarding future strategy for TRIX trail mix.

Keep this example in mind—we'll return to it in the upcoming chapter.

As we've discussed, once you've taken the time to form your Big Idea, you have a litmus test for any content you contemplate including in your ultimate communication. Simply ask yourself, "Does this help me get my Big Idea across?" Speaking of planning content, let's do that next.

chapter 3

compile
the pieces

In the previous chapter, I asked you to let go of a lot of detail in order to get succinct on your message. That may have felt uncomfortable. I'll venture to guess that it *did* feel uncomfortable. But don't worry. Now is when you get to think about your communication more broadly, including the various supporting elements that will help you get your message across.

In this chapter, I'll walk you through the process to create your plan of attack—a storyboard. We'll start by brainstorming and spend time generating ideas and enumerating potential pieces of content. Then we'll edit, arrange, and rearrange. We'll seek and incorporate feedback. All of this will culminate in an initial and robust plan for your presentation content.

What is a storyboard?

Storyboarding is a term I've appropriated for the business setting. A storyboard is a sequence of drawings that represent shots planned for a movie, television show, or commercial (for many people, this word conjures TV's *Mad Men*–style advertisement sketches). For use in the business world, I simply think of the storyboard as a visual outline for presentation content. You don't have to be an artist to reap the immense benefits of this strategy. In addition to organizing your thoughts and creating a plan that keeps you on track, taking the time to storyboard as part of the planning process often leads to shorter, targeted, and more effective communications.

The first piece of advice I have for you when it comes to everything we'll discuss in this chapter: keep it low tech. Let's begin with this.

Learn to love low tech

Resist any urge to turn to your tools at this point! This is not the right time to open PowerPoint, Google Slides, or Keynote and start making slides. We still have a good amount of work to do before then, and it will be entirely low tech. We will use pens, paper, and sticky notes.

Let's look at the reasons we sometimes use technology prematurely and the unintended negative consequences that will lead you to appreciate the benefits of staying low tech. First, there is a sense of accomplishment when we create in our tools. Making a slide *feels* productive. Expanding on this, making a lot of slides feels like great progress! Despite that, when you do this too soon, it can be counterproductive. You may spend time creating content that ends up not being right for the situation. A single unnecessary slide probably isn't the end of the world. But consider the case where you go into slide-generating mode and create an entire deck that doesn't get your Big Idea across. This is remarkably easy to do. The low-tech part of the process helps us to avoid this by ensuring every bit of content has been thoroughly vetted. This leads to my next point.

Another reason we are sometimes drawn to our computers is for the level of polish that comes with what we create. To a large degree, people have stopped writing with pen and paper. This can make doing so feel awkward and slow. Perhaps you don't consider yourself good at drawing or think you have sloppy handwriting—but if you are able to easily mock something up in PowerPoint, you might as well do that, right? No! This action is understandable, but there is a place for rough ideas, poor penmanship, bad sketches, and simply the process of committing pen to paper. As we put each of these things out into the world, we are testing content. We are thinking about it critically. In response to an idea you've written, you can feel your own reaction and solicit that of others in a way that focuses on the *meta approach* instead of the specific content (once a slide exists, it begs for the content and design to be critiqued; we'll need that, too, but at a later point). What we require first is a well-structured plan of attack.

Additionally, remaining low tech as we plan helps us avoid the attachment trap. Have you ever noticed that once you take the time to build something—a slide, for example—you develop a certain fondness toward it? In some cases, even if you know it could be better or would benefit from change, you might resist *because of the work it's already taken you to get it where it is.* Let's say I've just spent four hours creating a beautiful graph on a fantastic slide. I'm walking you through the deck, and we get to this particular slide. You say to me, "Cole, I don't think this one is relevant. Maybe you should push it to the appendix?"

This feels bad.

There are feelings of *loss* associated with this.

There is *real* loss associated with this when we take into account the four hours of work it took me to create the beautiful graph on the fantastic slide.

Now assume that I've remained low tech. I resisted the urge to open my laptop. I did not create any slides. Instead, I brainstormed ideas on sticky notes and organized them into a storyboard. Let's take the same scenario: I'm walking you through this plan, and we get to a sticky note that features a rough sketch of the graph I have in mind. You point out that it isn't relevant. I reflect on this, realize you're right, and recycle it. I didn't form attachment to or fondness toward the sticky note. There wasn't any feeling of loss involved. Nor was there time wasted creating and subsequently discarding content or relinquishing it to an appendix.

While working with presentation software makes you feel powerful and in control as you easily create slides, the low-tech planning is where the real magic happens. Let's take a closer look at how to do this, beginning with a brainstorm.

Brainstorm

I storyboard any time I'm going to cover new content or present something in a different way. I encourage you to do so, too. This active planning step helps you avoid doing things the way you've always done them out of habit by forcing you to critically consider the circumstances for a given situation.

Storyboarding best begins with a brainstorm, which for me always feels like a cathartic process. The goal is simply to generate ideas. Start writing. As you produce ideas, don't worry about whether the various topics will make it into your final deck or in what order they will appear. First, simply get your thoughts out of your head and into the physical world. Do this for a limited amount of time. For me, 10–15 minutes of concentrated brainstorming is typically sufficient. Then ideas will continue to arise as I work through the other parts of the storyboarding process.

My favorite storyboarding tool: sticky notes

I storyboard using small sticky notes. I opt for the 1⅞ inch (47.6 mm) squares and have them in a variety of colors that I'll sometimes use to categorize as I go along. I like sticky notes for their petite size, which forces me to be concise with my ideas. I also appreciate their stick to keep them in place as I begin to organize, which we'll discuss in the editing step.

Too constrained by sticky notes?

While I advocate using sticky notes for brainstorming and arranging ideas into a storyboard, they are certainly not your only option. I have friends who swear that index cards are the best tool for planning (they are just as easy to rearrange, *and* you can pack them up neatly with a loop or two of a rubber band for presentation planning on the go!). Once, in a workshop, a participant told me that sticky notes made them nervous. They felt too restricted because they were used to brainstorming on a full piece of paper (this method is totally fine, though I'd recommend cutting up the paper afterwards so you can move the pieces around). More important than the tool are the mechanics. The goal is to think critically about the content that will help you get your message across and arrange things in a way that will make sense for your audience. Use whatever device will help you do all of this with ease.

We'll get more detailed about what to put on a sticky note momentarily, but when I brainstorm, I usually write down topics and content ideas. As I brainstormed for this chapter of this book, my sticky notes focused on specific section titles and subsection content. When brainstorming for a presentation, imagine that each note eventually becomes a slide in your deck. But allow yourself flexibility: some single-idea stickies may become multiple slides, or you might combine several into a single slide. This will become clear when you edit. At the onset, it's mainly about generating a good number of ideas.

Change your environment for a creativity boost

The environment in which you brainstorm and storyboard has an impact. I work at a large black desk in the middle of my office, seated at a stool. When I storyboard, I physically stand up and walk around to the other side of the desk. It's a wide-open surface (practically begging to be filled with my ideas!). There's something about having a different visual perspective and standing as I do this that helps stimulate my creativity. After I've brain-stormed and arranged my ideas, I get a large piece of paper and transfer the sticky notes to it. This allows me to carry the plan back around to the computer side of my desk for when I start to write or create slides.

If you're ever feeling stuck, try changing your physical environment to spark new ideas.

What do I put on a sticky note?

I've said to generate ideas, but that's pretty general guidance. Precisely what kind of ideas, you might ask? There isn't a single *right* way to storyboard. You'll figure out what works for you by trying it and adjusting as you go through the process.

When I'm brainstorming, the sorts of things I write on my stickies tend to fall into the following categories:

- Historical or environmental context
- The problem statement, question, or hypothesis
- My Big Idea
- Assumptions I've made
- Biases to address

- Data points
- Graphs or other visuals
- Analysis details or statistical methodology
- Process steps
- Illustrative examples
- Findings or takeaways
- Alternative hypotheses
- Options to consider
- Discussion points
- Recommendations

This is a good place to pause and try it out. Do you have a current project where you need to communicate something to someone? Get yourself a stack of stickies or cut up blank paper. Set a timer for ten minutes. Using my list as a guide, brainstorm ideas for potential content that will help you get your message across.

Consider various perspectives

Most of the brainstorming we do is from our own perspective. Like communicating for yourself, as we've discussed, this is a natural—and reasonable—place to start. But it's not the right point to stop. We spent a good deal of time reflecting on your audience in Chapter 1. It wouldn't make sense to ignore them now as we plan our content!

After you've taken time to brainstorm for yourself, assume a different lens. Begin by imagining the viewpoint of your audience. Revisit the Big Idea that you formed in Chapter 2, and think about what *they* would want to know or see to better understand your message or be motivated to act in the way you want them to. If you're communicating to a mixed group, do this several times, assuming different perspectives from which to brainstorm and generate additional ideas. There may be other positions to take into account as well.

Assume the point of view of a colleague, your manager, or another stakehold-er. When it comes time to edit, one strategy will be to look for areas of overlap. Use those to create common ground and ensure the robust set of priorities are met.

Speaking of editing, once you've generated a ton of ideas—and perhaps even started to arrange and discard some of them—it is time to edit.

Edit: refine and rearrange

After brainstorming, take a step back. Begin to curate your ideas, picking out the ones that best suit specific needs. This editing step typically takes longer than the brainstorming part did, and you may continue to generate ideas as you work your way through it.

Think about what framework could help you pull everything together in a way that will make sense to someone else. How will you organize and order the content? Add new stickies to categorize themes and start to arrange. Where might you benefit from transitional content? Add notes. Are there opportuni-ties to combine similar ideas or topics that could be aggregated in the same section? Put those stickies together, and perhaps add a topic to group them. Identify where to incorporate data or illustrative examples. Continue to rear-range, physically lifting and moving sticky notes around. Add new ideas when necessary. Crumple up the ones that don't serve your purpose.

The importance of intentional discard

On the topic of eliminating, let's pause to discuss one of the biggest benefits of storyboarding: intentional discard. When we start in our tools (like Power-Point or Keynote), in addition to the issues I outlined earlier in this chapter, another problem is the false belief that what we create must answer any ques-tion that arises. Whereas when we start low tech, we can be thoughtful about each piece of potential content we consider including and ask ourselves an important question: does this help me get my Big Idea across? No? Cut it. Start a discard pile. Add to it without hesitation.

When I storyboard, I always have a discard pile. I'll sometimes write down the same idea five times and discard it five times because it takes this repetition for me to convince myself that it (whatever *it* is) doesn't belong in the communication. If the idea has come up this many times, it's probably good to know the content or answer to the question in the event it arises, but not every bit of relevant information has to have a home in my presentation. This process of intentional discard leads to shorter, more effective communications.

Storyboard at different levels for longer content

For longer presentations or written content, I often storyboard multiple times and at different levels over the course of time. This typically starts broad and then becomes increasingly granular as I plan the particulars. Let's take this book as an example.

First, I storyboarded the overall structure: the main sections and chapters (it was an iterative method rather than a linear one to get everything to align in a way that made sense to me). In some cases, I'd go a little deeper into content ideas for a given chapter to get a sense of overall balance and to keep track of the thoughts I had on what would best fit into a given area. As I write these words, the high-level plan lives in a readily visible sticky note outline on my office closet door. I reflect on it and periodically make adjustments (while I'm mostly set now on what I'm writing about in the *plan* chapters that include this one, I'm rethinking how to structure the *create* chapters that come next).

While that's happening at the meta level, I'm also focusing on a given chapter at a time. I start each by storyboarding. I brainstorm and then arrange section topics, content ideas, sidebars, illustrative examples, and anecdotes. For my writing, I don't generally solicit feedback at this point (whereas I often will if it's a presentation that I'm planning). If I'm unsure about the arrangement or approach, I'll talk through it aloud to work it out. Then I start writing, using the chapter storyboard I've created as my guide. There are points where I'll still get stuck and go back to the storyboard, rearrange, and then try again. However, most often at this point, the editing shifts to the written document (and continues there for quite some time!).

A similar strategy also works for longer presentations. Start by storyboarding the general layout and have this be your overarching guide. Then storyboard again at varying levels of granularity so you are able to see and vet your plan before committing to it and creating content. After storyboarding your general content, repeat the process for a given section. You may storyboard *again* to plan the content for a given slide. Yes, this takes time and effort. But as we've discussed, the amount of thought this forces you to put into everything will raise the quality of what you create and guide you to craft communications that better suit the given situation.

Where should my Big Idea appear in my storyboard?

When it comes to arranging content, one common set of questions that arises is, "Where do I put my Big Idea in my storyboard? Do I build up to it? Lead with it? Something else?" There's no single right path. Different scenarios will call for varying approaches. In some cases, these disparate methods will work equally well. There are a few things to take into account related to the placement of your Big Idea and general ordering of the components of your storyboard.

Frequently, when we initially arrange our content, it follows a chronological or linear fashion. This tends to come most naturally because that is the same general order as our experience. If I'm communicating the results of an analysis, I can start out with the question I set out to answer, then talk about the data I used (where it came from, what I did to clean it, etc.). Next, I could review the specifics of the analysis I undertook. This leads into my findings and recommendations. This progression comes as a matter of course; it's the same way I tackled the project.

When we arrange our content in a linear fashion such as this, the Big Idea typically comes at the end. This means we have to keep our audience's attention until the finale to get to our main point. Another option is to begin with the Big Idea. But what if we do that and others disagree with us? That might not be the best way to start. This leads me to some specific considerations to keep in mind as you determine where to put your Big Idea within your broader presentation.

One factor is the level of credibility you have with your audience. If you do not have a strong relationship with them and you start with your Big Idea *and they disagree*, you begin from a position of discord. This is not typically a fantastic starting point. In that case, going through the chronological ordering—the linear progression—could be a better option, so you bring others along with your logic as you go through it. By the time you get to the end, they are hopefully bought in or at least willing to listen.

On the other hand, there are scenarios when it absolutely makes sense to lead with the Big Idea. For example, if you already have established rapport or you think your audience is likely to accept what you recommend, starting with the Big Idea gets everyone into the right frame of mind and more quickly sets up productive conversations. You can also lead with the Big Idea if you're not sure you have time to go through everything from beginning to end or if you fear someone will interrupt and take you off track. If your audience cares more about the ultimate "So what?" than how you got there—then by all means, lead with the Big Idea. In some cases, if others buy in at the onset, you won't have to go through the rest of the details.

Generally, contemplate what order you anticipate working best given the specific situation: who your audience is and how you'll be presenting to them. Don't get too attached to your storyboard yet. We'll look at additional strategies for ordering content in Chapter 4 when we discuss story. At that point, I'll encourage you to return to your storyboard and make changes. Before we do that, though, this is a good place to pause and get input from someone else.

Solicit feedback

Getting feedback on your storyboard has benefits similar to receiving input on the Big Idea. There are advantages to talking through it out loud, articulating your logic, and answering questions to help assess whether what you're planning makes sense to someone else. After crafting your storyboard, grab a colleague and spend 10–15 minutes walking through it, discussing it, and getting feedback.

This early planning point is also often an excellent place to get client, stakeholder, or manager feedback. This isn't always possible and won't make sense every time, but when it does, it's an opportunity to make sure everyone is aligned before you've done a great deal of work. Preface your request with, "This is rough, but here's what I'm thinking," sharing your actual storyboard or even a bulleted list that walks through your plans. If you can get feedback indicating, "Yes, this is great, keep going," or "No, this isn't it; we should change direction," you haven't wasted a ton of time and effort. In general, the earlier in the process you get this type of directional feedback, the better. Flipping that around, if you are a manager of others and would like to be able to give feedback earlier in the process, encourage your team members to craft storyboards to share with you.

Storyboard as a team

Storyboarding as a team is an excellent exercise, particularly in the instance where multiple individuals will contribute to a deck or report. If you can, get everyone into a conference room with a whiteboard and markers. After you have agreement on general content and flow, draw large slide-shaped rectangles on the whiteboard (the oversized roughly slide-proportioned sticky notes are also fun to implement during team storyboarding, where each sticky note represents a slide). Add draft titles and sketch the supporting content to be gathered or created.

In this manner, everyone walks away with the same overall vision. It also allows people to understand how what they are tasked with will fit into the big picture, assists individuals giving each other feedback, and encourages cohesion across the communication. It helps ensure everyone is on the same page in terms of the deliverable.

Team storyboarding in a non-colocated environment

Getting everyone in a room with a whiteboard works great when you're all in the same office. But what happens when you need to storyboard as a team in a non-colocated environment? In this case, emulate the sticky note approach. Any type of shared document that multiple people are able to view and edit simultaneously can work for this (in Google Docs, your storyboard may look more like a bulleted list, which is fine). There are also applications that mirror this process, such as Miro, Evernote, or Microsoft OneNote. For smaller scale or free solutions, check out Storyboard That or Padlet.

Depending on your technology, sometimes brute force also works. For example, put ideas in large text on slides, then go to slide sorter view. Share the screen in a virtual meeting to drive discussion, moving around pieces to reflect the conversation. I also recall situations at Google where we'd have colleagues in the office and joining via video conference, and those physically present would aim the camera at the whiteboard where we were storyboarding so that everyone could participate.

Now that we've discussed how to storyboard, let's see it illustrated.

Compile the pieces: TRIX case study

Recall the example we've been working through at the close of each chapter.

As a reminder, my team has been contracted by the prominent food manu-facturer, Nosh, to conduct research and advise modifications to their popular TRIX trail mix to reduce cost without negatively impacting consumer sentiment. We've recently wrapped up the project and are planning the communication that I will present to the client team at Nosh outlining our findings and rec-ommendations. The desired outcome is a well-informed discussion and clear decision on what changes to make to trail mix ingredients and packaging, with the senior stakeholders in the group sufficiently impressed to advocate that Nosh shift future business to our firm.

Together with my colleagues, I've already crafted the Big Idea for our commu-nication: *Consider an alternative trail mix blend that balances consumer pref-erence with the desire to lower cost by decreasing macadamia nuts, adding coconut, and modifying the packaging so potential buyers can see the prod-uct.* This is the key point we want to get across to our audience. The actual communication will be a slide deck that I will present in a meeting. I will use it to convey the findings of our research and put forth our specific recommen-dation in context of a set of options for the stakeholders to discuss and set strategy for the TRIX trail mix product.

I begin by brainstorming. I get out mini sticky notes and start writing down ideas. I think through the project from beginning to end—from the context that led us to work with Nosh in the first place all the way through to the rec-ommendation and Big Idea. Due to this approach, my idea generation is linear in nature (roughly mirroring the progression of the project that was undertak-en). After doing this from my perspective, I attempt to assume various stake-holders' views and generate content ideas specific to their preferences as well. What will Vanessa (Head of Product) care about most, or what level of detail will Jack (divisional CFO) require to be satisfied? What information will Abbey and Simon (R&D) expect to be convinced that our methodology is sound?

After about 15 minutes of writing ideas and assuming multiple perspectives, I have a lot of sticky notes in front of me. Given the volume, instead of showing them all, I'll list what I've written on the various notes to give you a sense of quantity, breadth, and depth.

- Pilot project aims to assess ongoing partnership
- TRIX is Nosh's popular trail mix snack product
- TRIX sales over time (demonstrate success)
- Ingredients: macadamias, almonds, cashews, dried cherries, dark chocolate
- Desire to lower cost to manufacture
- Important: maintain high consumer preference
- Options explored: change size, price, packaging, ingredients
- Data: product sizes
- Data: packaging options
- Data: competitor pricing
- Data: competitor ingredients
- Component cost analysis
- Finding: macadamia nuts are expensive
- Price sensitivity analysis
- Finding: market not likely to bear higher price point
- Packaging cost analysis
- Finding: alter packaging at negligible incremental cost
- Ran tests with consumers to understand preferences
- Study 1: packaging testing
- Study 1: alternative packaging tested
- Study 1 details: locations, timing, participant demographics
- Intent to purchase data & analysis
- Finding: view window increases intent to purchase

- Study 2: taste tests
- Study 2: alternative mixes tested
- Study 2 details: locations, timing, participant demographics
- Preference scores data & analysis
- Finding: original mix preferred overall
- Finding: alternative A scores low on appearance & texture
- Finding: alternative B scores low on taste
- Finding: people love coconut
- What's more important: cost or preference?
- Nosh's risk tolerance?
- We didn't test a magic mix, but we do have good options
- Big idea: reduce nuts, add coconut, and modify packaging
- Other options: increase price, do more testing
- Discuss
- Determine next steps

If I had started in PowerPoint, I could have easily created a slide (or more!) for each of the preceding bullets. While the resulting presentation would probably make sense to me, given my intimacy with the project, it would be tough to take someone else through sensibly. While my team needed to process all of this context, data, and analysis to gain a full understanding of the situation and make an informed recommendation, my audience doesn't have to see every step we took along the way. Instead, I will curate these ideas into a path along which I'll guide them.

To achieve that, I start editing. Now that I see all of the ideas for potential content in front of me, I consider what framework I can use to organize the pieces. I start a discard pile and put stickies there that may not be directly relevant or help me get my Big Idea across. There isn't a single way to organize the ideas—this can be achieved in a number of ways. As I make decisions about what to include and how to structure it, I keep my audience and how

I'll ultimately communicate to them in mind. I imagine what success looks like, and then in light of the ideas in front of me, weigh different ways to pull them together to actualize it.

After I've spent some time rearranging and organizing, the final step is to solicit feedback. I talk through my storyboard with my colleagues. This is also a good point to seek input from someone less involved with the project or perhaps a friendly stakeholder who can provide insight on what the group will be expecting and assess whether my plan makes sense. Thinking about the specific audience members we described in Chapter 1, Matt, Vanessa's chief of staff in the Product organization, would be a good person to turn to for this.

After sharing my plan with several individuals (including Matt) and continuing to refine, Figure 3.1 shows my resulting storyboard.

FIGURE 3.1 Storyboard for TRIX market research project

I chose to lead with the Big Idea. The three blue stickies denote the main sections of the communication. These could turn into divider slides in the eventual deck. The initial section sets the context. I'll begin with the background on why we were engaged in the first place. From there, I will show the results of the various studies we designed and conducted. This will transition into the following section that highlights our learnings. At this point, I can convey data and analysis that yielded the various findings and how we think they should be put to use. Finally, I'll focus my audience on action. I'll frame a conversation on the relative importance of consumer preference weighed against cost. I'll reiterate our team's recommendation and also share a full set of options for the stakeholders to weigh and discuss. All of this will lead to their informed decision about the future strategy of the TRIX trail mix.

We've brainstormed, edited, rearranged, and iterated given input. While we could stop here with our planning, there is another important concept to discuss first: story. Story helps us bring our approach to an entirely new level. Let's pivot our attention to that next.

form a story

You've identified your audience, formed your message, and crafted your plan. Before we start building content, though, let's pause to spend time contemplating *story* and explore how we can incorporate the art of storytelling into our communications. I'll begin by outlining a typical approach for business presentations, then contrast that with the potential power of structuring with story. After discussing how I think about story and its shape, I'll highlight the important role of tension and walk you through how to use the narrative arc as a model for restructuring and further refining the plan we set for our communication.

Why did we just spend all that time creating a storyboard only to change it now? you might ask. That's a reasonable question. However, the work I led you through in Chapter 3 was not for naught. Brainstorming potential content immersed you in the full details of the situation and caused you to look at the specifics from multiple points of view. As you edited your sticky notes, you had critical debates with yourself (and possibly, with others) on why to include some pieces and which topics or paths don't aptly serve your intended audience or message. You curated a vast array of possible content into something more targeted and manageable. These will be the building blocks for your story.

Additionally, through sharing your storyboard for feedback, you articulated your logic: the pieces of the puzzle you've chosen to focus on and how they fit together to serve your purpose. As a result, you are now in a position where you are able to consider another structure precisely *because* of the thought you have put into everything thus far. The jump to story—and it is a jump, which we'll talk more about—might indeed have been too large had you not gone through all of this work first.

Before we dive into story, let's discuss a method that is often employed *instead*: the linear path.

A common approach: the linear path

The typical business presentation—whether communicated in a meeting or from a speaker on stage—often follows a predictable path. It begins with the background information to frame the topic or the context that led to the work that is being communicated. This may involve a problem statement that describes the purpose. Frequently, that's followed by a recounting of the various activities undertaken or methodology employed. This could include the timeline and project scope, meetings held, experts consulted, data collected, analysis undertaken, and so on. After these specifics are fully detailed, they are followed by a summary of the lessons learned. The session ends with findings, recommendations, or next steps. Think back to the last presentation you sat through in a meeting or at a conference. Did it look something like this?

FIGURE 4.1 Typical business presentation linear path

There is nothing wrong with the linear path I've described, which is also depicted in Figure 4.1—but there's not anything particularly awesome about it, either. I've been known to describe it as *selfish* on the part of the communicator to organize content in this manner. When I do so, I am being intentionally provocative to make a point. This is the approach we tend to default to when we communicate because it mirrors the same steps, in roughly the same order, as we experienced during the project or process. It's chronological. It is logical. It feels familiar. I'll repeat a sentiment I mentioned early in the book: it's easy for me to communicate for myself. But is that framing particularly inspiring or memorable for others?

You know that the answer is no. You've been in the audience, suffering through presentations like this in the past. A key thing was missing in that instance—*you*. One failing of the linear path to explanatory communication is that we are able to follow it perfectly while simultaneously giving little or no thought to the people to whom we are communicating. This can yield a resulting communication that is ineffective for our audience. That's a problem!

Contrast that with story. Stories have a pronounced shape, involving the audience in a climactic rise and fall. Stories appeal to us on an emotional level. Stories engage. All of this together renders communications that follow a story structure much more interesting than the logic-inspired flat line of the linear path. Let's explore *story*, beginning with some discussion of what exactly I mean when I say that word.

What is story?

Story, storyteller, storytelling—these concepts have long existed but relatively recently become business buzzwords. They are thrown around frequently and loosely. While I love that communicating with story has become a legitimate topic of discussion, the overuse and misuse of these terms also dilutes what story truly is, misinforming how it can be used.

When I think about story as it relates to communicating in a business setting, I really mean *story*. I often refer to children's books to illustrate. Why? They are relatable. Every adult has a personal childhood experience they can draw upon to engage with my explanation. Some have children they read to on a nightly basis. Children's stories also often perfectly illustrate what I mean when

I say *story*. There is a plot: characters and a sense of place and time. Something occurs that throws things out of balance. There are ups and downs as the story progresses. These things-gone-wrong draw us in and keep us paying attention to find out what happens. By the end, the issues have typically been overcome or resolved in some way. Stories I've used to discuss these concepts include *The Cat in the Hat*, *Where the Wild Things Are*, *Harold and the Purple Crayon*, *Red Riding Hood*, *The Wizard of Oz*, *Charlotte's Web*, and recent favorites from reading to my own children, the *Larry Gets Lost* series. Are you familiar with any of these stories? Did my simple listing of the titles prompt you to remember or feel something?

Let's take that idea a step further and examine the utility of story through a quick thought exercise. Bring one of your own favorite childhood books to mind. What is the title? Recall the primary storyline. Who was the main character? What dilemma did they face? How did the story end? Close your eyes. Can you picture some part of it—perhaps the cover or a scene from the book—in your head? How does doing this make you feel?

Reflect for a moment. When was the last time you gave any thought to this particular story? Yesterday? Last year? A decade ago? Longer? Isn't it amazing that, no matter how much time has passed, you are able to recall it now?

This is partly due to the shape. Because there is one event that leads to the next and intensity often increases and then decreases, an effective story told well provides specific anchors. These are things that happen in the context of the narrative that can be recalled. This, in turn, makes it easier to remember and retell.

A good story also appeals to us—the audience—on an emotional level: both as the events of the story unfold and often afterwards as well. We may have laughed or cried. Perhaps we were entertained or learned an important lesson. In some cases, we might reflect on how we would act ourselves in a similar setting or express empathy for the characters and what they go through, feeling sad on account of their sorrows or sharing in the joy of their happy ending.

That is the kind of story I want you to have on your mind throughout this chapter as we study story from different angles and how we can use components of storytelling to inform how we communicate. No, we won't always be able to make people laugh or cry. But if we can use story to gain attention and get people to engage in productive ways, that's pretty powerful, too.

The structure of story

One key part of the storytelling process is *you*—the storyteller. I mean this both from the standpoint of the story you conceive when you plan and build your materials (our focus currently and in the following section) and how you ultimately tell that story (which we'll delve into in the final section of the book). As is the case when learning almost anything new, start simple. With time and practice, your comfort, experience, and skills for using story to communicate will build. As they do, you can refine your approach, becoming increasingly nuanced while better meeting the needs of your various communication situations.

I've observed this progression directly. The way I think about and teach story has changed over time, following my own learning and development in this space. Given that, I thought it would be helpful to walk you through a couple of specific characterizations of story that I have found useful. This brief exploration will give us a common language and structures to model as we think about applying story to our business communications.

A basic story: plot, twist, and ending

You may recognize the pieces of this basic story structure; they are the same ones I asked you to consider when we discussed the 3-minute story in Chapter 2. Here, rather than arrange the components linearly, I'll make a shape with a rise and fall—a small story mountain, as depicted in Figure 4.2.

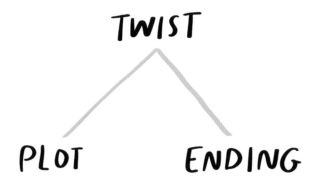

FIGURE 4.2 A basic story structure

The plot is context. This encapsulates what is happening at the onset of the story, where setting and characters are introduced. Things get carried, onward and upward, to the twist. This is the tension that lends shape to the story, something gone wrong that needs to be addressed. The ending solves that thing-gone-wrong and brings the story to its close, wrapping everything up neatly.

The simplest story: beginning-middle-end

When my oldest son was first learning about story at school, his first-grade teacher described it as being made up of a beginning, middle, and end. This is elementary (literally, for elementary school students) but a decent place to start. Aristotle is believed to have introduced this basic idea, proposing a three-act structure for plays. Following this model, Act One (the beginning) is the set-up. It lays out the plot and the characters. Act Two, the middle and typically longest segment, builds upon this, introducing complications, twists, and turns as the action escalates. Act Three (the end) is the resolution that brings the play to its close.

Note that this general structure is similar to the linear path introduced earlier in this chapter. Things move naturally forward in a logical manner. This is one progression we can follow for our business communications. As discussed, however, there is often an opportunity—and some serious accompanying benefits—to push beyond this, explicitly highlighting tension and bringing shape to our story.

The basic story structure of plot-twist-ending was what I focused on in my first book, *storytelling with data: a data visualization guide for business professionals* (Wiley, 2015), and it is the approach we commonly employ when we teach effective communication in a shorter workshop setting. The simplicity is useful, and many business scenarios can be mapped directly to it. It's a great way to get people to *start* thinking about story. If you hesitate at the idea of using story to communicate at your organization, this is a terrific first step. We'll come back to this idea and lay out specific tactics when we revisit tension later in this chapter.

Before we do that, let's examine another well-known story structure that builds on this basic version.

The narrative arc

One common way of depicting the path that a story takes is the narrative arc. Similar to the basic story structure, the beginning of the story is the plot: where we are at the start. Tension is introduced through an inciting incident. This tension escalates in the form of rising action that reaches its maximum peak at the climax, where there is a significant turning point in the story. Things relax over the falling action, a buffer that leads us to the resolution at the story's end. This is the general structure that the children's books I listed earlier each follow. Bring to mind the familiar story you conjured. I bet its primary storyline can be plotted along this path as well (shown in Figure 4.3).

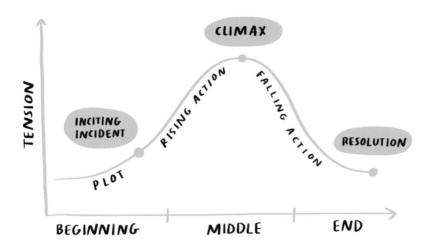

FIGURE 4.3 The narrative arc

When I first encountered the narrative arc, I experienced one of those eureka moments: *I've found it—the simple and relatable construct that's going to help me explain and teach story!* It's more complex than the basic plot-twist-ending but still simple enough to explain in mere minutes. Both familiar stories and real-life business scenarios can be mapped against it for illustration purposes. It can also be used as a schematic to plan future presentations. I will walk you through how to use it as a guide for your business story soon. Before that, let's look at some of its advantages.

There are a couple of important distinctions I want to highlight between the narrative arc and the linear path we touched on earlier. Perhaps the easiest difference to see is the shape. The linear path is a simple progression from left to right compared to the rise and fall of the arc. Tension is the magical component that lends form to the latter. That's perhaps the biggest single benefit of shifting how we generally address presentation organization from a linear path to the narrative arc—it forces us to identify the tension present in the situation. This is not the tension that matters to us, as the creators of the content, but the tension that matters to our audience. Whereas it's easy to organize our communication in a linear fashion without giving thought to others, it is almost impossible to neglect them when modeling after the narrative arc. To do the latter, we are forced to think about our audience and the tension relevant to them. We'll talk further about this when we discuss tension in the context of planning your own presentation.

Something perhaps less obvious is that it's easy to treat the various topics or sections of content in the linear path as discrete and disconnected. The shift from one piece to the following can be abrupt. The narrative arc, on the other hand, forces connectedness. There is something about the shape that causes us to think about how we transition from one topic to the next in a way that the linear path doesn't invite. When we organize ideas using the arc as our guide, each component brings the story naturally forward. Things flow better when we plan content this way.

Freytag's Pyramid

An older dramatic structure is likely the predecessor to the modern-day narrative arc. Nineteenth-century German novelist and playwright Gustav Freytag expanded on Aristotle's three acts, outlining a five-part model for successful storytelling. Commonly known as Freytag's Pyramid, it has similar components to the narrative arc but is usually illustrated in a more angular form (depicted in Figure 4.4).

While the pyramid has basically the same pieces as the arc, different words are typically used to describe them. *Exposition* feels more robust than plot. The middle three sections are commonly expressed using similar language to what we saw with the narrative arc. I am partial to the French *denouement* (believed to be introduced post-Freytag), which suggests an unraveling of complexities (literally, "untying the knot").

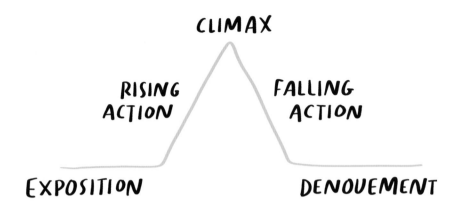

FIGURE 4.4 Freytag's Pyramid

Whether the simple plot-twist-ending or more elaborate narrative arc, these constructs are each simplifications of the full story. In the same way that the storyboard we created in Chapter 3 was a subset of the vast array of potential content that we brainstormed, our communication mapped against these structures will also be a curated path. They won't include every single detail. That version would look more like a jagged mountain.

Reality is a jagged mountain

Rather than a single smooth ascent and descent, the way things play out in reality is often more complicated. This is also true in the longer narratives of books and movies. There are ups and downs throughout that move the story forward, carrying us, entertained and engaged, from plot to ending. While the twist or climax might reflect the primary conflict or maximum point of tension, there are typically numerous other issues introduced and resolved over the course of the broader narrative. It is precisely because of all of these ups and downs that the story holds our attention, keeps us guessing, and provides points of satisfaction along the way.

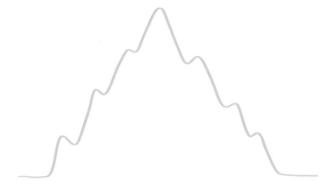

FIGURE 4.5 The jagged mountain

This jagged mountain could encapsulate every up and down over the course of a narrative—or, bringing this back to business, every oscillation through the duration of our project. While all of these ups and downs may be critical to keeping our attention over a 400-page book or two-hour movie, it's rare that you have this much time with or attention span from your audience in a work setting. Additionally, we don't necessarily need to convey the comprehensive story.

Different audiences will care about disparate levels of detail. The exec might only want the basic story or high-level arc. The finance partner will be interested in a completely distinct set of peaks, merging into a widely varying storyline or narrative, than what you would use to communicate to the marketing lead. A mixed group of stakeholders or conference attendees will require a separate combination of detail to suit their individual and shared goals. When we are the ones communicating, we generally must have a good sense of all or most of the peaks; from them, we should be able to identify and weave together the specific subset that will work for others. To say this another way: *you* are not telling *your* story—you are *forming a story for your audience.*

This seems like a good point to transition to the practical. We can use strategies extracted from story and the structures we've explored to communicate our work. Let's discuss that next.

Bringing story into business

Memorability, emotional appeal, and the ease with which we retell them are characteristics of story that we can tap into when communicating in a business setting. I have encountered many diverse circumstances for communicating, and I am hard-pressed to recall those that didn't benefit in some way from thinking about story. To fully consider story means reflecting on your audience and how they fit into that story so that it best resonates with them.

When you're initially beginning to incorporate components of story—particularly if this feels uncomfortable or countercultural at your organization—look for places where it is likely to work. Start there. There is too much risk to begin from a place of resistance. If it doesn't work, it could deflate your confidence, hurt your credibility, or discredit the method. None of these are good outcomes. They don't mean the approach can't be effective; they indicate that it didn't work in that situation, either due to the specifics of the scenario or the way it was executed.

When story can work...and when it may not

I'd characterize the ideal scenario for using story to communicate as follows. You want to lead people on a journey. You've done something—finished a project, become an expert on a topic, had a unique experience, conducted research, or completed an analysis—and are ready to take others through it to help them understand something in a new way, have a conversation, make a decision, or be inspired to make a change. Story is the path along which you can guide your audience to help make the action you seek transpire.

One instance where you might question the use of story is when it simply feels like too big of a leap from the way communication typically happens in your team or at your organization. If the status quo is to always present information in a certain manner, others may reject this departure from the norm. I once worked with an organization that had a required template for communicating project results. There were set components meant to be addressed in a specified order (roughly mirroring the scientific process: observation, research topic, hypothesis, experiment, analysis, and conclusion). The consensus of the group I was working with was that any change to this would be unacceptable to their stakeholders. That may indeed have been the case; those inside an organization will typically have the contextual knowledge to take into account and use to guide their decisions.

That said, if you aren't getting the attention or driving the action you seek in a situation like this, perhaps addressing things differently is exactly what is warranted. One way to form a bridge between what people expect and a new approach is to do both. Complete what is mandatory (for example, create the normal communication that follows the set template). Pair this with the new format and let others know that's what you are doing. You could say something like, "Today, I want to try something a little different. I've still provided the expected documentation, and I'm happy to walk you through it. But first, I want to spend a few minutes telling you the story of our project." Obviously, it takes careful consideration to determine when something like this will work and when it runs the risk of backfiring. Spend your time crafting stories for the situations where it will help, not hinder, you.

As you begin using components of story to communicate, another place to tread lightly is in high-stake scenarios. Let's say you have an upcoming presentation to make to your company's senior leadership. Please don't do what I've just suggested—this is not the best setting to start incorporating story. Instead, test it out first in lower risk spaces, where you have others' support or where you are otherwise more likely to be successful. This will boost your confidence and credibility. Over time and with success, positive momentum builds and you can harness it, becoming increasingly proficient in how you use story in higher risk settings.

When you've identified a suitable situation to use story to communicate, start by identifying the tension.

Identify the tension

Tension is a critical—and oft overlooked—component when we share information in a business setting. When I teach the lesson on story in our workshops, I tend to get quite dramatic in my delivery, particularly in the discussion about tension. This is to emphasize the point but shouldn't be taken as a call to create drama for our stories to be effective. It's not about making up tension. If there weren't tension present, we'd have nothing to communicate about in the first place. Rather, it's about figuring out what tension exists in a given situation and how we can illuminate it for others. When we do this well, we get their attention and are in a better position to motivate them to act.

Think back to some of the lessons covered in Chapter 1. I cannot emphasize enough the importance of getting to know our audience and what matters to them. It's easy to concentrate on what is meaningful to us, but that's not a good way to influence. We need to step outside of ourselves and think about what tension exists *for our audience*. This relates back to one of the Big Idea components that we discussed in Chapter 2: what is at stake? When we've effectively identified the climax of the scenario and related it to the stakes for our audience, then the action we want them to take resolves the tension we've brought to light in our story.

Identifying the tension is a useful undertaking even if you don't go full-blown story and use the narrative arc to structure your communication. In the planning process, step back and ask yourself: what is the tension in this instance? What is the thing-gone-wrong or the thing-that-could-go-wrong that others will care about?

What's the tension in this situation?

As we've discussed, tension is a key component of story. But what should you do if the tension isn't obvious? First, identify what is at stake for your audience. I outlined a strategy in Chapter 2 for playing things out to extremes. Revisit that to see if it helps clarify. Focusing on the gap between the current and desired state is another tactic to help define the tension. Also try jumping ahead to the action—what do you want people to do? The steps you wish them to take will resolve or ease an issue. Starting with the action can help you back into the identification of tension. If you're still having trouble articulating the tension, talk through the scenario with someone else—a colleague, manager, or stakeholder. The conversation may enlighten you. Don't give up if the tension isn't immediately obvious; keep working to identify it. This will become easier with practice.

Once you've identified the tension, it's time to return to your storyboard and arrange it along the narrative arc.

Arrange along the narrative arc

When you need to get and maintain the attention of others, a well-structured story can help you do it. As we've discussed, arranging your communication using the narrative arc as a model assists with memorability and gives your audience something to retell to others, helping them spread your message.

One noteworthy aspect of the narrative arc is its shape. However, the smooth, steep, and symmetrical rise and fall depicted won't necessarily be the exact structure of your business story. Allow yourself leeway (we see stories in everyday life veer from this path, too, through flashbacks, foreshadowing, and so on). Your story might be flatter; the climax may merely be a small bump.

The highest point of tension might not come in the middle of your presentation. You could lead with it or build up to it over a longer period of time. Your general plan should incorporate the pieces of the arc (especially tension, as I've detailed). More important than following the exact form when we think about applying story to business communications is that it has a shape, one you've planned taking into account the context of how, what, and to whom you'll be communicating.

At this point, I typically clear off working space on my desk (or if I'm traveling, I'll do this on or transfer it to a large piece of paper for portability). I secure a stack of stickies and write one for each primary component of the narrative arc: plot, rising action, climax, falling action, and resolution. I arrange these sticky notes in the shape of an arc, with some space around each so I have room to add multiple stickies if necessary.

FIGURE 4.6 My sticky note narrative arc

This is one of the reasons I love the stick of sticky notes: I can easily relocate them from their storyboard and arrange them along the narrative arc. This step helps me confirm that each element of story is present. Let's review the components of the arc, with some related thoughts and questions to use when rearranging your storyboard in this manner. The following is excerpted from my second book, *storytelling with data: let's practice!* (Wiley, 2019).

- **Plot:** What do others require in order to be in the right frame of mind for what you'll be asking of them? Identify the tacit knowledge you have about the situation that would be helpful to communicate directly to ensure people are working from the same set of assumptions or understanding.

- **Rising action:** What tension exists for your audience? How can you bring that to light and build it to an appropriate level given the circumstances for them?

- **Climax:** What is the maximum point of tension? Remember, the tension isn't for you—the tension is for your audience. Think back to the Big Idea and conveying what's at stake. What does your audience care about? How might you use that to get and maintain their attention?

- **Falling action:** This is perhaps the fuzziest of the components when it comes to application in a business setting. The main purpose is so that we don't go abruptly from the highest point of tension—the climax—to the ending. The falling action is a buffer to ease this transition. In our business stories, it may take the form of additional detail or further breakdown (e.g. here's how the tension plays out by business unit or region) or potential options you've weighed, solutions to employ, or discussion you'd like to facilitate.

- **Ending:** This is the resolution, the call to action. The ending is what your audience can do to resolve the tension that you've illuminated. Note that it isn't typically as simple as, "We found X; therefore, you should do Y." Our stories are often more nuanced than that. This ending could be a conversation you seek to drive, options to choose from, or perhaps even input you desire from others to fully flesh out your story. In any case, identify the action you want your audience to take and how to make it clear and compelling.

As I arrange my ideas along the arc, I frequently find myself reaching into my brainstorming pile from my storyboarding process and adding back (or forming new) ideas that will help me transition smoothly from one part of the arc to the next.

Sometimes, remapping my ideas in this manner means only slight changes to how I envisioned things in my storyboard. On other occasions, it's an entirely different path. In every case, I find that looking at what I'm planning through the lens of the narrative arc causes me to make some improvement over what I had previously. My hope in sharing my process is that it will help you to refine what you've planned for your presentations as well.

Once I've arranged my ideas along the arc, confirmed that each of the components are present, and perhaps made additional edits by adding or removing stickies, I step back and think about how it will work.

Using stories within a presentation

While I've outlined how to use the shape and components of story to structure your business presentations, there are also opportunities to use stories *within* a presentation.

I have incorporated personal and illustrative stories many times over the years, both on stage delivering keynote addresses and when teaching workshops. The specific stories I've told have run the gamut of topics: back-to-school shopping with my mom, a memorable childhood Christmas, my time working at Google, my son learning to read, and more. While the stories have been diverse, my motivation for telling them has been consistent. I use personal stories to share something about myself that others can relate to, engaging them on a deeper level. Each story is also meant to pique interest and illustrate or frame something important that I want people to remember.

Consider when you might tell a story to connect with others, illustrate a concept, make a point, build credibility, gain support, drive change, or inspire. To be successful integrating your own stories, look for ways to do so that will feel authentic to you. Map your intended story against the narrative arc. Determine which information to include or emphasize and which to leave out. Practice and get input from someone else. Use additional strategies outlined in Chapter 9 for refining through practice to ensure you tell your personal story masterfully.

As we've discussed, the narrative arc is a simplified schematic of the complete story. The full picture looks more like that jagged mountain we saw earlier. I'll use this opportunity to reinforce that you don't have to communicate ev-ery*thing* to every*one*. Get your specific audience and message in mind, and assess which points they have to know and what order will work best to convey your message and prompt the action you seek.

Once you're happy with the path you've outlined for your story, talk through it aloud. We'll discuss this strategy in the context of honing your delivery in Chapter 9, but for now think of it as a simple test to see whether the way you've arranged things creates a story that can be told. Make adjustments as necessary after completing this exercise.

After you have refined it on your own, discuss the story you've formed with someone else. As we saw with the Big Idea and storyboard, the process of explaining your strategy to another person is invaluable. Give an influential stakeholder visibility or seek input from a manager who can confirm whether you're on the right track. The conversation that ensues will almost always help you continue to polish your approach.

Now that we've explored how to apply story in general to structure our busi-ness communications, let's make use of it in a specific scenario.

Form a story: TRIX case study

We closed Chapter 3 with a storyboard showing one way to arrange the communication to my client team at Nosh. Let's take another look at that plan now and apply what we've learned in this chapter about story. Figure 4.7 shows the storyboard I created.

FIGURE 4.7 Storyboard for TRIX market research project

First, I clearly identify the tension. This scenario has tension at its core: the current mix of the popular TRIX trail mix isn't sustainable due to rising costs. That part of the tension is built into the context, the plot of my story, but it is distinct from the tension in the story I am communicating. What is the thing-gone-wrong that I can bring to light and use to prompt action among the client group at Nosh? The issue here is that there isn't a single clear fix—there were things we hoped would play out a certain way that didn't. The original mix was preferred overall. Yikes! That unwelcome news is going to get people's attention and appeal to something important to them.

I get a new stack of sticky notes and write the components of the narrative arc: plot, rising action, climax, falling action, and resolution. I remove individual stickies from my storyboard and arrange them along the arc that I've just created.

As I do so, I realize that I have cut out too much content in my simplified storyboard. In considering the arc, I'm reminded of my audience. It's our first time working with Nosh. I need to establish credibility in both our team and our methods. I must sufficiently impress them so that they want to continue to work with us.

In order to make that happen, this means some of the potential content I brainstormed and discarded originally may work its way back into my story. I have to find a good balance between the overarching story that will frame the discussion and ultimately drive my client team's decision with the detail that illustrates the robustness of our team's work. These goals feel at odds.

How should I move forward given this?

When I feel stuck—which I do here—there are a couple of strategies I typically try. First, I step back from the work and create some physical and temporal space to allow my perspective to develop. This could take the form of leaving my office and going for a walk or run. When I have the luxury of additional time, I turn my attention to other work, letting things ruminate in the back of my head until an idea sparks or I'm ready (or deadline constrained) to go back to it.

In this particular case, the sticky notes, in the form of a rough arc and also with a number of uncategorized ideas, sit on the unused side of my desk over the course of a few days. The entire time, ideas are brewing in my brain. I periodically visit the sticky notes: rearranging, adding, and taking away ideas. At one point, I am convinced that it should be a choose-your-own-adventure story, where I would begin by outlining the various streams of work that our team undertook and let the client team at Nosh dictate what direction to take. Upon further reflection, I realize this isn't a great idea. Given my familiarity with the project, our work, the data, and what we found, I am in a unique position to guide others through it. Putting them in control runs the risk of subverting my expertise and credibility. After discarding that idea, a useful one struck me. What if I *combine* my story arc with the linear path that outlines the full detail of all of the work the team undertook?

Another strategy I employ when I'm stuck or testing ideas is to discuss it with someone else. Doing this will often extricate me faster if I don't have additional time and have to push forward and meet deadlines. In this case, I vet my new idea with a colleague on the project team and then determine my plan. I'll start by telling the story of TRIX: what we learned through our in-depth research and analysis and the steps we believe should be taken. Then in the appendix, I will include the full detail of our work, organizing it in an easy-to-navigate fashion as evidence of the robustness of our undertaking. The latter is more than we might require for an ongoing client who already trusts our expertise and methodologies but makes sense given this specific scenario. This highlights what we should always aim to do—identify what success in the given situation looks like and plan an approach that is likely to bring it to fruition.

After deciding this, arranging the story along the arc becomes a quick exercise. I no longer felt the pressure to jam everything into the storyline, since we will also provide a comprehensive appendix. I identify the path I want to guide my audience on when I present our work and findings to them. See Figure 4.8.

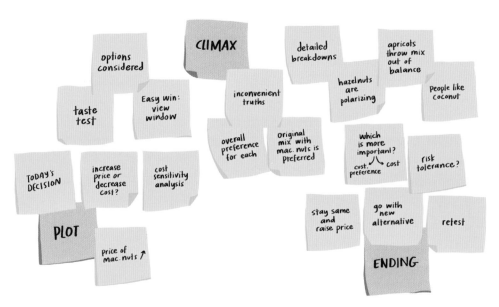

FIGURE 4.8 Narrative arc for TRIX market research project

Similar to what I'd originally planned in my storyboard, I'll start with the ending—the decision I want to frame for the group. Then I'll set the plot: a key ingredient's increasing price means the trail mix recipe needs to be changed. In the rising action, I'll introduce the studies we ran and the options we explored, culminating in the climax that reveals some inconvenient truths: the original mix is preferred, and there were clear issues with both alternatives tested. In the falling action, I'll reveal that not all hope is lost; there were some interesting and unexpected findings from our studies. This will bring me to the end, the resolution, where my stakeholders will weigh our recommendation along with some other options for deciding how to move forward.

This isn't a huge change from my original storyboard. However, forming my approach using the construct of story helped me think about things in a different way. It brought my audience clearly into the picture. It helped me figure out the right balance of detail given our goals. As a result of all of this, I have a better plan now than the one with which I started.

I want you to feel empowered to do this as well. Critically think about your audience—who they are and how to identify and meet their needs. Craft your message. Compile the pieces you will communicate in support of that message. Form the story, the path along which you will take people to build understanding and inspire them to act. You've fully considered what success looks like and how you can align all of the components we've addressed so far to put yourself in a winning position.

You now have your plan of attack—the story you will tell.

It's time to create the materials that will help you do it.

create

set the style & structure

You've thoughtfully planned your communication. Now, it's time to create the materials that will support you. This section focuses on content that will be organized into a slide deck, which I find is the most common form of business communication for meetings and presentations. For those communicating in different ways, many of the following strategies will be transferable to other scenarios; I encourage you to apply your thoughtful judgment.

I'm also working under the assumption that the content will be *presented*. You or someone else will talk through the materials you create. This could be in person or in a virtual setting, and we'll cover strategies to use in each of these situations. In either case, there is an important idea to keep in mind when developing the deck: **your slides are not what will do the communicating— you are.**

This runs counter to how we typically operate, aiming instead to make slides that stand on their own. That's a reasonable goal for material that we will disseminate. However, when creating content to present live, your slides are there to support you, not the other way around! Because of this, there are different design considerations for material that you will present. Think of your slides as a useful assistant. They can provide visual illustrations of concepts, aid you in explaining details, remind you of the next topic, or reinforce the ideas that you raise. But *you* are the one who will do most of the communicating. Your slides should augment you as the presenter.

When it comes to our slide decks, they may contain a combination of words, graphs, and images. These are the main types of content that we'll explore in this section (Chapters 6, 7, and 8, respectively). Before we do that, in this chapter we'll get super practical and set the foundational style and structure.

Set the style and structure first

It's time to open your presentation software. However, you *aren't* going to make slides quite yet. First, spend time actively setting the style and structure of your communication. While this might seem like a superfluous step, it is this action that will set the content you generate apart in positive ways and ensure the slides you create support the story you have planned.

When it comes to style, I'm referring to slide design, primarily: color, font, and layout. In the same way that we think about what experience we want to create for our audience in the context of story, keep this in mind when making stylistic decisions as well. Perhaps there is existing branding to incorporate, or you might want to start from scratch. We'll discuss each of these situations and how, in either event, your design choices should be congruent with the subject matter and desired tone of your presentation.

Setting the structure, or framework, of the presentation allows us to bring the output from our low-tech planning process into our tools. This breaks the development of our materials into manageable chunks so we can optimize our content creation time. When working in a team, doing this step up front helps get everyone on the same page and imparts an understanding of how individual pieces will be woven into the overall presentation. This lends visible harmony to the communication.

In this chapter, I'll share the pragmatic, three-step approach that I use and teach for setting the design and framework for your presentation:

1. Determine the style;
2. Make the slide master; and
3. Set the structure.

Let's begin with step one.

Determine the style

Color, font, and layout: these design aspects come together to create the overall look and feel of your materials. In some cases, these decisions have already been made for you. In other instances, you'll make your own choices. There are pros and cons to each of these scenarios.

Brand-driven style

Your company or organization may have already spent time establishing and defining their brand. This likely translates into designated colors and specific fonts that are suggested or required. It's possible a style guide exists that outlines these and other particulars, like proper use of your company logo. There might even be a pre-designed template for your presentation software with set colors, fonts, and layouts.

If this exists, use it.

While some balk at the idea of using branded templates due to the perceived constraints they impose, I suggest reframing. Using something that already exists is an easier starting point (particularly if you aren't a designer). This will make your process more efficient because there are far fewer decisions to consider. Standard templates also lend professionalism and consistency.

Conference slide templates

Large-scale conferences often provide speakers with presentation templates. In spite of this, when I prepare slides for a keynote address, I typically *don't* follow my own advice to use the provided template. This is because first and foremost I want to represent myself, my company, and my topic when I am speaking and not the conference. I understand organizers' desire to bring consistency to the various sessions and promote their brand. To meet my goals while also satisfying those of the organizers, I'll begin and end with the provided title and closing slides. Then I design my own slide template for my presentation (including my own title slide to transition into my content), in some cases tying in colors or fonts from the conference version so they feel cohesive. To see this in action, check out my 2019 Tableau Conference presentation, *low-tech super powers for data storytelling* (storytellingwithyou.com/superpowers).

The exception would be if the standard template really is awful. When people complain about presentation templates, the top gripes voiced have to do with color and visual distractions. Personally, I don't buy the our-brand-colors-are-horrible argument. This is perhaps true if you use multiple colors together, but thoughtful integration of black and gray to augment a single brand color will almost always alleviate this issue and is generally accepted, even given a required color palette. I'll show examples of this in forthcoming chapters.

Harder to overcome is when the slide template is already visually busy before you've added any content to it. This could be due to a vibrant background color or pattern, added embellishments, or a prominent logo. If you have to use something with a challenge like this, it means you have to be even more careful about what you add to the slide and generally put fewer elements than you would otherwise. You'll also have to be thoughtful to create sufficient visual contrast to direct attention without completely overwhelming your audience.

If you find yourself fighting with the existing slide template, look for avenues to delicately provide feedback to those requiring or creating it. Alternatively, you may have leeway to make minor changes directly.

Practice designing in style

As we've discussed, there are benefits to integrating branding into your visual communications. However, eloquently incorporating these elements into your slides takes practice. Here's an opportunity to practice in a low-risk manner through an exercise excerpted from my second book, *storytelling with data: let's practice!*

Identify two recognizable brands. You might choose company brands or sports teams, for instance. It will be more fun and increase the learning potential if you pick two that are quite different from each other in terms of style. Research images related to the brand and list ten adjectives that describe the look and feel of each.

Next, select a slide you've created. Remake it twice, incorporating components of each of your chosen brands, respectively. After you've finished, compare the two iterations. How does each feel? Were you successful in bringing the adjectives you outlined to life? How would you generalize brand components to take into account when communicating? What are the benefits of doing so? Are there scenarios where it *doesn't* make sense to be consistent with branding?

In the event that multiple presentation templates are available to you, I suggest opting for the simplest. The emptier your starting point, the more flexibility you'll have when it comes to adding content to each slide. If no standard template exists, consider making one.

Let's discuss one of the first steps in that process.

Setting your own style: color

When you start from scratch, there are more decisions to make. This can be a fun but overwhelming process, particularly for those who aren't confident in their design ability. I *don't* recommend using the preset templates in your presentation software. They tend to be busy and use questionable color and font combinations.

Instead, start simple and find something from which to take inspiration. When I'm setting a new style for a slide deck, the first choice I'll often make is color. There are a number of online resources that can help with this. Adobe offers color combinations based on current trends and tools to build your own color palette at color.adobe.com. Google, as part of their Arts & Culture Experiments, provides palettes based on thousands of artworks at artsexper-iments.withgoogle.com/artpalette. The US National Park Service circulates park-inspired color palettes on Twitter and Instagram tagged with #NPScol-orforecasting. This is merely a sampling of resources for generating color schemes. There are also numerous online color palette generators that will extract colors from pretty much anything. For example, at degraeve.com/color-palette you can upload the URL of any image (a stock photo, a picture of your favorite shirt...the possibilities are endless!).

When selecting colors, keep your purpose in mind. Are you creating a tem-plate that will be the new standard across your company or team? If so, the color combination should work with the established logo and brand and be adaptable enough to meet multiple needs. On the other hand, if you are designing a bespoke presentation, choose colors that relate to the topic or match the mood or perceptions you wish to impart.

People are inclined to feel certain ways when elements of our visual com-munications are rendered in particular hues. Figure 5.1 shows common color associations held in the United States.

serious distinctive elegant bold powerful sophisticated expensive night death conservative classic responsible dull somberness authority neutral logical rich practical reserved trust authority dignity security confident classic stability trust calming patient cool water contentment trusting serene sophisticated water coolness healthy fertile freshness environmentally conscious nature reliable appetite calm soothing refreshing young youth friendly positive feelings sunshine surprise cowardice energetic caution fun cheeriness sunset exuberance spontaneous optimistic speed history autumn earthiness richness tradition conservative earthy wholesome delicious rich rustic warm natural rich refined tasty expensive luxurious aggression passion sexy strength powerful assertive vitality fear speed danger exciting playful tropical flirtatious romantic sweet tasting femininity innocence softness youthful sophistication mysterious spirituality dramatic wealth royalty youth creative romantic sentimental nostalgic

FIGURE 5.1 Common US color associations

Many color associations vary by region (for an overview, check out the "Colours in Culture" visualization by David McCandless at informationisbeautiful.net). Take into account how all of this plays into the colors you set in your template or that you select for a given communication.

Also include a sufficient variety of hues and intensities so you have options to make things visually distinct. I recommend incorporating black and a range of grays. These will provide options for using single-color emphasis as well as de-emphasizing select visual elements in your slides. We'll revisit these strategies in the context of visual hierarchy and look at specific instances in Chapters 6 and 7.

Establishing the *storytelling with data* style

I created the *storytelling with data* company brand in 2010. It began with a simple blue text title on my blog. Both color and font were extracted from Microsoft Excel's standard options, where I made all my graphs. When I decided I needed a logo, I made it myself, integrating a bar chart into the words and updating the font from Arial to Avenir to match my first book. In time, we also shifted from the basic blue to a bolder, brighter version.

While the logo has gradually changed over time, the adjectives I'd use to describe our brand remain steadfast: *approachable, accessible, clean, clear, consistent, encouraging, friendly, human, polished, quality, simple, thoughtful, trusted,* and *welcoming.* These guide both how we act and how we communicate visually. We have set slide templates that are used for our workshops and often play with fresh presentation designs for new content. The TRIX case study design that I walk you through in this chapter is an archetype of the latter.

FIGURE 5.2 The *storytelling with data* logo

Once you've selected your color palette, add the colors directly to your slide-ware application. You can watch a video tutorial where I walk you through how to do this at storytellingwithyou.com/slidecolors.

Setting your own style: font

There is an entire field that focuses on the design of printed materials called **typography**. Fonts are an important component. I am by no means an expert on this topic (nor am I on color; the advice I share is based on my practical use of these design aspects). Most typographers would shudder at the fact that I employed the commonly used Arial font for as long as I did! I believe this is another facet of communication—like many others we've covered—where it makes sense to start simple and, if needed, get more nuanced over time.

Learn more about typography

Font, or typeface, also invokes feeling, albeit typically to a lesser degree than color unless it's something especially stylized like *script* or **PERMANENT MARKER**. A common early decision when choosing a font is whether to opt for a serif (with a decorative stroke that extends off the end of a letterform, such as Times New Roman) or sans serif variety (the more minimalist Avenir font that this book is set in is a sans serif typeface).

There are three main ways to obtain fonts: system fonts, free fonts, and professional fonts. System fonts are the ones available on your computer (Arial, mentioned previously, is a prime example of this). You can download free fonts at no cost from fonts.google.com. Professional fonts are those you must pay to use.

An excellent resource and entertaining read if you'd like to learn more about typography is *Butterick's Practical Typography* (practicaltypography.com).

When it comes to font in business communications, I am an advocate of prioritizing legibility above all else. I recommend selecting a simple typeface and ensuring the text is sized so that it is easy to read. I tend to prefer sans serif fonts due to their clean look. I opt for font families that have a markedly distinct bold option to use for sparing word or phrase emphasis. I don't tend to mix different font families, but I have done this on occasion (my second book, *storytelling with data: let's practice!,* was printed in a mix of Avenir and a bespoke handwritten font to promote a less formal feel).

If I'm going to share the slides I create or if they'll be projected from someone else's computer, I'll select a system font (one that is pre-installed). When slides are viewed from another computer and a special font hasn't been downloaded, a system font will be automatically substituted. This both means the design will differ from what was intended and other formatting problems may arise since fonts vary in size. To avoid these issues, save the file as a read-only PDF before sharing or opt for a system font if the deck will be presented. In cases where your slides will only be viewed from your own computer, you have more options.

I have a hard time choosing fonts without seeing slides formatted in them. If I plan to use a new one, I often postpone my selection until I'm actively creating slides in order to compare different options side by side. I'll outline the process I go through for the TRIX case study later in this chapter.

Make the slide master

At this point, if you have a company or team presentation template, make use of that and skip this step; move ahead to the *Set the structure* section later in this chapter.

If you don't have a standard template or you have decided to create something new, it's worth investing the time to make a slide master. The slide master stores information about the theme and slide layouts of a presentation.

This is where you input your chosen colors and fonts and also make decisions about the general layout of the slides. When designed well, the slide master helps bring a cohesive feel to presentations and makes individual slides faster to create.

Presentation tools

The most common slide applications that I encounter in a business setting are PowerPoint, Keynote, and Google Slides. No tool is inherently good or evil; how you use the product and present the materials you create with them determines whether your communication will be effective. My general advice is to get to know your chosen slideware so it doesn't constrain what you are able to do. If you encounter challenges, a good Google search will usually bring up numerous resources to help guide you.

I'll walk you through the process that I use to make a new slide master for a presentation. While my instructions refer to PowerPoint (the presentation software with which I am most familiar), you can apply a similar approach in any slide application.

Start with a blank slate

I begin by opening PowerPoint and creating a new presentation. Then I view the slide master and undo everything that is there. First, I delete all of the provided layouts (save those that Microsoft won't let me remove—the first two, which are the upper-leftmost Theme Slide and the Title Slide that immediately follows it). Then I delete each of the individual placeholders (for titles, bullets, date, page number, etc.) from the remaining two slides.

Why go through this work? I don't want layouts that have been designed by someone else that are meant to meet the basic requirements of many scenarios. Rather, I want to thoughtfully design slide layouts that will meet *my exact* needs for *my specific* situation.

After deleting everything that is there, I am left with two empty master slides: a blank slate. Next, I design these layouts and add the additional ones to meet my objectives. Together, these will become the template that I will use to create my slide deck.

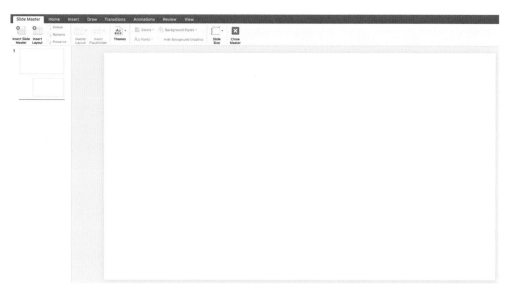

FIGURE 5.3 My blank slide master in PowerPoint

The upper-leftmost white rectangle in Figure 5.3 is where I'll set the overarching theme. Each element that is added to this slide (whether a static element or placeholder; I'll walk through that distinction momentarily) will show up on every other layout in the given theme. When we want to depart from this, we can cover up individual pieces as necessary. This will make more sense in the context of an actual example, so let's build a slide master, starting with that top theme slide.

Design the theme slide and content slides

Let's assume I'm preparing to give a presentation on behalf of my company, *storytelling with data*. This means a number of design decisions have already been made. I use the SWD color palette, which includes the bright blue from our logo and a number of complementary hues. I'll stick with the Avenir font family, the typeface you are reading now (a free font that I already have installed on my computer).

I'll keep things simple. On my theme slide, I'll introduce a placeholder for the title at the top left. I'll format the color to be blue and select Avenir Medium for the font. On the bottom right, I'll add an icon version of my company's logo.

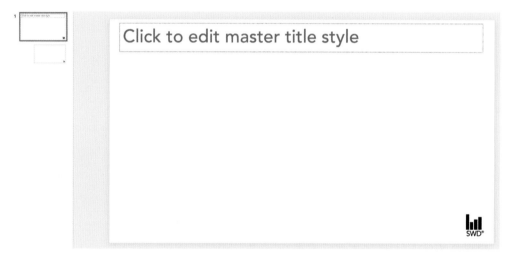

FIGURE 5.4 Slide master theme slide

Now I have my theme slide set. When I insert a new content layout, it will look exactly like this. If I want this exact formatting every time a new slide is created, I can add a single new layout and stop there.

If I'd like some different set formatting options from which to choose, I will add additional layouts and make the desired modifications to each. For example, I could include an option that has black title text instead of blue. Perhaps on occasion, I'll want a version that *doesn't have* the black SWD logo: I can place a white rectangle over this element on the given layout slide to achieve this. Figure 5.5 shows my master slide view after I've added a layout that mirrors my theme slide and the two slide variations I've just described.

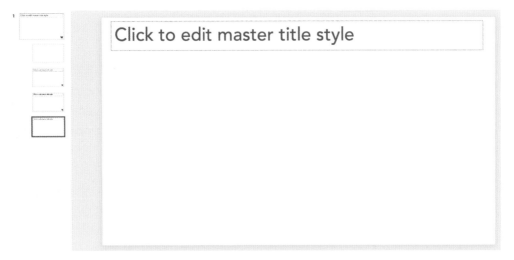

FIGURE 5.5 Slide master with various content slides

Notice that the second-from-the-top slide is still blank. This is my title slide. Let's design it, plus some divider slides, next.

Design title and divider slides

What comes first in a presentation deck? The title slide. If we think ahead to our delivery of the materials, it's possible that this initial slide will be visible for some amount of time—projected onto a screen as people walk into the meeting room, log on to a virtual meeting, or take their seats at a conference. As a result of this, often it's our title slide that makes the first impression on our audience. Use it to set the stage visually for what's coming.

The title slide is where I first introduce my selected colors, font, possibly a logo or image, and other stylistic choices. I will use it to set expectations for the topic of my communication as well, an approach we'll review when we discuss use of words in Chapter 6.

In practical terms, within the slide master, I'll navigate to the title slide (which appears second, following the theme slide), insert a title element, and position the placeholder where I want it. I'll increase the size of the text and set the color and font to match my general style. If desired, I'll add a subtitle placeholder as well and format it to work with the rest of the design.

At this point, I'll typically also add divider slides. These can be used to emphasize a point or to visually demarcate the sections within my presentation. I like to have them in a variety of colors that work with my general theme. To achieve this, I'll add additional layouts and format the background in my desired colors (in this case, blue, orange, and teal). I'll also add title placeholders, then format and position them. I didn't love the contrast of black on color, so I reformatted both title placeholders and logo to be white for my divider slides. I'll add a plain black and a plain white layout (formatting the background to the desired color and covering the black logo on the white slide with a white rectangle), because I find I use these frequently.

Figure 5.6 shows my slide master after making all of these changes.

FIGURE 5.6 My new master slide template

I also renamed the theme and individual layouts. Now, when I exit the slide master and insert a new slide into my presentation, I choose which of my preset layouts to follow from my new theme, as shown in Figure 5.7.

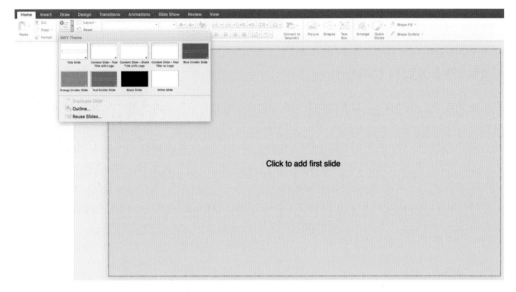

FIGURE 5.7 Select a layout from the new theme

While I've outlined this as a linear progression—creating one type of layout and then the next until you have a complete template—in reality, it's often an iterative process. I'll create my slide master and then make adjustments to those layouts as I start to build out actual content and see how it looks in my various set formats.

Your process and layouts may look different from mine, and that is totally fine! I share these specifics from my approach simply in case they are useful. One quirk of my process is that I tend not to create any layouts that have set content placeholders (bulleted text or a placeholder for graphs and images, to name a couple) because I like to position elements on each slide individually. That said, there are likely consistency and efficiency gains to be had, particularly if multiple people across your team or organization are using the template, and especially if different individuals will be contributing slides to a single presentation. Design it all in a way that makes sense to you and works for your situation.

Once you've developed your slide master, it's time to set the structure of your presentation.

Set the structure

I'm a big advocate of building the skeleton for a presentation before adding content to individual slides. You already have the bones for this from the story-boarding and story formation processes that we discussed in Chapters 3 and 4. Now is the time to start to realize it in your presentation software. Setting up the structure after you've created your slide master but *before* putting content on your slides helps keep your attention on the overall flow. This way you don't get distracted when it is time to start fully fleshing out your content.

Title your slides

With your storyboard or narrative arc handy, create a new presentation using a provided template or the one you designed. Add a title slide. We'll discuss effective titling in Chapter 6 when we explore using words well, but for now title it with the topic. Add a content slide. Refer to your plan, and add what you've written on the first sticky note as the slide title. Fight the urge to add *anything else* to the slide at this point—this process of setting up the structure first allows you to continue to vet the overall approach through a different lens. If there's detail you feel you absolutely have to capture (for example, if a thought related to an individual slide strikes you and you don't want to lose it), add it to the slide notes of the given slide. Then you'll have it as reference once you do start to build content. Continue this process until you've transferred all the ideas from your curated sticky notes (or whatever method you used) into your presentation software. I'll share some examples later in the chapter.

Takeaway titles and horizontal logic

I am a big advocate of takeaway titles. We'll talk more about this concept in Chapter 6 (and look at a variety of examples), but here's a teaser to prompt you to think about it as you add initial titles to your slides. Identify the main point you wish to make on a given slide. Articulate it in a sentence. Work to make it more concise—aim for simple and direct. Once you've arrived at something that is clear and pithy, title your slide with it.

Transferring ideas from storyboard or story arc to slides makes this process easier given that you likely already framed the pieces of your narrative in a way that answers the question, "So what?" Continue to do this when you transition from stickies to slides, forming titles that don't set up the *what* (descriptive title) but rather the *why* (takeaway title) for the given content. When you read through only the titles of your deck, together they should convey your overarching story. This is called horizontal logic.

After completing this process, go back to the beginning of your deck. Flip through, reading the slide titles that you've just added. Does it accurately reflect what you want to communicate?

If you answered yes and have a short communication with a simple story arc, jump ahead and start to build content on the individual slides. In a longer presentation—and in particular if there are various facets to the story you want to tell—it may be worth creating and integrating a navigation scheme.

Create a navigation scheme

Like the table of contents in a book, a navigation scheme sets the structure of your presentation so others know what to expect and in what general order. Presentation creators often overlook this basic and important step. When you are creating a communication, you know it well, so it's easy to jump straight in. But your audience is never as close to your work as you are. Letting them know the general plan up front helps ground their expectations in helpful ways. As an added benefit, it keeps you, the presenter, on track both as you create and deliver the content as well.

In addition to setting the stage for what's coming, a navigation scheme employed well will also help orient people in the midst of content. When making use of one, I advocate introducing it somewhere close to the beginning. Then return to it as you transition from one section or topic to the next. In this manner, you can make it clear to others where you are in the presentation as it relates to both where you've been and where you're going.

Let's get more concrete. Presume that you're preparing a communication to present the results of a supplier analysis you've undertaken. You've plotted your story arc and divided the content into five sections. You could use a simple slide with numbers and text to introduce these topics. See Figure 5.8.

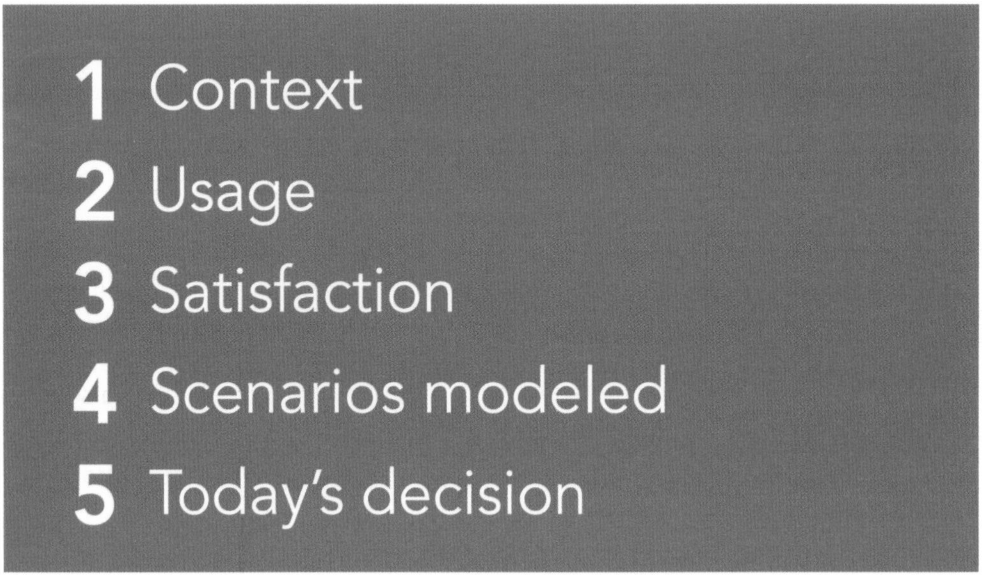

1 Context
2 Usage
3 Satisfaction
4 Scenarios modeled
5 Today's decision

FIGURE 5.8 Navigation scheme from supplier analysis presentation

After talking through the particulars of section one with the various slides you will have built to assist you, you would repeat this slide, with some minor formatting adjustments that draw attention to the following topic. See Figure 5.9.

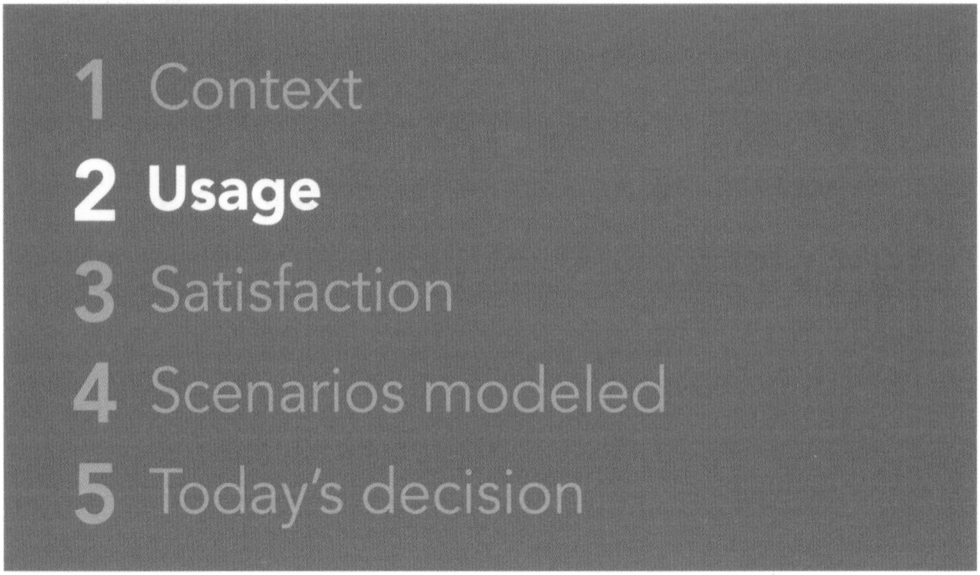

1 Context
2 Usage
3 Satisfaction
4 Scenarios modeled
5 Today's decision

FIGURE 5.9 Transition into section 2

You'd follow a similar process to transition from each section to the next as you progress through your content.

The specific look and feel of your navigation scheme will vary by situation. For a business presentation, the slide you use as your navigation scheme might be simple numbers or text, as we've just seen. For a conference session, you likely have more leeway to be creative, perhaps integrating images or other visual stimuli. In the Tableau Conference presentation mentioned earlier in this chapter, I kicked things off with a story about my kids (made relevant to what I planned to cover in the session). I used images of them on a slide to introduce three lessons, then revisited this slide when I transitioned from one lesson to another. Figure 5.10 shows the navigation scheme that I introduced after my story to set up the three sections.

FIGURE 5.10 Navigation scheme from my Tableau conference presentation

After introducing the lessons briefly, I focused attention visually on the first one—Super Writer—to transition into the details.

FIGURE 5.11 Transition into first lesson

After the slides in this first lesson, I repeated the original slide, this time with attention drawn to the middle panel introducing the second lesson we learned from the Curious Cat. We'll look at this particular example again momentarily, where you'll be able to see this progression.

Whether simple or more creative, I recommend making your navigation scheme aesthetically distinct from the body of your communication. This acts as a visual cue to your audience (and you) that something is changing. Use one or more of the divider slides you designed in your slide master for this.

Vet the flow in slide sorter view

Whether using a navigation scheme or not, viewing your presentation framework in slide sorter view—where you see all the slides at once as small thumbnails—will give you yet another lens through which to see your planned content.

I recommend doing this after adding slide titles and then, if using one, again after incorporating your navigation scheme. When you've used a visibly distinct layout (a slide with colored background or images, as we just reviewed), this allows you to see chunks of planned content at a glance. Assess relative order and see whether the length of each section feels balanced for what you need to get across and how you want to spend your time.

Figure 5.12 shows an early slide sorter view for my Tableau Conference presentation.

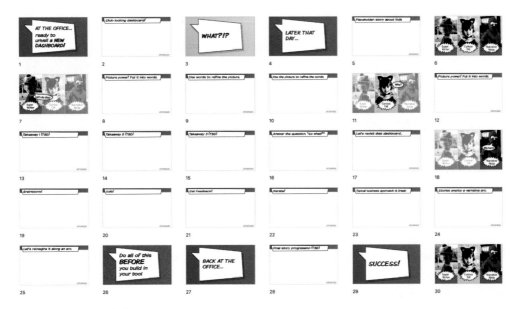

FIGURE 5.12   Slide sorter view

My initial framework was a combination of divider slides (those with colored backgrounds and cartoon-like text), my navigation scheme (the repeated image with my kids, with respective emphasis), and blank slides with only titles or placeholder titles for planned content. A number of these placeholder slides turned into longer progressions—my final slide deck was 174 slides! Building this structure up front helped ensure that it all came together in a way that made sense.

Seeing and talking through your presentation outline in slide sorter view helps you continue to assess your approach. This is another excellent place to seek input and refine. Confirm you are on track before you start building individual slide content. We will turn our attention there soon.

Before we do, let's look at one more example.

Set the style & structure: TRIX case study

Now that you've read an overview of my process, let's see how it plays out step by step in the case study we've been working our way through.

My first step is to determine the style. I start completely from scratch. To anonymize this example for use here, I invented the TRIX brand (a step to ensure that the original company, product, and team remain undisclosed). I'm pulling back the curtains on this piece to detail my inspiration for the colors: an image of Arches' famous red rock formations in Moab, Utah, shared as part of the National Park Service's #NPScolorforecasting. (You may recognize this color scheme—I liked it so much that it influenced the design of this book!)

FIGURE 5.13 Color inspiration from #NPScolorforecasting

Figure 5.14 shows the logo I created based on the color palette I pulled from the image. I even took inspiration from the way the color palette is shown in the original image, integrating multi-colored rectangles into my logo!

FIGURE 5.14 Logo created using Arches image colors

I program the brand colors into PowerPoint for easy use (like I did in the instructional video mentioned earlier in the chapter). While I used a bold font for the logo, I know I want something easier to read and with more options for creating contrast in the main typeface of my presentation. I save that decision to make for when I create my slide template so I can compare different options side by side.

In the slide sorter view in PowerPoint, I delete all of the preset formats and start with a blank slate. First, I design the title slide. I play with different placements of the logo and various background colors. In the end, I opt for a mostly white slide, with a large blue rectangle for my title and subtitle. See Figure 5.15.

Click to edit master title style

Click to edit master subtitle style

FIGURE 5.15 Title slide

Next, I try various font options. I consult *Practical Typography*. I want a system font so I don't encounter issues if the deck is shared. Author Matthew Butterick isn't a fan of system fonts due to their overuse; however, he does indicate a handful that are "generally tolerable." I add text to my slide title and quickly test out each of the 21 typefaces on the tolerable list, saving a copy of the ones I like the most.

Book Antiqua

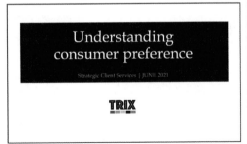

Gill Sans MT

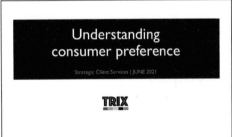

Helvetica Neue

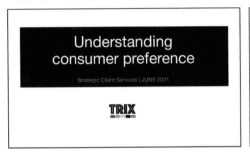

Optima

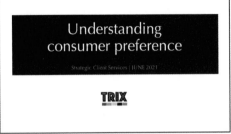

FIGURE 5.16 Comparing fonts

I narrow my options down to a single serif font (Book Antiqua) and three sans serif fonts. I'm after something that feels fun but professional that will stand out against my strong color palette. The serifs of Book Antiqua feel too formal. Helvetica Neue is quite similar to Arial, which I've used a lot in the past. I want to go in a different direction. The thinness of Optima means there's less contrast of white text on a dark background, which I don't love. By process of elimination, I choose Gill Sans MT.

After setting my title slide and deciding on a font, I design the content slide. I am a fan of a prominent title space at the top of each slide. This can be used to highlight the primary takeaway. I add a placeholder for this title text and leave the rest of the slide blank, save a small logo at the bottom right. My audience in the Western part of the world is conditioned to start at the top left of my page or screen and move their eyes in a zigzagging "z" shape. This means the bottom right of my slide is the last place they'll look—the perfect spot for a logo to remind them of the brand without it being a distraction from the other elements that I'll add to each slide.

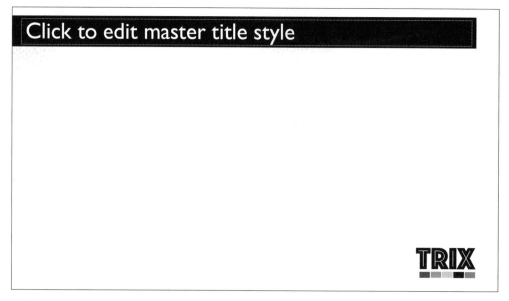

FIGURE 5.17 Content slide

I begin the dark blue title bar at the far left of the page. This is to grab your attention and draw it rightwards to the title. Rather than continue the title bar across the entire slide, I stop it short, leaving some white space on the right.

I right align the TRIX logo at the bottom in this same spot. This leaves me a natural margin on the right-hand side of each slide. I'll leave the areas on the right and to the left of the title text and below the bottom of the logo free of elements when I design my actual slides. A clean margin around each will ensure there's enough whitespace for the slides to breathe.

I design my divider slides. These are simple full-color slides with basic text placeholders. I create one in each of the Arches theme colors. Figure 5.18 shows the dark blue version.

FIGURE 5.18 Divider slide

At the end of this process, I have a template that I name Arches Theme. It contains a title slide; content slide; section slides in bright blue, orange, yellow, dark blue, and turquoise; a plain white slide; and a plain black slide.

FIGURE 5.19 My new Arches Theme

Next, I start a new presentation using my Arches Theme and begin working on my navigation scheme.

You may recall an idea I had and abandoned as part of my low-tech planning process: a choose-your-own-adventure story. I still have this in my mind as I start playing with a navigation scheme. I want to be able to visually illustrate that we took a long and winding path—diving into numerous aspects, collecting and analyzing data thoroughly, to come up with our ultimate recommendation.

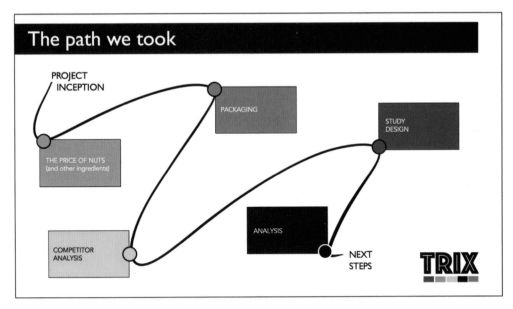

FIGURE 5.20 Initial navigation scheme

I create the slide shown in Figure 5.20. Still toying with the idea of building this full detail into my deck, I add divider slides for each of the sections shown in my navigation scheme, then add titled slides within each section. Figure 5.21 shows the slide sorter view after doing this.

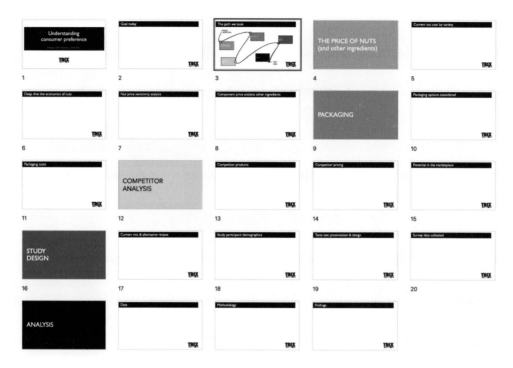

FIGURE 5.21 Initial slide sorter view

Seeing the content mapped out this way and turning back to my story arc, I realize that I've gone a little off track. Rather than go through all of this detail, I could use the slide I had initially planned for my navigation scheme to talk through at a high level the robust process we undertook. I'll let my audience know that the full detail is in the appendix (where I'll repeat the navigation scheme and use the color-coded divider slides to denote the respective sections), and that I will be happy to walk through any of that—*after* I tell them the TRIX story.

Turning back to my arc, I plot out the slides that will tell this story, shown in Figure 5.22.

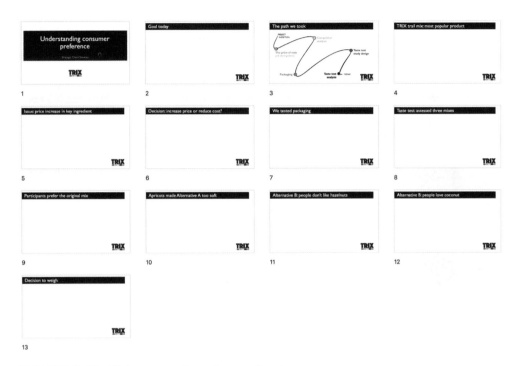

FIGURE 5.22 Slide sorter view of my refined story

I'll start by setting the context, sharing the goals for the project generally and for our meeting specifically. Then I'll use a variation of the visual path I created to discuss the numerous lines of work we undertook at a high level. The rest of my slides will tell the TRIX story. Here are the slide titles from slide four onward for easy reading:

- TRIX trail mix: most popular product
- Issue: price increase in key ingredient
- Decision: increase price or reduce cost?
- We tested packaging
- Taste test: assessed three mixes
- Participants prefer the original mix
- Apricots made Alternative A too soft
- Alternative B: people don't like hazelnuts
- Alternative B: people love coconut
- Decisions to weigh

Now with my slide style and structure slides in place, it's time. Let's begin creating the actual slide content.

We'll start with a basic—and important—element: words.

say it
with words

Words on slides play a critical role in our visual communications. They can pique interest, set expectations, illuminate, explain, and reinforce. Words can also overwhelm, complicate, irritate, and distract.

We all use words on a daily basis in our speaking and our writing. But the way to employ text in your presentations doesn't necessarily follow the conventions of these activities. Have you ever thought critically about how to best title a presentation? Or debated whether the number of words is too few or too many on a given slide?

Perhaps it's because words seem simple that many people don't give much thought to them. In a presentation setting, when we *don't* carefully examine how we use our words, they can easily work against us. Most of us have experienced a common abuse: the dreaded slide filled with bulleted text. We'll dissect why this technique doesn't work and introduce alternative strategies. There are more nuanced considerations when it comes to utilizing words wisely, too. Harnessing the power of words in our presentation materials is the focus of this chapter.

Let's begin by exploring how to use words to title our visual communications.

Words to title

You've surely set a presentation or slide title before. How did you approach it? For many, the tendency is to opt for a *descriptive* title—one that introduces the topic. There's nothing inherently wrong with this; however, I see it as a missed opportunity. We can use words in powerful ways to title our presentations and slides.

Foreshadow with your presentation title

Let's start at the beginning of your deck, with the title slide. Descriptive presentation titles would be things like "Supplier Analysis," "Competitive Landscape Update," or "Quarterly Business Review."

As we discussed in Chapter 5, the presentation title is the first thing others encounter in your communication. Use it to capture your audience's attention, foreshadow an interesting point you're going to discuss, or introduce something you want to prime others to ponder. Consider the following titles: "Changing our supplier strategy could reduce costs," "We are winning across the competitive landscape," or "(Mostly) strong results last quarter." How do they compare to the descriptive ones listed previously?

There are a couple important distinctions to note between the titles I just suggested and those introduced in the prior paragraph. Instead of topics, the revised titles are more complete thoughts. In some cases they are even full sentences. Related to this, while the original titles were written in title case (where the first letter of each word is capitalized), the modified iterations are in sentence case (the first letter of the first word is capitalized, and the rest are written in lower case). This is personal preference, but sound logic encourages that the title be a full idea and go beyond a simple topic. The reworked titles each foreshadow something about the forthcoming content. In some cases, the revised titles bring the audience (and presenter) into the picture, through use of words like "our" and "we," making things more personal and less abstract.

If moving entirely away from descriptive titles feels like too big of a leap, try a combined approach. Make your primary title descriptive but add a foreshadowing subtitle (or vice versa). Figure 6.1 shows what the title slides could look like for the series of titles I've introduced, as well as a bonus fourth example. The first one (upper left) has a descriptive main title and explanatory subtitle, while the others illustrate the opposite, emphasizing the more intriguing part but also keeping the descriptive title present to help set the context.

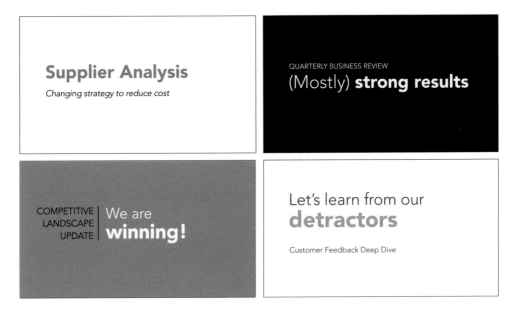

FIGURE 6.1 Business presentation title slides

The preceding examples are business-meeting-type titles. Imagine how the same shift from descriptive to more refined titling would work in a formal presentation setting, too. Instead of titling my conference keynote with the topic "Data Storytelling," I might use "Bringing data to life through pictures and story." This provides a peek into what I'll illustrate and how I'll inspire. View that actual presentation title slide, together with a few others I have used (including the Tableau Conference presentation referenced in Chapter 5), in Figure 6.2.

FIGURE 6.2 Conference presentation title slides

Whereas the business title slides simply featured text and perhaps a prominent color or two, there's often more freedom for creativity in conference presentation design. There are two noteworthy differences that I observe when
comparing and contrasting Figures 6.1 and 6.2. First, there is greater variety
in typeface. Whereas a business presentation likely leverages your company's
chosen font (mine do—those shown each use Avenir), there's more room to
play and try different styles in a conference setting, where eye-catching is
a reasonable goal. An additional distinction is the integration of pictures or
other visual elements into some of the conference presentation title slides.
Whereas I don't typically suggest this in an ordinary business meeting, this can
work well for materials delivered from stage. We'll talk more about the use of
images in each of these settings in Chapter 8.

Communicate the key takeaway with your slide title

Another important set of titles to think about is your slide titles. Similar to what
we have discussed with presentation titles, I find that people often default

to descriptive titles for their slides. More missed opportunities! If this is your habit, break it. Determine what you want others to remember about what you will say or show and title your slide with that. I refer to this as the **takeaway title**. It is helpful to start by articulating your main point in a single, complete sentence. Then shorten it as necessary, both to make it pithy and so it fits cleanly in the space. Avoid slide titles that extend onto multiple lines, which look messy and compete for attention with what you are saying.

Let's make this concrete through an example. Consider the descriptive slide title "Net Promoter Score." The Net Promoter Score, or NPS, is a common metric used in voice of customer analytics. The higher the NPS, the better. Imagine that I turn the primary idea I want to express on a given slide into the following sentence: "NPS has increased; however, when we dig deeper, we see an increasingly polarized customer base, with a higher proportion of both promoters and detractors than earlier in the year." While I might say those words, they would take up more room than I'd like at the top of my slide. I will adapt this into something punchier for my slide title, such as, "NPS up; however, customers are increasingly polarized." Or if I really want to emphasize the latter point, I could take things a step further, with something like, "Concern: increasingly polarized customer base." Then the fact that NPS has increased is something I can address as context but with clear emphasis on the area in need of attention.

A good takeaway title allows me to set people's expectations. As I illustrated with the NPS example, we can use a slide title to let others know how they should feel about the topic. You may also use the slide title to prompt the action you seek. Incorporate action words like *understand*, *discuss*, or *decide* to make it clear to your audience what exactly you want them to do. Priming with titles helps your audience get focused and act in the way that you desire. You'll see more of this in Chapter 7.

Let's revisit horizontal logic

Do you recall the concept of horizontal logic introduced in Chapter 5? We discussed it as a way to set the structure of your presentation. Now, with a better understanding of the takeaway title, is a great time to review it. We've discussed how important effective titling is for a given slide. When you've crafted a thoughtful narrative flow and employ takeaway titles on each slide, you can read only the slide titles of your presentation to get the overarching story. If you test this and it doesn't work, it may indicate where you are missing a piece or need transitional content or additional fine-tuning.

Now that we've covered thoughts related to presentation and slide titles, let's shift to some strategies for using text as primary slide content.

Words as content

Sometimes it feels like every slide we create should have a slick diagram, image, or graph. But words themselves can *be* content. Don't overlook the power of simple text.

One way to bring story structure directly into presentation design is to think of the slides we will create along the path of the story we plan to tell. As a reminder, Figure 6.3 shows the narrative arc (introduced in Chapter 4).

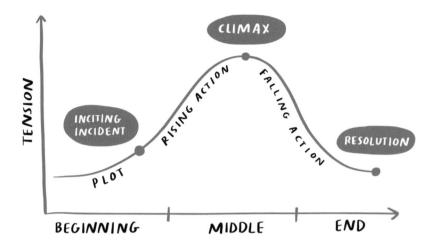

FIGURE 6.3 The narrative arc

Let's consider what text slides could look like along this path.

The story begins: plot slides

At the onset of our communication, there is often context to set. Perhaps you want to remind people where things left off when you last met, create common ground by bringing those who haven't been involved in the project up to speed, emphasize an important fact or stat, or simply let others know what you plan to talk about and why.

Words can help you do each of these things. That said, it is important to keep in mind that the majority of those words will be through what you *say*, not what you show.

Let's first look at a few examples of **sparing text**. When there are only a few words on a slide, those few words feel important. That's the power of blank space at play (the limited elements that *aren't* blank space stand out). When you have something critical to say, also putting *only* those words in text on their own slide both reinforces what you've said and helps ensure the important point isn't missed. Perhaps there is a notable number to highlight:

"Only 1 in 10 customers would recommend our service to their friends and family." Think of how that would feel if you underscore this context by making it the sole text on an otherwise blank slide.

Figure 6.4 shows a couple of iterations of what this could look like. Note the different design decisions made in each, and contemplate when and why you would choose one version over the other.

FIGURE 6.4 Sparing words on slides

As another example of sparse words on slides to set the stage, think back to the Big Idea that was introduced in Chapter 2. We discussed it primarily as a tool for you to become clear and concise on your message. However, once you've taken the time to form it, it may also make sense to communicate it directly to your audience. One way to do this is by devoting a slide to it.

Imagine that my Big Idea is: *We have an opportunity to achieve high patient satisfaction at a reasonable cost by shifting our supplier strategy.* Given this, I might create a slide like the following.

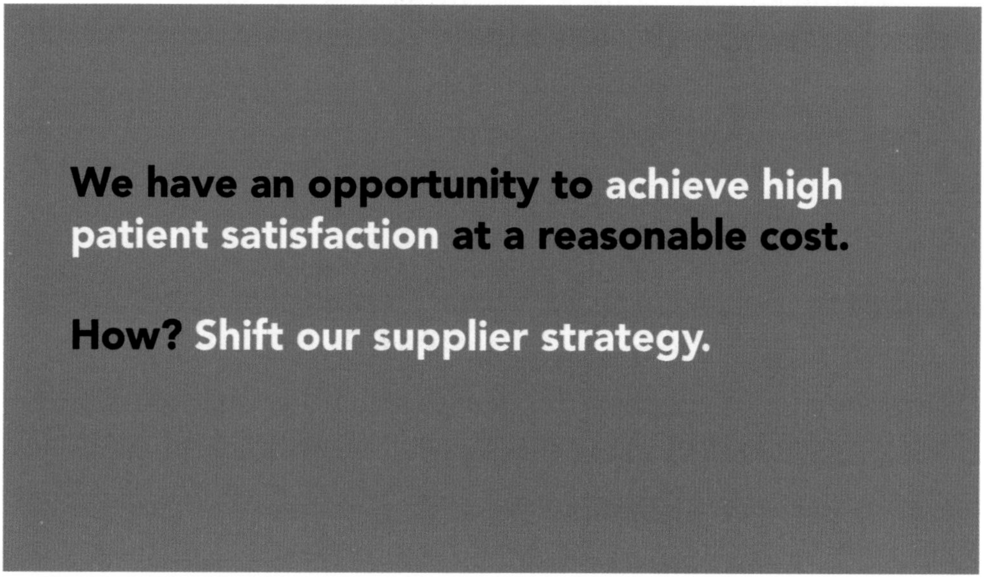

We have an opportunity to achieve high patient satisfaction at a reasonable cost.

How? Shift our supplier strategy.

FIGURE 6.5 Big Idea on a slide

Depending on how I want to approach it, I might begin with a slide that shows only the first sentence to set the context (the opportunity we face). Then I can decide whether to foreshadow where I'd like to drive the conversation or if it will make sense to build to it over the course of the overarching story. I often use my Big Idea as an introduction to the rest of my content before I return to it at the end. Using it up front helps set expectations. Returning to it after the full details have been revealed can drive robust discussions among stakeholders focused on the issue at hand or help them frame thoughtful questions. The repetition is also useful to reinforce the main point so that people are able to recall and repeat it more easily.

Create visual hierarchy on your slides

Thoughtfully establishing visual hierarchy on a slide means designing the information so that not all elements are treated equally. Highlight the most important aspects so they stand out and garner attention. This can be achieved through size, boldface, sparing color, or placement on the page. While you draw attention sparingly, also work to push less critical pieces to the background so that they are there for reference without distracting. In the case of text, this can be accomplished through use of gray, smaller size, and de-emphasizing placement at the bottom of the slide. This way of visually signaling to the audience how to process information helps denser content from overwhelming by making it scannable. We'll look at a number of instances of this with words in this chapter and in our data slides in Chapter 7.

We've seen a couple illustrations of sparing words on slides. But how should we approach it when there are more than a few words we'd like to share? People can't read and listen simultaneously. If they've started reading, it means they've stopped listening. You don't want to compete for attention. Does this mean we can't use more than a few words on a slide? No. It does mean we need to intentionally design and present—either formatting our slide to make it easily scannable, only showing some text at a time, or pausing to give others time to read. Let's look at an example.

Figure 6.6 shows a plot slide. It's intended to create a common understanding of the purpose of the meeting.

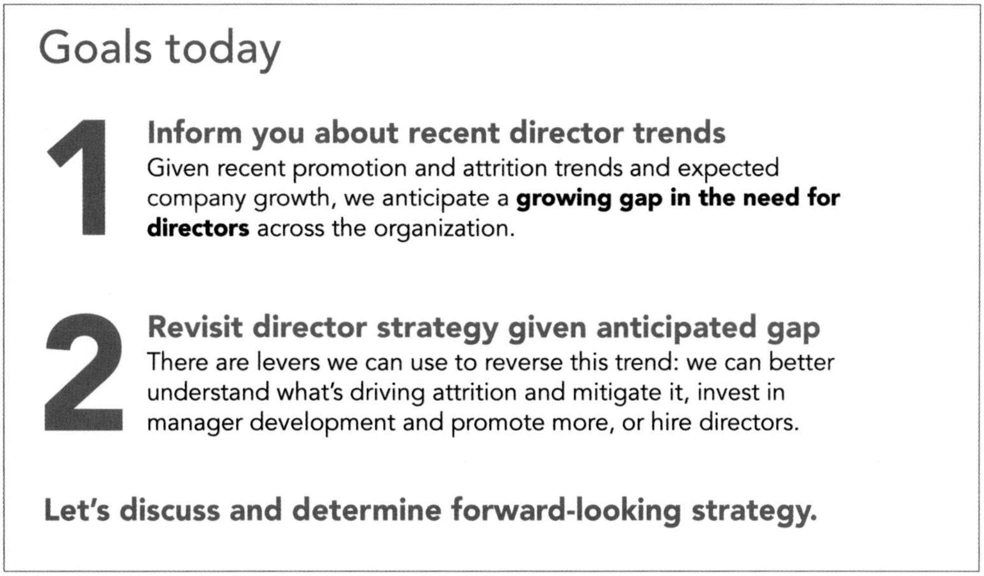

FIGURE 6.6 More words on a slide, formatted for easy scanning

A slide like Figure 6.6 could be used early in my presentation to introduce the general structure of my content and set clear expectations for what I hope to accomplish. There are many words on this slide—some might argue too many. However, I've taken careful steps to make the content scannable. People can quickly read just the colored and bold text to get the gist. Note that this approach does give me the ability to have additional context present, which is useful in the scenario where I'm worried I'll forget something important or if I'm preparing content that someone else will be presenting. You can also imagine a lighter version of this slide, where I remove most or all of the smaller black text (which would then become my planned speaking notes).

Don't use your slides as a teleprompter!

Perhaps the most common instance of words employed *ineffectively* in presentations is the dreaded slide filled with bulleted text. I'd venture to bet that anyone who makes presentations has created one of these slides (I know I have). Most of us have also experienced this as an audience member, and it is painful. That's because we read in our heads much faster than any presenter is able to read out loud. After we've scanned the text—not really listening since it's difficult to do that while we're reading—we tune back in to realize the presenter is still several bullets back. It's an invitation to turn our attention to something else!

If you find yourself making this type of teleprompter slide—whether for yourself or for someone else to present—stop. Determine for each bullet: what is the primary topic or main point? How could you state it in a pithy, or short and punchy, way? Put *that* on the slide and preserve the context by adding it to the speaker notes section below the slide. We'll look at a specific example in the case study at the close of this chapter.

We've looked at a few plot slides where the primary content is words. Let's examine what text slides look like once we get into the story.

The story continues: mid-story slides

While I find that most of the text slides I use are in the plot and ending of my presentations, there are definitely cases where mid-story slides have words as primary content, too. When this is the case, I typically employ one of three strategies: pause to let people read, reveal piece by piece, or selectively highlight. Let's look at each of these approaches.

Imagine there is a fantastic verbatim quote from one of our customers that we want to use to lend evidence to a point we're making. I could design a slide like Figure 6.7. Before turning to it, I would say something along the lines of, "I'm going to ask you to take a moment to read a comment we recently received from one of our customers."

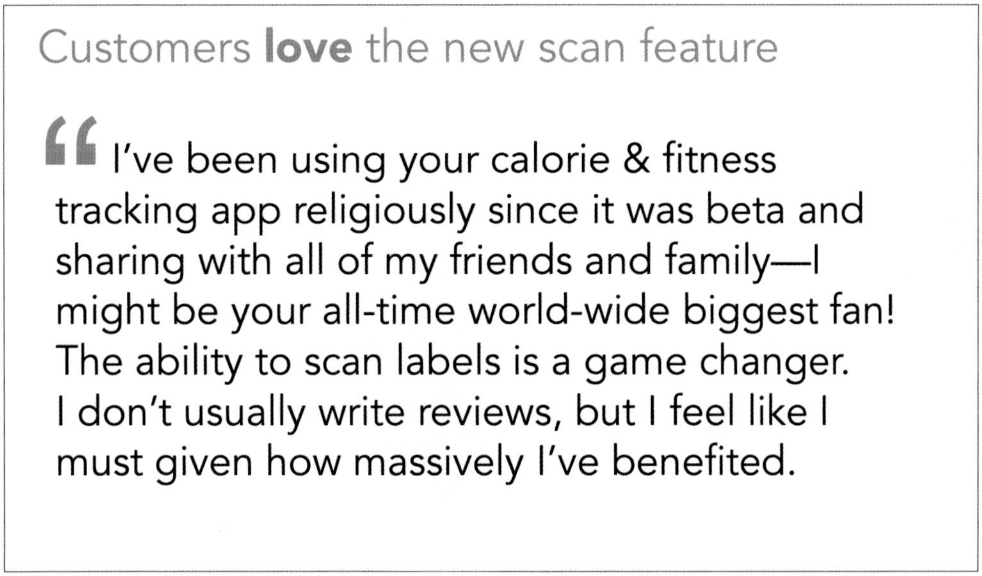

Customers **love** the new scan feature

❝ I've been using your calorie & fitness tracking app religiously since it was beta and sharing with all of my friends and family—I might be your all-time world-wide biggest fan! The ability to scan labels is a game changer. I don't usually write reviews, but I feel like I must given how massively I've benefited.

FIGURE 6.7 Take a moment to read this comment

I'd put up the slide and then pause to allow my audience time to process it. In an in-person session, you can gauge how long it takes others to read by watching them: note when eyes stop moving back and forth. Or if you don't have the benefit of seeing your audience, read the words yourself slowly in your head (more leisurely than you think is required—you can easily scan your words because you are familiar with them, whereas others encountering them for the first time will process more slowly). After a sufficient pause to allow their attention to return to you, make your point.

Alternatively, rather than show the entire quote at once, I could introduce it line by line or segment by segment. This technique works well when presenting virtually. The visual motion of text building gradually helps maintain viewers' attention as you talk through it (we'll take a closer look at this strategy with more varied content in Chapter 7). Take care with this paced strategy, which might feel overly controlling in some scenarios.

As another approach, if I don't need my audience to read the *entire* quote to make my point, I can reduce the effort and time to process by selectively highlighting. This draws on the visual hierarchy concept introduced earlier in this chapter. Figure 6.8 shows two designs that employ selective highlighting to draw attention to a few choice words through color, size, and position.

Customers **love** the new scan feature

❝ I've been using your calorie & fitness tracking app religiously since it was beta and sharing with all of my friends and family—I might be your all-time world-wide biggest fan! **The ability to scan labels is a game changer.** I don't usually write reviews, but I feel like I must given how massively I've benefited.

Customers **love** the new scan feature

❝ I've been using your calorie & fitness tracking app religiously since it was beta and sharing with all of my friends and family—I might be your all-time world-wide biggest fan!

The ability to scan labels is a game changer.

I don't usually write reviews, but I feel like I must given how massively I've benefited.

FIGURE 6.8 Selective highlighting

Compare the two designs in Figure 6.8. What does each say to you when it comes to how you are meant to consume it? To me, the first iteration seems as though I'm meant to read it all while paying special attention to the bold black text, whereas with the second version, I'm inclined to believe I only need to read the blue text. In either case, I am able to make my point as the presenter sooner than the initial two strategies described. Just be aware when using this method that some people will still want to read everything and won't be fully attentive to you while they do so.

Using words well also comes into play when we are using other types of primary content for our mid-story slides (for example, together with graphs and diagrams). We'll explore the use of text to help make other visual content more easily understood in Chapter 7.

The story ends: closing slides

The end of your presentation is a great place to reiterate your primary take-away or concentrate attention on what you want your audience to do next. Words can help you do both of these things.

As I mentioned before, in the case where I've shared my Big Idea to set the stage early in my presentation, I'll often come back to it at the end. It's useful to reflect on where people are at during each of these points. When I introduce my message up front, it's before I've fully supported it; I've put forward an idea or foreshadowed where we're going, but not yet in a way that others will necessarily know what to do with it. Contrast this with the experience when I restate it later in my presentation. I've gone through the necessary detail and supporting evidence during the story I've been telling. Now, when I show my Big Idea again, if I've done my job well, my audience should be equipped to do something with it. Let's look at an example.

FIGURE 6.9 Big Idea slides for the beginning (left) and end (right) of my presentation

Early in my presentation, I will introduce the opportunity. Over its course, I can illustrate exactly what that means—the *who*, *when*, *why*, *where*, and *how* of the situation. At the end, I will return to my Big Idea, perhaps in a more direct and pithier manner (note how I've shortened the message on the right in Figure 6.9). I'll leave this latter slide up after my planned content ends during the discussion that follows or as I answer questions.

Form a pithy, repeatable phrase

Repetition helps form a bridge from our short-term memory to our long-term memory. We can make use of this in the actual words we use to communicate our story in a business setting by articulating our main point in a pithy, repeatable phrase. Revisit the Big Idea explored in Chapter 2. Turn your Big Idea into a pithy, repeatable phrase. This can help you get clear on your goal when communicating and can also be incorporated into your materials to help increase memorability for your audience. The pithy, repeatable phrase is short and catchy, and it may incorporate alliteration. It doesn't have to be cute. It does need to be memorable.

In a live presentation, you might begin with the pithy, repeatable phrase. You could also end with it, or you might weave it in different ways over the course of your presentation so that when your audience leaves the room, they've heard it a few times. This means they are both more likely to remember *and* be able to repeat it.

Let's consider another scenario. Imagine I've decided against beginning with my Big Idea in favor of building up to my recommendation. I use simple words to state the action I would like my audience to take: to discuss the recommendation that I have just made. See Figure 6.10.

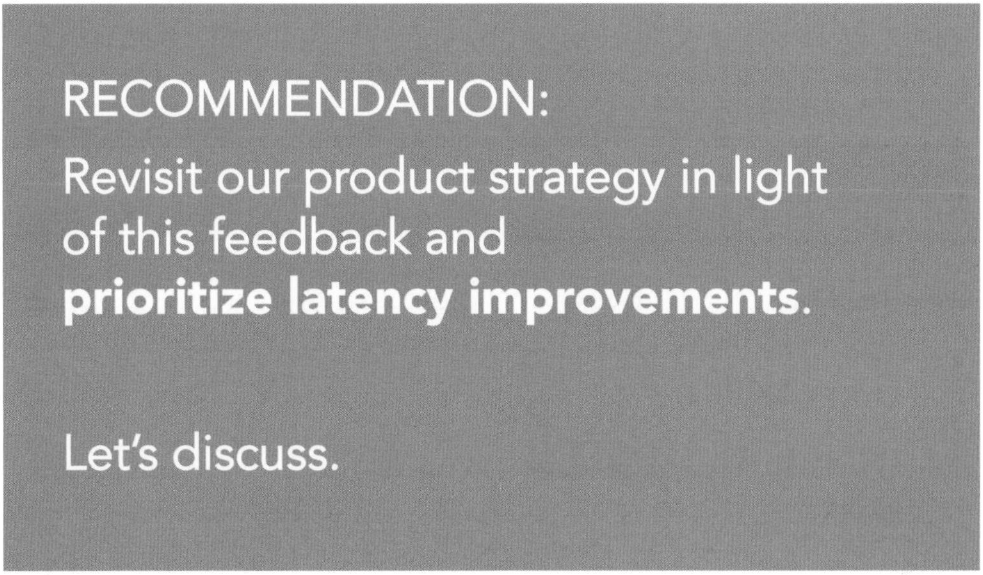

> RECOMMENDATION:
> Revisit our product strategy in light
> of this feedback and
> **prioritize latency improvements.**
>
>
> Let's discuss.

FIGURE 6.10 Words to outline recommendation and drive discussion

We've looked at a number of slides where text is the primary content. These certainly aren't the only ways to use written words in our presentations but should give you some ideas upon which to build. Whether words or other content, for each slide you create, step back and think about what exactly you hope to accomplish. Then design the slide in light of how you'll be presenting, who your audience is, and how you can best achieve your goal.

We'll revisit this idea of creating content along our story arc in the context of data and image slides in the upcoming chapters. Before we do that, let's look at another example of using words wisely.

Say it with words: TRIX case study

Recall that we closed Chapter 5 with my framework for the TRIX presenta-tion. This will be the focus when I meet with the client group at Nosh to share the results of the market research our team has undertaken and our related recommendations. As a reminder, the structure I set in Chapter 5 is shown in Figure 6.11.

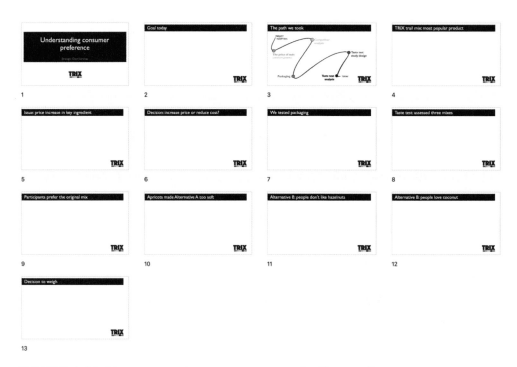

FIGURE 6.11 The presentation structure we set in Chapter 5

It's time to start filling in the content.

Just as we did at the onset of this chapter, let's start at the beginning of our slide deck with the presentation title. The placeholder title in Figure 6.11 is "Understanding consumer preference." This is fairly descriptive. What if, instead of merely introducing the topic and what I want to do (help them understand consumer preferences), I give a glimpse of something of what we found? Perhaps I can use my title to get people's attention and introduce a sense of intrigue.

When it comes to exactly what I aim to communicate, I review the Big Idea from Chapter 2: *Consider an alternative trail mix blend that balances consumer preference with the desire to lower cost by decreasing macadamia nuts, adding coconut, and modifying the packaging so potential buyers can see the product.* We talked in this chapter about actually communicating the Big Idea as a slide. As another strategy, from my Big Idea I can create a pithy, repeatable phrase and then use that to title my presentation.

In this scenario, the crux of the matter centers around macadamia nuts. They are a key ingredient in the original mix, and it's their rising cost that was the impetus of this work in the first place. We found that consumers love them. Our recommendation is to keep this key ingredient, albeit in lower quantity, to balance consumer preference and cost. Taking this all into account, I transform my Big Idea into a simple statement: *the magic is in the macadamia nuts.* I will title my presentation with this.

I spend time on each of my slide titles to ensure they highlight the takeaway as I flesh out the individual content. Speaking of which, let's focus on one of the early planned slides where words will be the primary content.

We know from Chapter 1 that my audience is a mixed group who has different levels of familiarity with the background, how my team got involved, and the study and research we've undertaken. At the beginning of the presentation, I want to share context to get everyone on the same page and frame the overarching goal for the meeting.

To address this, I create the following slide.

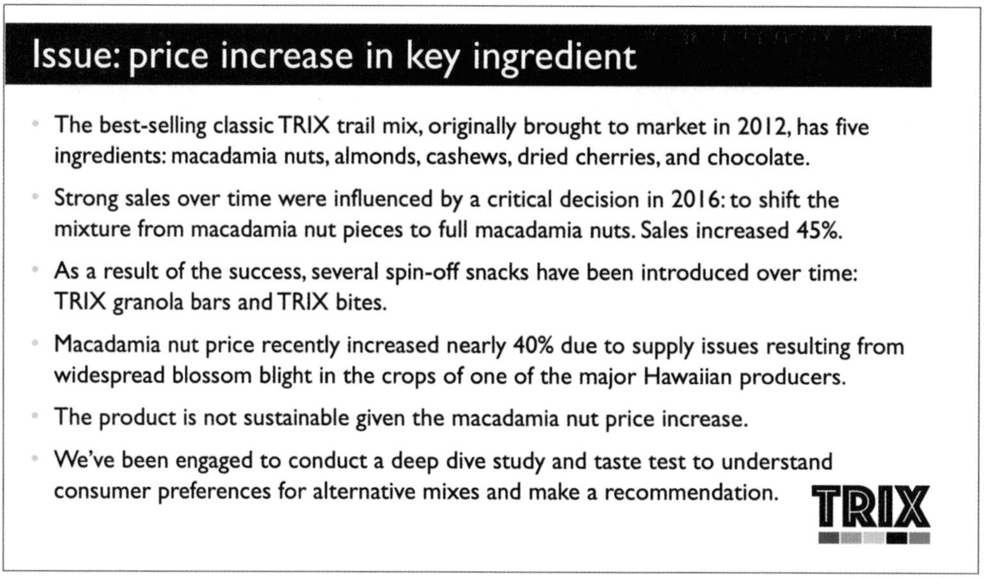

Issue: price increase in key ingredient

- The best-selling classic TRIX trail mix, originally brought to market in 2012, has five ingredients: macadamia nuts, almonds, cashews, dried cherries, and chocolate.
- Strong sales over time were influenced by a critical decision in 2016: to shift the mixture from macadamia nut pieces to full macadamia nuts. Sales increased 45%.
- As a result of the success, several spin-off snacks have been introduced over time: TRIX granola bars and TRIX bites.
- Macadamia nut price recently increased nearly 40% due to supply issues resulting from widespread blossom blight in the crops of one of the major Hawaiian producers.
- The product is not sustainable given the macadamia nut price increase.
- We've been engaged to conduct a deep dive study and taste test to understand consumer preferences for alternative mixes and make a recommendation. **TRIX**

FIGURE 6.12 A text-heavy slide

Review Figure 6.12 in light of the lessons we've just covered. Have I used words wisely?

I turn my attention first to the slide title. It calls out the issue of increasing price. This is a takeaway title, but is it the one I want here? Rather than orient people around the issue, perhaps I should direct them toward a potential solution.

When it comes to the text on the body of the slide, it does describe the context. Someone could read through this to get a good understanding of the plot of my story. However, I don't want my audience to do that. I will be there; I'll simply *say* these words. The slide that helps me do this should augment me as the presenter, not compete with or replace me.

With these ideas in mind, I transform this issue-focused teleprompter slide into something more. It centers on what we will accomplish together: rework the mix. I can still use text to remind myself of the upcoming content (and reinforce it for others) but in a way that their attention will remain primarily on me through this process. See Figure 6.13.

Let's rework the TRIX mix

- 5 simple ingredients

- Whole macadamia nuts are key

- Issue: macadamia nut price increase

- We've assessed alternative mixes

- Today: you decide next steps

FIGURE 6.13 Fewer, punchier bullets

Note how much easier and faster Figure 6.13 is to process than the text-heavy version. But I can take things a step further. I want to pause on each of these bullets to fully explain the ideas and weave them together as I lead people through this content. Rather than show them all at once, I'll introduce them one at a time. Then I will add relevant context through my spoken words. My audience won't be tempted to read ahead, because I won't give them the ability to do so. I'll achieve this through light animation in my slide application.

When I initially show this slide, it will be blank, save the title and logo. On my first click, the initial bullet will appear while I outline the five ingredients in the original TRIX mix. When I click again, the second bullet will appear, and the formatting of the first bullet will change to transparent. Figure 6.14 shows what the slide will look like when I discuss the macadamia nut price increase (the third bullet point).

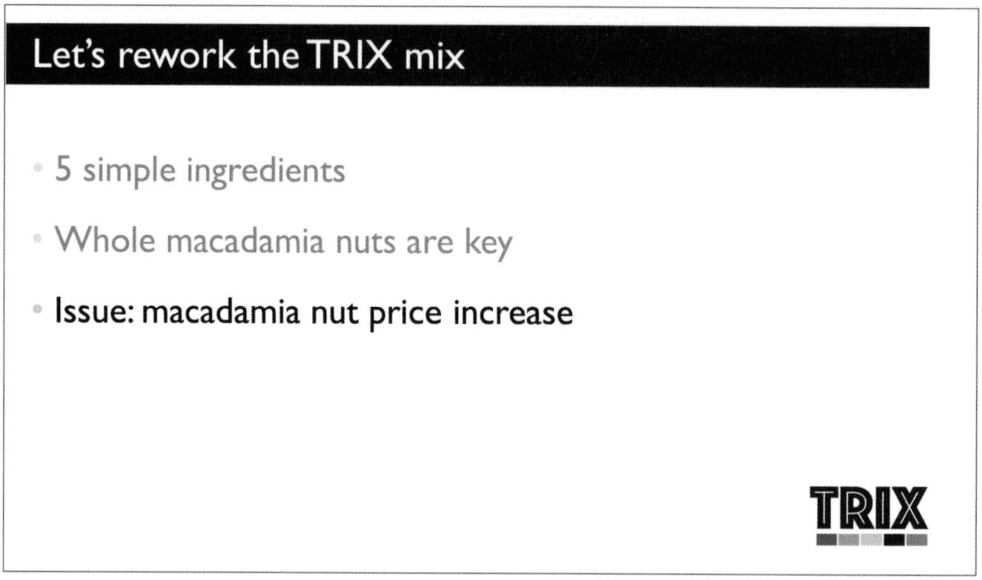

Let's rework the TRIX mix

- 5 simple ingredients

- Whole macadamia nuts are key

- **Issue: macadamia nut price increase**

FIGURE 6.14 Animate progression to make current focus clear

I will continue in this manner through each of the points, pausing to lend additional context through my voiceover as I go. My audience can see when they turn their attention from me to the slide, both at what point we are currently and the path we've taken to get there.

This is an example of rethinking how we use our words in a presentation setting—designing the text on our slide to work with us instead of against us. Take a look at the before and after.

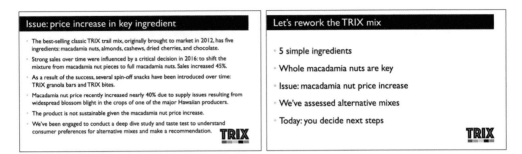

FIGURE 6.15 Transition from teleprompter slide to using words wisely

This isn't the last you'll see of this content. We'll look at strategies for transitioning text to more visual content in Chapter 8. Before we do that, let's examine another scenario where words play a critical role: in our communication of data.

chapter 7

show data
in graphs

We use data to inform, build credibility, support ideas, battle false precon-ceptions, help people understand something in a new way, and drive change. Executed well, a graph brings an awesome "aha" moment of understanding, turning data into information that can be used to make a smarter decision, have a more robust conversation, or act with greater confidence.

Before we get into how exactly to do that, I have one important caveat: just because you have data *doesn't* necessitate its inclusion in your presentation. When integrating numbers and graphs into a communication, step back and ask yourself why precisely you are doing so. What will the given data point or graph achieve? This practice will help the data you incorporate be more effec-tive. Also, when you clearly know the reason for communicating specific data, it is easier to create data visualizations that accomplish what you intend. We'll discuss practical ways to do this over the course of this chapter.

For more on data visualization, read my first book

For a foundational review of communicating effectively with data, check out my first book, *storytelling with data: a data visualization guide for business professionals.* You'll encounter some concepts that will be familiar from your reading here (in particular, the importance of audience, message, and story), plus greater depth on communicating with graphs in particular. This includes thorough discussion of common business visualizations, graph design considerations, and many illustrative examples. The follow-up, *storytelling with data: let's practice!*, shares additional case studies and strategies through a plethora of exercises, inviting you to take a hands-on approach and hone your data communication skills via guided practice.

You do not need an advanced quantitative degree to make a good graph. You also don't have to use fancy graph types or special tools to communicate effectively with data. It is helpful to possess an understanding of some visual design concepts specific to graphs, which we'll develop in this chapter. Before we do that, let's talk a little more about typical goals for visualizing data in general and in a business setting in particular.

Why we visualize data

I characterize data visualization as turning numbers (data) into pictures (graphs). We graph data to answer a question, create beauty, entertain, evoke feelings, experiment, explain, explore, grab attention, influence, inspire, make someone laugh, or aid understanding. This is not a comprehensive list of motives, by the way—there is a spectrum of reasons that drive people to visualize data.

When I graph data, it is most often in a business setting. My main objectives are typically to create understanding and drive others toward a specific action.

I use graphs for speed, comprehension, and memorability. Our visual system is fast at processing information (faster than our verbal system, which means an effective picture or graph has the potential to get an idea across more quickly than written text, a concept we'll discuss further in Chapter 8). A good graph also facilitates the explanation of something more complex, particularly when it's useful for people to be able to see something in order to understand it better. Finally, visual recall is something we can use when we display data in graphs. When I make a statement and show a graph that illustrates it, not only is my audience able to remember what I said but also what they saw.

Given these goals, I actively simplify my data visualizations. This generally means showing my audience where to look, what to see, and how each piece fits into the broader picture. While these are things we should aim to do with any content we create to communicate to others, there's a process I follow for graphs specifically: articulate the takeaway in words, iterate on the visual form to select a graph that will help me bring those words to life, refine the graph, and finally, weave that graph into the overarching story. Let's talk more about each of these steps.

Articulate: put your point into words

What do you want someone else to see when they look at your graph? You already know the answer to this question—it is why you've chosen to include the data in the first place. We've seen the benefits of iterating to refine the words we use in the context of our overarching message and the way we title our presentations and slides. This practice can be applied to our graphs, too.

Articulating observations for yourself about the data you plan to show will help you make better graphs. I'm a fan of a simple exercise to do this. For any graph that you plan to include in your presentation, form a few sentences about it. Determine which is the most important and improve it. This sentence should describe the specific takeaway that you want people to know. In other words, if someone looked at your graph and asked you the question, "So what?," your sentence should answer this. Don't just do this activity in your head: write it down. Often, the initial sentence formed is longer or more complicated than it needs to be. Edit your sentence. Say it out loud. Make it as simple as possible.

Shouldn't the data speak for itself?

The instruction to put data into words runs counter to the misguided notion that data speaks for itself. Sure, a graph can speak for itself, but without our help, it runs the risk of saying something different to each person who looks at it!

When you are the person who is communicating data, you are in a singular position to help others derive greater value from that data. You likely know it better than anyone else. It is your job to convey that understanding and the viewpoint you have developed based on it. Don't ask your audience to undertake this work. Note that this doesn't mean others will necessarily agree with you, but it sets the best stage for understanding and a productive conversation. Put your data into words!

If there are a number of observations that are important, it's possible that you'll end up with multiple sentences. Undertake this process as many times as needed to ensure the sentence outlining each individual takeaway is concise. (More than one sentence often means you'll have various iterations of your graph on your data slides to walk through these nuances—an approach we'll look at soon.)

The graph you use to form your sentence doesn't have to be perfect. It can be rough, may have some clutter, or not be the ideal graph form. That's okay. The words you choose to describe it are going to help you refine it. It's an iterative process. The more time you spend with the graph or iterating through various potential views, the better you'll understand the data. Use this increased understanding to continue to enhance the words you use to describe it, then use those words to further improve the graph.

Let's look at an example. Spend a moment studying Figure 7.1. What observations do you make? How would you put those into words—what sentences would you form about this graph to answer the question, "So what?"

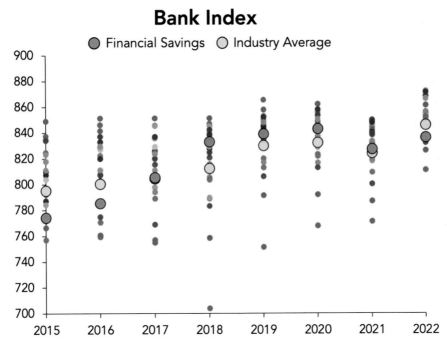

FIGURE 7.1 Study this graph

If you're struggling, fret not—this one is challenging. To further complicate matters, I haven't provided any context, so it's not surprising if you have more questions than observations at this point. Check out what happens, however, when I start formulating statements about the graph. Doing this forces me to explicitly call out some of the tacit knowledge I have due to my familiarity with the data that you do not. There are a number of observations I could articulate. As you read through the following, refer back to Figure 7.1. Determine whether you see what I describe.

- There is variance in customer satisfaction across banks and over time.

- Satisfaction has generally increased across the industry, and the range from low to high is smaller in 2022 than in prior years.

- The industry average satisfaction is higher than Financial Savings in 2015–2016, at or below Financial Savings in 2017–2021, and then higher again in 2022.

Let's presume that Financial Savings is my client, and this final sentence is the main takeaway I want to convey to them. It's time to refine it. I could simplify it and make Financial Savings the focal point with something like, "Financial Savings is below the industry average for the first time in five years." I would be better off saying those words than communicating the visual in its current form. Rather than throw out the graph, however, let's use the clarity of what we want to communicate to improve it.

Visualize: let form follow function

You may be familiar with the adage "form follows function." Suppose that you are designing a chair. This idea dictates that you would start by determining what function you want the chair to perform. Is it a desk chair that should promote good posture in an office or a lounge chair to relax in the sun? Obviously, these two uses will drive different designs. The same is true for our graphs. When we start by outlining the specific function we want a given graph to serve, it makes the process of choosing an effective one much easier.

Whether a data novice or an expert data wrangler, people often unintentionally overcomplicate the function they expect their graph to perform, which in turn convolutes its form. For those who haven't worked much with data, making a graph can feel intimidating, like it has to answer every possible question that could arise. Those who work with data regularly might feel that visualizing it is an opportunity to showcase all the complicated work that took place or to demonstrate prowess in their tools.

These perceived constraints lead people to design a table of data that is overwhelming, a busy graph that is difficult to understand, a visual that is comprehensible only to those involved in the technical analysis or with an advanced quantitative degree, or other issues. Because the function we expect the graph to perform has been overcomplicated, it's not surprising that the form that follows is unnecessarily intricate as well.

This is why we put our takeaway into words as the first step for making an effective graph. When we do that, it's easier to be explicit and specific about the highest priority function we need our graph to perform. When visualizing data in a business setting, there are a handful of graphs that handle common tasks:

- **Show a trend over time:** line graph, slopegraph, area chart
- **Compare across categories:** bar chart (vertical, horizontal, stacked, diverging), dot plot
- **Express a relationship:** scatterplot, waterfall chart, pie chart

There are numerous existing resources on these and additional graphs. Instead of repeating that here, let's revisit the example from the last section and see how we can visualize the data to illuminate the point we want to make.

Tip: focus first on line graphs and bar charts

Whether you've been visualizing data for years or are building your very first graph, when communicating data to others, you will be best served by getting really good at making effective line graphs and bar charts before spending time expanding your graphical lexicon and visualization skills beyond these basics. Lines and bars are common—for good reason. Their broad familiarity renders them straightforward to interpret. There are some twists on these basics and also use cases for other visuals, though those will be rarer.

When you use a less common graph, you introduce a hurdle: you have to keep your audience's attention while you explain how to interpret the graph before you even start to talk about the data and what it shows. There will be instances when this makes sense—when the additional time and effort will be worthwhile because it allows you to highlight or explain something that is otherwise difficult to see or when organizational familiarity with a less common visual has been built over time—but those are exceptions, not the norm. In general, when communicating with data, keep things as simple as possible. This often means sticking with the basics: line graphs and bar charts.

You'll find many more examples of lines and bars in my other books. For a deeper exploration of additional common visuals, check out the SWD chart guide at storytellingwithdata.com/chart-guide. To further expand your graphicacy and see use cases for a wide variety of visuals, I recommend the book *Better Data Visualizations* by Jonathan Schwabish (Columbia University Press, 2021).

Recall that I articulated the key takeaway as "Financial Savings is below the industry average for the first time in five years." This means when it comes to the function, it will be important to show industry and Financial Savings' satisfaction over time. Let's look at this data in a line graph. See Figure 7.2.

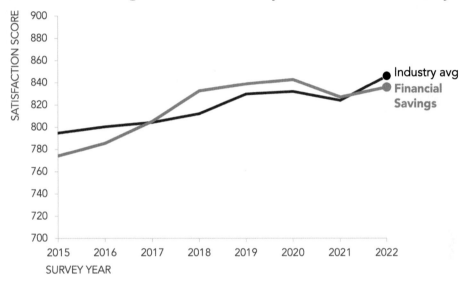

BRANCH SATISFACTION

Financial Savings is below industry for the first time in 5 years

FIGURE 7.2 Form follows function

Choosing a graph form that works for the point is merely one consideration. To create the magic that allows an idea to come to life through a graph, take steps to make the process easy and enjoyable for your audience. This means identifying aspects that will feel like work to others and alleviating that effort to the extent possible through your graph design.

Figure 7.2 incorporates a number of improvements relative to Figure 7.1 that can be expanded to some general good practices for communicating with graphs. Each of these has to do with words and how we use them together with our graph to make things easy to understand.

- **Put the key takeaway into words.** Once you've articulated your key idea for yourself, integrate it into your graph to make the takeaway clear to others. Words have an amazing ability to prime. When you say something or write words about a graph, it sets expectations for what others should look for or see. Further, studies have shown that if you title a graph with the relevant message you'd like your audience to remember, they are more likely to remember it. Powerful stuff!

- **Include axis titles.** You know what is being plotted, so it seems obvious to you; this will not be the case for most others who encounter your graph. Take the simple step to include axis titles (in Figure 7.2, this is Satisfaction Score on the y-axis and Survey Year on the x-axis), so others are able to easily understand the data. I am an advocate of aligning graph and axis titles at the upper left to create visual structure. It's for the same reason that I often use all caps for axis titles: they have a clean rectangular shape compared to mixed case, which frames my graph nicely.

- **Label the data directly.** Rather than have a separate legend, when possible label data directly. See the placement of the Industry avg and Financial Savings labels to the right of the lines in Figure 7.2. This eliminates the labor of going back and forth between the legend and the data to decipher the graph.

I have also improved the graph by creating visual hierarchy, eliminating distractions and focusing attention on what remains. We'll talk more about that next.

Unsure which graph works?
Sketch or iterate in your tool and get feedback

Much in the same way we found benefit in beginning presentation planning in a low-tech fashion, making a good graph can start with pen and paper, too. Particularly in cases where you aren't sure which visual works best or believe a less common view may be worth the tradeoffs, sketching to brainstorm and get a glimpse of how things could work is useful. When drawing, you don't form attachment to what you create like you do when you build in your spreadsheet or presentation application. This makes the iteration process faster due to the relative ease of letting go of less desirable options.

Data drawings are also a great point at which to get directional input from others. When concepts are rough, it's easier to assess the overall form and function rather than get caught up in individual design considerations. Additionally, drawing frees you from tool constraints. Get things right on paper, then figure out what tools or experts can help you realize your ideas. Remain open to making changes. Often, when we conceptualize on paper, we aren't precisely plotting every data point. Continue to evaluate the effectiveness of your chosen route and modify as needed.

You can also iterate through different views of data in your graphing application. Let it be a quick and dirty process—the graphs don't have to be polished at this point. Create a few different ones and determine which will help you best make your point. If you are still uncertain, solicit input from others.

Refine the graph: declutter and focus

We touched on visual hierarchy in Chapter 6 in our discussion about communicating with text. By de-emphasizing or removing less critical components and selectively highlighting the important aspects, we make it easier for our audience to process the information we communicate. When I'm refining my visuals in this manner, I typically start by identifying and eliminating clutter.

Declutter your graphs

Let's explore the power of decluttering through an example. Imagine you work for a company that conducts an annual corporate fundraiser. Monetary donations and food donations are brought together to prepare meals to feed those in need in the community in which your organization operates. You track a simple metric over time: the number of meals served per year. The initial graph you create to visualize this data might look something like Figure 7.3.

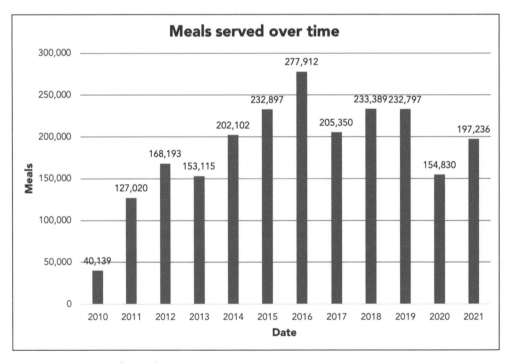

FIGURE 7.3 Initial graph

Figure 7.3—like all of the graphs in this book—was created in Microsoft PowerPoint. (An identical version could be created using Excel, which historically has been my primary graphing tool; I've transitioned to making graphs for presentations directly in PowerPoint to save the step of copying and pasting from Excel.) Because the default settings of any tool have been modified to address many different scenarios, there will almost always be details you can tailor to better accommodate your specific situation.

If you work with a different application for visualizing data, I encourage you to create a basic graph and undertake the process that follows.

Before proceeding to learn what changes I make to declutter this visual, spend a few moments considering Figure 7.3. How does this graph feel to you? In an effort to simplify, which elements are you inclined to deemphasize, eliminate, or modify in other ways?

Download files and access additional resources

You can download the slides shown throughout this book at storytellingwithyou.com/downloads. If you're curious about how particular design components were built, I encourage you to explore these files. Additionally, you'll find many resources specific to graphs, including tutorials, on the *storytelling with data* blog (storytellingwithdata.com/blog) and YouTube channel (storytellingwithdata.com/youtube). For ways to practice graphing and telling stories with data and exchange feedback with other members, I invite you to join our online community (storytellingwithdata.com/community).

To me, the graph in Figure 7.3 feels messy. While this version would be totally fine to use behind the scenes to get a better understanding of the data or in a casual conversation with a colleague, it is not something I recommend presenting in a formal setting. This would be lazy because there are quick and easy things we can do to make it easier for our audience.

Figure 7.4 shows my decluttered version of the graph.

Meals served over time

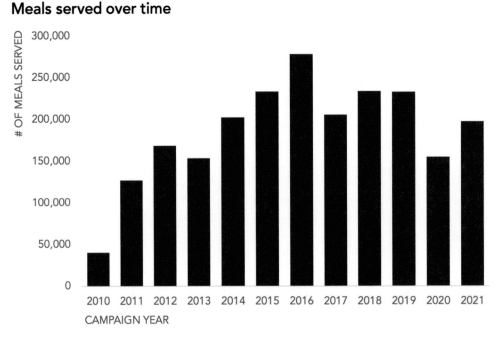

FIGURE 7.4 Decluttered graph

I made a number of changes, which you can identify by comparing the versions. Below, I'll outline common forms of clutter to remove when refining a graph.

- **Graph borders:** These are usually unnecessary. Instead, use white space to set your graph apart from other elements on the page or screen.

- **Gridlines:** Eliminating the horizontal or vertical lines that cross your graph is a simple step that makes the data stand out more. If specific numerical values are important, label the data directly (after doing this, sometimes it will make sense to get rid of the axis altogether).

- **Axis lines:** You won't *always* do away with the x- and y-axis lines (at minimum, you may push them to the background by making them gray); they lend visual structure to graphs. However, there are instances where you can remove them without losing anything (the same goes for tick marks, the small demarcation lines on an axis line—assess on a case-by-case basis).

- **Trailing zeros:** If every number on your axis has zeros past the decimal place, round to the nearest whole number. For large numbers with many zeros, think about whether scaling to hundreds, thousands, or millions will make the information easier to digest and discuss. (I opted not to do this in the previous example because thousands has always seemed like an awkward unit to me, but you may feel differently, and that is fine.)

- **Data markers:** These shapes (often on line graphs) are usually not necessary on every data point. Used sparingly, they can help direct attention.

- **Data labels:** Only include the numerical labels that specify the value when you have a clear reason for doing so. Often, even when you opt to include data labels, you don't need them on every single data point (in bar graphs with sufficient space, I recommend embedding labels in the interior of the bars to combine the elements visually and decrease perceived clutter).

- **Diagonal text:** This looks messy, grabs attention, and is slower to read. Aim for horizontal text when possible (if you have a bar chart with long category names, try changing the layout from vertical to horizontal to orient the text in a likewise manner).

- **Center-aligned text:** Such text is often floating in space, and when it flows onto multiple lines, it looks sloppy due to the jagged edges. I'm a fan of left- or right-justified text that is aligned with other elements to create visual order.

- **Unnecessary color:** More than a couple colors in a graph make it difficult to concentrate and can cause unnecessary work for others. Sparing color is an excellent tool to focus people's attention, an idea we'll revisit soon.

Note that there will be exceptions. Always evaluate the specific scenario in which you are communicating and what will work best given the data, the audience, and your time and tool constraints. If you're able to explain why you've elected to include items or done something in a way that runs counter to the tips in the preceding list, odds are you've put enough thought into it to make that a reasonable choice.

Is a little clutter in your visual communication going to be the end of the world? Probably not. Each individual piece of clutter on its own is relatively minor. However, when there are many unnecessary elements, they add up to create a less-than-ideal experience, distracting attention from our data and our message.

Good graph design: it's the little things

In our conversation about clutter, I've framed it mainly in terms of extra stuff to eliminate. Another way to think about making an effective data visualization is to start with a blank slate and build it piece by piece and with a critical eye on each element you add. There are many little decisions we make every time we graph data—some explicitly through our design choices and others implicitly when we don't modify our tool's default settings. Constructing a graph one element at a time forces you to contemplate each decision and its impact on the visual. Watch me do this in the video *it's the little things: ten tiny considerations when designing a graph* (storytellingwithyou.com/littlethings).

After taking the time to declutter your data visualization, also spend time intentionally directing attention to add value in its place.

Focus attention

When you make a graph or a slide, you are familiar with it. You know where to look and what to see. For this to be as obvious to others, we must take intentional steps in our design. We've already seen how words help us make our point clear. Pair this with sparing contrast to indicate where to look, and you have a potent combination. Let's review another example of this strategy, and then I'll outline a variety of methods to focus attention.

Did Figure 7.4 leave you dissatisfied or with a feeling that it was unfinished? It was. Making it clear where to look can't be achieved by simply eliminating clutter; we also need to intentionally direct attention within the content that remains. Let's assume that the primary message we want to highlight is that the number of meals served has increased since the dip in 2020 (due largely to the COVID pandemic) but has stayed lower than other recent years.

Figure 7.5 shows one way to achieve this.

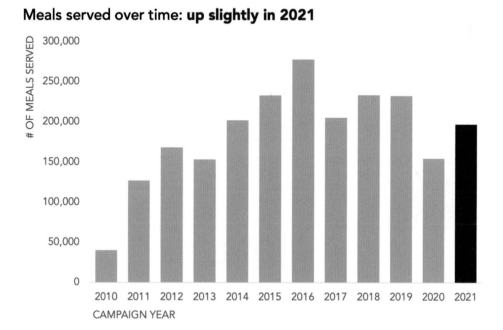

FIGURE 7.5 Focused graph

I chose to de-emphasize meals served from 2010–2020 by making them gray. They are there for context, but the navy bar at the right (this color was chosen to align with the branding of the organization) calls for the audience's attention. When you make it clear where to look and what to see, this helps overcome potential issues. Even if it's not the perfect chart choice or some clutter is present, your graph can still be effective.

To achieve this focus, contrast is key. Below, I've listed some common ways to create visual contrast within a graph.

- **Color:** Use a bold, bright color to emphasize a specific data series or data point. This works especially well when the rest of the graph is black, gray, or otherwise muted, as illustrated in Figure 7.5.

- **Intensity:** Render the focal point(s) in full intensity and push the rest visually back by making them less intense. A brute-force way to achieve this (that is particularly useful if you don't have the ability to make formatting changes to your graph) is to cover less critical components with a semi-transparent shape.

- **Thickness:** In a line graph, make the primary data series you want people to look at thicker, the others thinner, or combine these two approaches. You can similarly use thickness with important text (e.g. titles, labels, annotations) by making it boldface.

- **Size:** Relative size visually indicates relative importance. If something is important, it may make sense to make it larger than other features in the overall design.

- **Added elements:** In some cases, pointing an arrow at, circling, or otherwise enclosing pieces of interest can be effective (still, there are often more eloquent ways to highlight through how you design the graph). Some items that add information in addition to signaling importance include sparing data markers and labels or annotation.

- **Animation:** Motion captures attention. The simple act of a data point not being present and then appearing will steer eyes in the right direction. This is particularly useful in live presentations, and we'll look at examples of this soon.

This isn't a comprehensive list of ways to direct attention, but it is a good start and hopefully gets you thinking critically about how to prompt others to look where you'd like them to in your graphs and other visuals. It may also make sense to layer various elements of visual contrast. If I want you to look at a given bar in a bar graph, I could render it in a different color, add the data label to the bar, and bold the data label text. To achieve clear focus, contrast should be sparing—if you make everything different, nothing stands out!

Study shows benefits of focusing attention in data viz

Is there a study that proves this stuff works? That's a question I've received about decluttering and directing attention in data visualization more than once. While I have plenty of observational evidence, it's only as of 2021 that there is a prominent study to cite as well.

I partnered with the Visual Thinking Lab at Northwestern University on research summarized in the paper titled "Decluttering and Focus: Empirically Evaluating Design Guidelines for Effective Data Communication" (by Ajani, K. et al.). Participants were shown a mix of 1) cluttered, 2) decluttered, and 3) decluttered *and* focused data visualizations. They were asked to evaluate the designs on aesthetics, clarity, professionalism, and trustworthiness and also to redraw and recall topics and conclusions of the previously seen visuals.

While decluttering the designs led to higher ratings on professionalism, adding focus to the design led to higher ratings on aesthetics and clarity and improved memory and recall. Bottom line: there is measurable benefit to focusing your audience's attention.

The examples we've looked at in this chapter have been single snapshots of data to illustrate common practices for making a good graph. Once you've done so—taken steps to make it clear to people where to look and what to see—it's time to incorporate that effective graph into the overall story.

Weave graphs into your story

You may recall that in Chapter 6 we discussed using word slides along the path of our story, following the narrative arc introduced in Chapter 4. We started at the beginning of the story with plot slides to set the context; the story continues via mid-story slides and then ends with closing slides. While there will always be exceptions, I find that the majority of data slides presented in a business setting fit best in the *mid-story* section of the overall path. This is because there is often situational context that must be detailed before jumping into the data. By the closing of the presentation, we've typically moved past the data into the more actionable realm of what to do in light of the improved understanding we've helped facilitate.

Successfully presenting data involves more than simply showing a well-designed graph. Have you ever been in a meeting or presentation where a graph is put on the big screen and you're so busy trying to decipher it that you've stopped listening to the person speaking? This happens frequently. Rather than create data slides that distract, aim to build slides that work seamlessly with the spoken words of your presentation, reinforcing the points you make and the story you tell.

We can do this by designing slides that set the stage for our data and then building and progressing through a given graph. In the meals-served scenario that we've looked at several times in this chapter—after setting the general context or plot but before showing any data—I could incorporate a slide like the following.

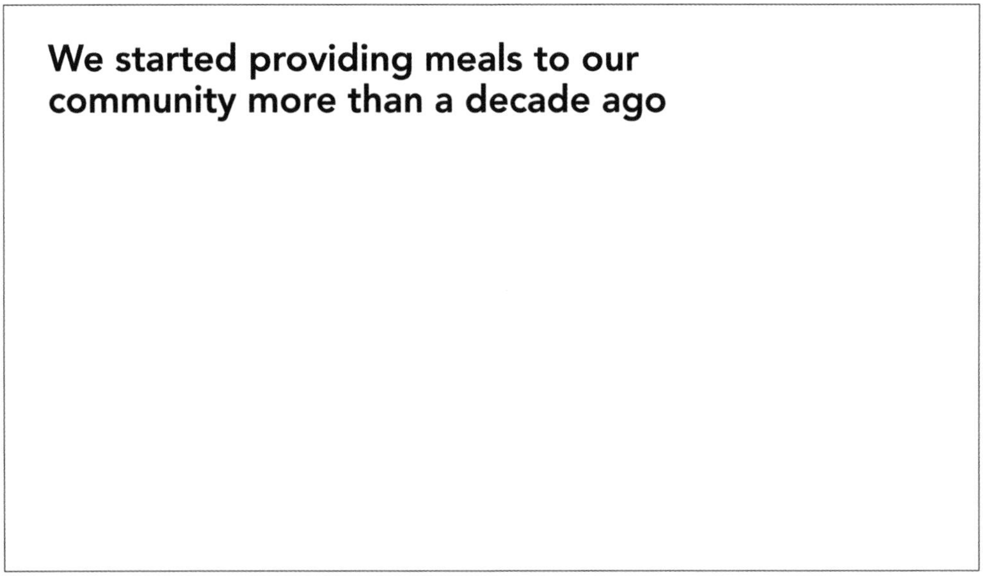

We started providing meals to our community more than a decade ago

FIGURE 7.6 Mostly blank slide to set the stage

Figure 7.6 is a blank slide, save the slide title. That is by design. This will remind me when I'm presenting to set up what will come next (which can either follow on the next slide or be animated to appear on this one). Thinking ahead to my presentation, on this slide I will say something like, "Back in 2010, we launched an exciting new program with the goal of feeding those in need in our community. I'm going to show you just how many meals we've served over time."

Because my audience won't have anything to distract them after they quickly scan the title, I'll have their full attention when I set the context. This helps ease the transition into the graph.

In the same way that we animated small sections of text to appear on our word slides in Chapter 6, I will build my graph in steps as I explain it. After setting up what I'm going to show, I *could* simply introduce the bar chart from Figure 7.5. I might do that if the history was well known by others, and I only wanted to focus on the recent year relative to the rest. However, in the event that I want to walk others through the data and lend insight to explain what has driven the ups and downs over time, this wouldn't be a smart approach. If I show all the data immediately, it's too easy for people to look at it and then direct their attention elsewhere altogether or at a different point in the graph. We can ease the latter through selective highlighting, but if you'd like your audience to accompany you as you tell the story of your data, set up your graph first. Then progress through the data step by step, revealing only what you want them to see while you verbally make the relevant points.

While this strategy can be used for a simple graph—which we'll see momentarily—it is *especially* useful when communicating something dense or unfamiliar. Introducing and discussing one or a couple of components at a time allows you to build to a complex visual that doesn't feel complicated. We'll look at an instance of this when we return to the case study later in this chapter.

Back to meals served over time: after my set-up slide where I seeded the expectation for what's to come, I'll introduce the first iteration of the graph. See Figure 7.7.

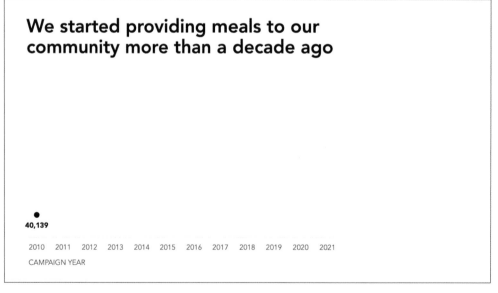

FIGURE 7.7 Start to build the graph

As I put up this slide, I will say, "On the vertical y-axis, I'll be plotting the number of meals served. Back in 2010, we launched the pilot program. We served *over forty thousand* meals that first year, markedly more than our twenty-five thousand goal." To tell the story of meals served over time, I will start with this single data point and then build a line graph (instead of the bar chart that we looked at previously for this data). This will make it easier for people to see the increase or decrease from year to year through the relative slopes of the lines that connect the data points. I've also stripped away some of the graph details (graph title, y-axis title, and y-axis labels). I will share these particulars through my spoken words. (If I were sending these slides out to be consumed on their own or was worried this might confuse, I would retain them for clarity.)

My subsequent slide could look like Figure 7.8.

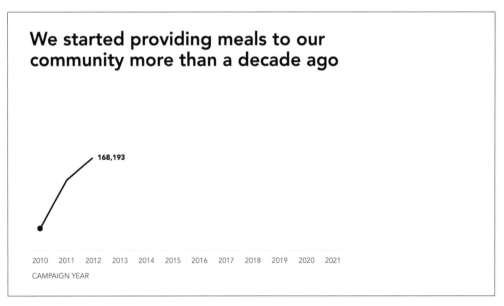

FIGURE 7.8 Continue building the graph

I would present Figure 7.8 with the accompanying voiceover: "Given the wild success that first year, we decided to make it an annual campaign. As word spread, more and more colleagues got involved, including our executives, who made some sizable donations. We served one hundred and sixty-eight thousand meals by the third year of the program." Anticipate how I could continue to build the graph in this way, revealing only a year or two of data at a time to highlight specific points and lend additional context and information as necessary. Eventually, this would culminate in my final, complete graph.

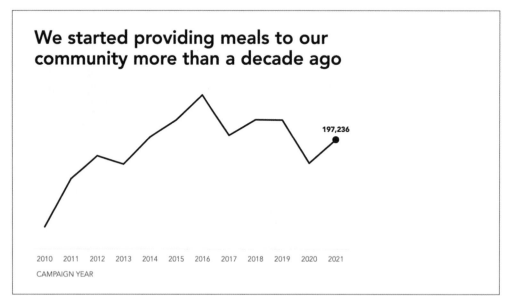

We started providing meals to our community more than a decade ago

197,236

2010 2011 2012 2013 2014 2015 2016 2017 2018 2019 2020 2021

CAMPAIGN YEAR

FIGURE 7.9 The complete graph

Upon progressing to the final graph in Figure 7.9, I'll highlight the takeaway that we identified when we looked at this data initially in this chapter: "Meals served increased in 2021 relative to the COVID-dampened support in 2020; however, they remain below recent years." I could then transition into the end of my story—my intended call to action or the discussion I wish to frame. Or, if this is a single piece of a more robust story, I would move from here into the next chapter of what I want to communicate.

Animate data for the virtual setting

This strategy of setting the stage and then building and progressing through a graph is particularly useful in a virtual environment. Many things compete for attention when your audience is sitting behind their computer—don't give them an excuse to tune out! Putting a complicated graph in front of them is an invitation to do exactly that. On the other hand, when you don't show them everything at once, it helps keep them focused. They won't want to miss the point of your graph. The simple visual motion of elements appearing helps maintain attention. Also, as we've discussed, others are more likely to actively listen to you because they aren't spending brainpower figuring out where to look or how to decipher—you are telling and showing them! You are leading them through the story of your data. That sounds much more pleasant for everyone than simply showing a graph, right?

When presenting data, you should almost always have only one graph per slide. This is for a number of reasons. It's hard to talk about multiple graphs simultaneously and easier to direct attention with fewer things on the screen. There is also a size consideration: multiple graphs on a single slide means the details are small. With a single graph, you have more space to make titles, labels, and the data itself large enough for everyone to see. The exception is when related graphs are so important to view together that you lose too much by breaking them up across multiple slides. Still, this can generally be addressed by making it clear how the different visuals connect.

When we build a single graph, as you saw in the previous example (Figures 7.7–7.9), it's pretty explicit how each one connects to the following. The audience literally sees how the data points relate as the line builds from left to right. There is benefit to doing this because the familiarity you've established means that later iterations of the graph will be faster for people to grasp and understand. Building on this idea of familiarity breeding comfort and efficiency, starting from something known is a great strategy when you want to depart from the norm, too—an idea we'll see employed soon in the case study.

Frequently, there are multiple different graphs that we want to communicate as part of our broader narrative. In some instances, there are still data points that we can highlight in one and then also in the next to make how they relate to each other obvious. More often, it's our words and the framing of our presentation slides that will create this bridge for others. It's the overarching story that will help make things clear.

This is one of the reasons that all of the planning we've done up to this point is vital. As we storyboarded, arranged our ideas along the narrative arc, and set the structure in our slideware, we thought about how the pieces were connected at each of these points. As you're creating your data slides, you'll want to refer back to this planning to make sure you incorporate transition slides, slide titles, and verbal segues that will make these connections straightforward for your audience.

Let's revisit the case study. I'll use it to reinforce a number of the lessons we've covered in this chapter and highlight how to connect different visuals as we build our data slides.

Show data in graphs: TRIX case study

You'll recall that in Chapter 5 we set the structure for the presentation to our client team at Nosh. In Chapter 6, we framed the plot for the story we plan to present by creating word slides to support our communication of the general project context. Now, let's determine how we can build slides with graphs to discuss the results of the taste test we conducted.

Figure 7.10 shows a summary of the data.

Taste Test Summary

Measure	Original	Alternative A	Alternative B
Product Overall Liking	8.1*	7.2*	6.9*
Overall Appearance Liking	8.3*	6.8**	8.0**
Amount of Nuts JAR / Skew	89% JAR	67% JAR	71% JAR / 18% Too Much
Amount of Fruit JAR / Skew	80% JAR / 13% Not Enough	65% / 27% Too Much	89% JAR
Amount of Chocolate JAR / Skew	93% JAR	85% JAR	88% JAR
Overall Texture Liking	7.9**	6.9**	7.2*
Level of Crunchiness JAR / Skew	79% JAR	71% JAR / 20% Not Enough	85% JAR
Level of Chewiness JAR / Skew	83% JAR	67% / 31% Too Much	89% JAR
Overall Taste Liking	8.4*	7.4**	6.2**
Level of Saltiness JAR / Skew	89% JAR	77% JAR / 17% Not Enough	68% JAR / 27% Too Much
Level of Sweetness JAR / Skew	83% JAR	72% JAR / 19% Too Much	76% JAR / 14% Not Enough

N = 257 *Indicates significance at the 95% level. **Indicates significance at the 90% level.
Liking: How much do you like or dislike the sample overall? JAR: Thinking of the sample you observed and consumed, what is your opinion of the [amount of or level of] [nuts / fruit / chocolate / crunchiness / chewiness / saltiness / sweetness]?

TRIX

FIGURE 7.10 Summary table

Never present a slide like Figure 7.10 in a formal setting! This data dump is fine as the basis of a casual discussion with your colleagues in a working meeting or possibly in the appendix of your materials. It does not, however, meet the goal of communicating data when you have a specific story you want to tell.

The first thing I do is get clear about what I want to say and put specific take-aways into words. There are a number of different points of this data that I'll use throughout the presentation, but I won't show them all at once. I'll weave them into a connected narrative that helps it make sense to someone unfamiliar.

At this juncture, let's focus on a single takeaway to illustrate and apply the lessons we've learned. The original mix is preferred over the alternative trail mixes considered both overall and across the independent measures (appearance, texture, and taste). Figure 7.11 shows the initial bar graph I create with this data.

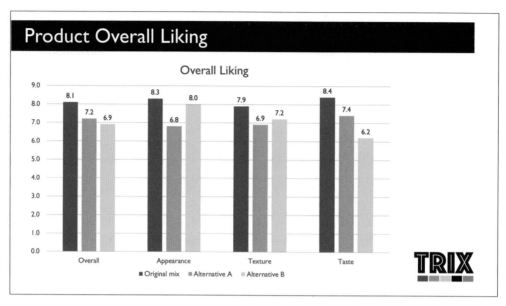

FIGURE 7.11 Initial graph

Next, I modify the visual to transition from a generic graph with default settings to one that is designed to meet my specific needs. I declutter, eliminating unnecessary elements so the data stands out more. I put my point into words and use contrast sparingly to indicate to my audience where to look for evidence of those words. See Figure 7.12.

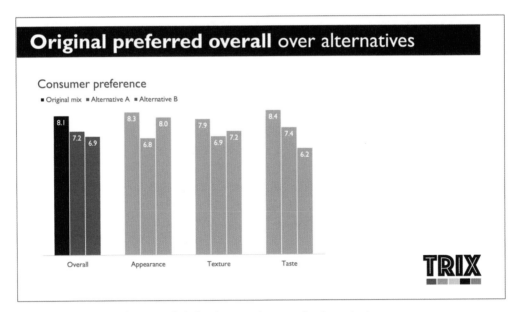

FIGURE 7.12 Redesigned slide shows where to look and what to see

Now is a good time to think about how I will lead people through this data. It's worth mentioning that the presentation structure I set in Chapter 5 (Figure 5.22) included a single slide to illustrate this point. I could simply use the bar chart from Figure 7.12 and be done—but I'd be doing everyone a disservice. As we discussed in this chapter, I don't simply want to show the graph. I want to weave data into my overarching story.

That single slide in the planned structure was only a placeholder. It's going to take more than one slide to accomplish my goals. I want to set the stage and build each graph to feel intuitive to my audience while maintaining their attention as I progress. I also want to connect the various views so everything fits together and makes sense.

As I step back and look at this data not on its own, but in light of everything I want to convey, I make a directional change. I recognize that I will want to show more data at once than is going to work well with the bar chart I initially designed. After realizing this and then brainstorming alternative approaches and discussing with colleagues, I decide that a more novel view will work better to show the high-level taste test data and connect it to the details I plan to communicate.

I start by highlighting that participants preferred the original mix and introduce the 9-point hedonic scale—which ranges from dislike extremely to like extremely—along which participants assessed the samples. See Figure 7.13.

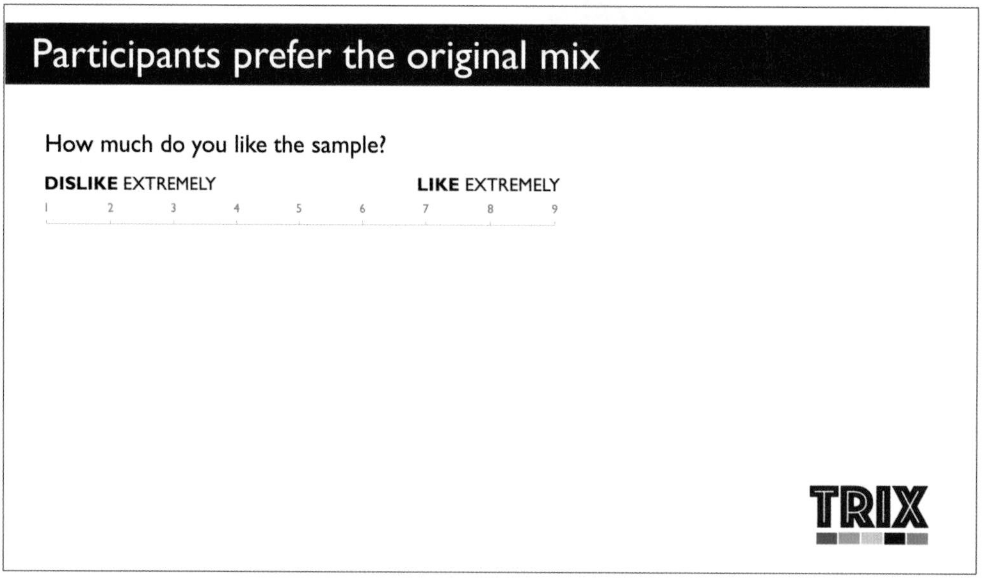

FIGURE 7.13 Set the stage

Then I layer data onto the graph so I can talk about each point. I start with the original mix, then add Alternatives A and B. Figure 7.14 shows what it looks like after these three pieces have been added.

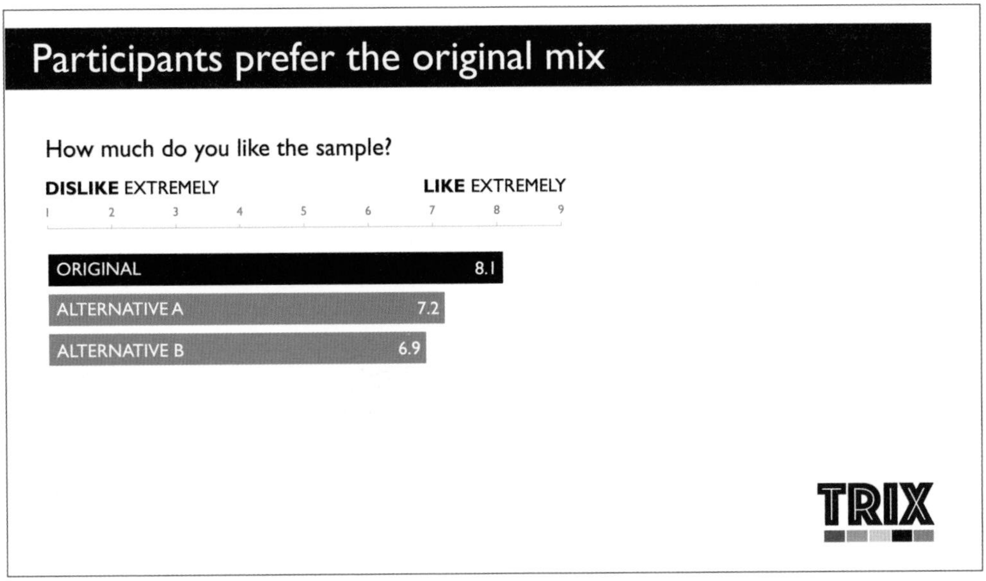

Participants prefer the original mix

How much do you like the sample?

DISLIKE EXTREMELY   **LIKE** EXTREMELY

1   2   3   4   5   6   7   8   9

ORIGINAL   8.1

ALTERNATIVE A   7.2

ALTERNATIVE B   6.9

TRIX

FIGURE 7.14 Build the graph

You'll notice that I'm plotting the data in a horizontal bar chart this time (rather than a vertical column chart with the liking scores on the y-axis that we saw previously in Figures 7.11 and 7.12). This is to set up the more novel approach I alluded to—a dot plot—but ensure the data is understood by connecting it to something commonly known (the bar chart). I begin by replacing the ends of the bars with circles. This works particularly well in a live setting, where the audience sees the circles replace the ends of the bars in the transition.

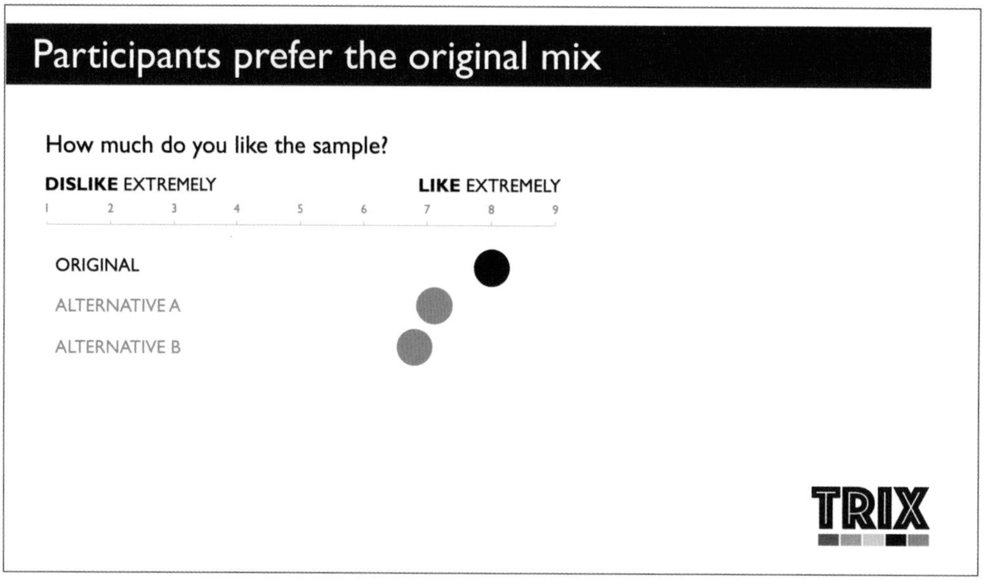

FIGURE 7.15 Transition to dot plot

Next, I collapse the dots onto a single line. This is another step to lead my audience through how to interpret the data.

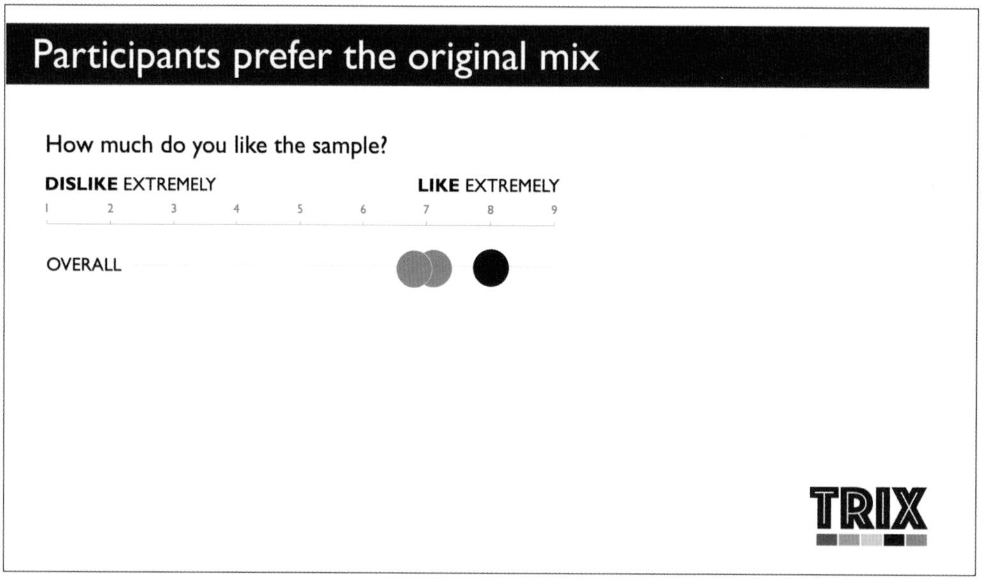

FIGURE 7.16 Collapse onto single line

After collapsing onto a single line, I have sufficient space to add the other dimensions from the taste test. Figure 7.17 shows what that looks like for the original mix.

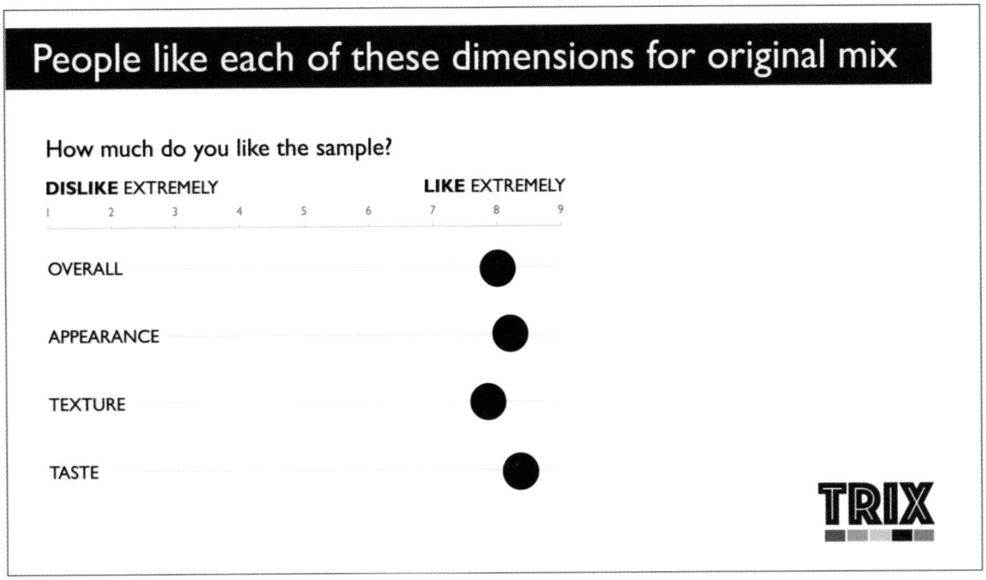

FIGURE 7.17 Layer on additional data

Now that I have the structure fully set up, I can layer on various data points and discuss them one or a few at a time (this is the part that would have been difficult with the bar chart I had originally planned that drove my decision to pivot to the dot plot).

I start with the original mix, as depicted in Figure 7.17. Then I layer on the liking scores for the alternatives tested. Figure 7.18 shows the liking scores for Alternative A.

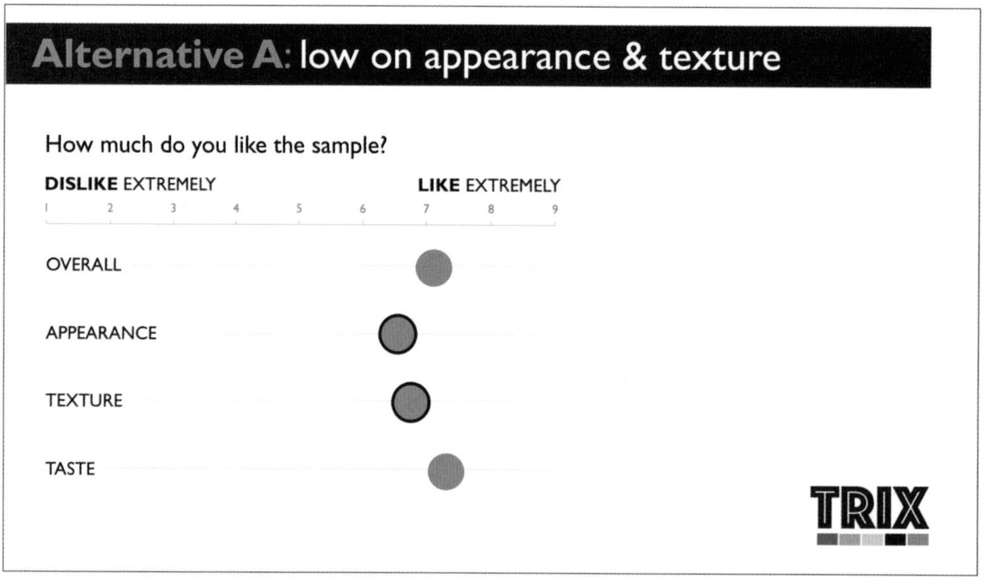

FIGURE 7.18 Make it clear how the views connect

With this step-wise approach, I make it clear to others how the various data points I am communicating all relate. I highlight through both my text and the contrasting formatting for the lower scores on appearance and texture (shown in Figure 7.18). I use this to transition into the subsequent level of detail from the taste test for Alternative A, which will allow me to share further insight into why these scores were low. The format of that data is different, so I'll use another graph there. I'll follow the same process of setting the stage and building it step by step to lead people through how to interpret the data and direct their attention to specific points of interest as I continue to progress through the story. You'll see how it all comes together later in the book.

Before we do that, there's an additional type of visual content that I'll integrate into my final presentation: images. Let's shift our attention there next.

chapter 8

illustrate with images

When may your topic or message be best served by an image? If you've ever presented from a stage, it's likely that you've contemplated and perhaps used pictures in your presentations. But what about in your normal day-to-day meetings with slides: when and how might you effectively use images there?

You've seen examples of what *not* to do. A stretched photo that has the sole purpose of filling empty space on the page, a stock image of hands shaking on a slide about partnerships, clip art or comic strips that are only tangentially related to the topic and distract or annoy rather than play any role of utility—these are instances to avoid. I have heard the directives that lead to these misuses: "We have some extra space on that slide; let's put something there," or "You should spice up your deck with some pictures!" These statements illustrate both the wrong reasons to use images and the incorrect manner in which to use them.

Pictures used well are extremely powerful. They can help you explain concepts, increase understanding, maintain attention, reinforce content, improve memorability, and more. I'll mention that I'm using the words *image* and *picture* interchangeably. We'll explore a variety of specific image types soon, demonstrating through examples and sharing practical tips that will help you effectively integrate images of all types into your visual communications. Before we do that, let's get specific about why we might integrate pictures into our presentations in the first place.

Reasons to use images

There are a variety of reasons to use images in your visual communications. While not fully comprehensive, I've organized common ways to use pictures into four broad categories—to help explain and understand, aid memorability, set the tone, and improve the design. Let's discuss each of these in detail.

Images can help *you* explain and *your audience* understand

Put simply, incorporate a picture when it's helpful for others to *see* something. Use an image when looking at the thing will help your audience comprehend it better or the visual aid makes it easier for you to explain a subject or concept. For instance, imagine you work at a start-up and are putting together a pitch deck to help secure funding. You could include a sketched or computer-generated prototype of your flagship product for your venture capitalist audience, assisting your explanation and ensuring their understanding.

You can also use images to help frame your communication. We discussed setting up a navigation scheme in Chapter 5 in the context of plotting out the slides in a presentation (I shared an example using simple words and another that integrated photographs of my kids). To recap this approach, the image you'd use in this instance would encapsulate the primary sections or topics in your presentation. You'd introduce it near the beginning to set up what you will talk about and in what order. Then you'd revisit it as a transition point between sections to keep people oriented on where you've been and where you're going. Finally, you'd use it again near the end of the presentation to recap your main points.

Let's look at an example presentation from my work that employs this technique. I once put together a short session on the importance of decluttering data visualizations. I started with a story about how I used to get in trouble for not cleaning my room. It was part delay tactic that drove my childhood transgressions, but the resulting chaos made me realize that I had a difficult time concentrating in a disorganized environment. I used this anecdote as a metaphor for how visual clutter in a graph translates into an inadequate viewer experience. Then I showed the following image of a messy desk to introduce the specific content I would cover.

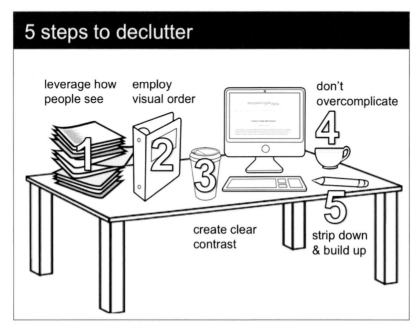

FIGURE 8.1 Navigation scheme with images: initial view

After talking through the visual navigation scheme shown in Figure 8.1, I transitioned to my first point using Figure 8.2.

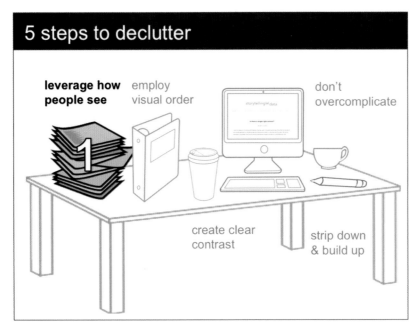

FIGURE 8.2 Navigation scheme with images: transitioning to first concept

I returned to versions of this image after each step, highlighting sparingly in a similar manner as a visual transition to close out one topic and introduce the next. (If you're interested in seeing the presentation, you can watch it at storytellingwithyou.com/declutter.)

This is another way to use images that will both assist you as the presenter and help tie things together in a manner that makes it easier for others to understand. As a bonus, the repetition of continually returning to the image and concepts makes it easier for others to remember what you've covered. Speaking of memorability, this is one potent power of pictures.

Images can aid memorability

An image used well improves your audience's ability to recall a concept or point. This is due to something known as the **Picture Superiority Effect**—people re-member pictures better than words. This is thought to be due to the double encoding that happens with images (in both visual and verbal memory) versus the single encoding in verbal memory with words. Numerous studies have found that recall is improved when an effective picture is combined with words compared to words alone.

The key word here is *effective*. You may have a great picture, but is it right for reinforcing your idea or message? Does it help others *see* something in your head? For the ideal picture-message combo, when your audience later recalls the picture, they are reminded of what you said when you showed it.

We incorporate a number of images into our *storytelling with data* workshop slides. In the context of directing attention, we often introduce the "Where are your eyes drawn?" test. As part of this exercise, we present various pictures and have participants shout out where their eyes are drawn first. This practice illustrates what happens to our visual attention in a number of different scenarios.

One set of images starts with a full screen of multicolored balloons. See Figure 8.3.

FIGURE 8.3 Where are your eyes drawn?

Colorful isn't a good goal when you would like your audience to look at one thing in particular. Contrast Figure 8.3 with the following image.

FIGURE 8.4 Sparing contrast focuses attention

I don't have to say the words, "Look at the blue balloon." When presented with Figure 8.4, you are already looking at it before I can even get them out of my mouth. Striking contrast—in particular, the sparing use of color—garners attention. If my audience later recalls either picture, they should remember the associated lesson. That is an example of an image used to illustrate *and* reinforce a point to aid memorability.

Images can set the tone

Carrying on with the topic of color, you may recall in Chapter 5 that we discussed how hue evokes feelings and can help you set the tone for a communication in the context of presentation design. Pictures do this as well—and have the potential to do so to a much greater degree.

I once began a workshop with the story of my daughter's birth. While this might seem like both a highly personal and unexpected experience to share in a business setting, I had concrete reasons for doing so. I was speaking to a group of physicians. Specifically, they were brain surgeons who spoke on behalf of a medical device company. My assignment was to convince them to approach things differently than they had done in the past. (How's that for a potentially intimidating audience and scenario?!) The setting was a hotel ballroom; I was in the front of the room presenting to about fifty surgeons.

In my story, I was hooked up to an electrocardiogram, watching the printed results unspool from a reel of paper beside me. I saw a peak, then a valley, a peak, then a valley—the data going up, then going down—and I was thinking to myself, that's an interesting graph. The doctor looked at the same piece of paper and proclaimed, "This is what active labor looks like!" Throughout this narrative, I had a blank slide at my back to focus the surgeons' attention on me. Then at the end, I put up two pictures of my beautiful daughter, Eloise: one in the Neonatal Intensive Care Unit and another roughly a year later.

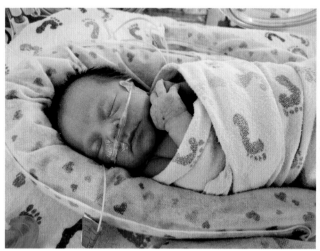 

FIGURE 8.5 Eloise, newborn and at one year

This before-and-after that demonstrated the marvels of modern medicine— something my physician attendees could certainly appreciate—was a dramatic way to hint at the transformation I planned for the attendees that day. I was going to ask them to be vulnerable and look at things in a new way. By doing that myself at the start of the presentation, I got the undivided attention of every person in the room and began to build their trust. The story and the pictures helped them relate to me, establishing a rapport that set the foundation for the day.

I incorporate images of my children into my presentations in ways that some might find surprising. For me, it's natural. Because I learn a great deal from them, often the stories I tell within my presentations include them. I mention this not to encourage you to share personal photographs specifically. However, when you relate strongly to an image in some way, it is more likely that you'll be able to talk about the associated concepts and present that image in a way that will get others to connect with it, too.

For a less dramatic illustration of how pictures can help establish tone and align people, I'll draw on a client example. I once worked with an energy company, helping a group in operational risk with communications they were building for the leadership team. While reviewing a draft deck on the big screen in a working meeting, we flipped to a slide titled "Why do we purchase insurance?" There was a small picture at the top of the slide, followed by a lot of text. The words were organized into categories: to transfer the risk, to meet statutory requirements, and to meet contractual obligations. Each category contained several bullet points with more details.

I didn't know what the picture was showing because we were well outside the realm of my expertise. I started asking questions. It depicted a multi-million dollar machine breaking, highlighting the need for insurance. I could tell simply in the way that the group discussed it that the image was evoking the desired reaction. Unfortunately, the impact was being dampened by the current approach that incorporated a small image with many words. As part of the revamp, we made the image the focus of the slide, with the statement "Why we need insurance." The text in the original slide became talking points (preserved in the speaker notes section) for the communication.

Images can improve the design

There will be some instances where it might make sense to incorporate an image simply for the sake of aesthetics. Thinking back over my own use of images, I've done this more often with conference-style presentations than run-of-the-mill business presentations, though there may be opportunities in that setting, too.

If there is a powerful image that you make central to your communication, you can use it to set colors, fonts, and other design aspects to lend a cohesive and professional look and feel. In one of my favorite keynote presentations, I told a story about encountering my two-year-old son, Dorian, reading a book. He wasn't actually *reading* the words. He was retelling the tale aloud using the images to prompt his recall of the story he had heard many times before (another illustration of the power of pictures!). As part of my presentation, I shared that book and told an abbreviated version of the story to the audience.

The book is titled *Larry Gets Lost in Seattle*. It was written by John Skewes, who has authored an entire series based on Larry and his misadventures. Figure 8.6 shows a sample two-page spread.

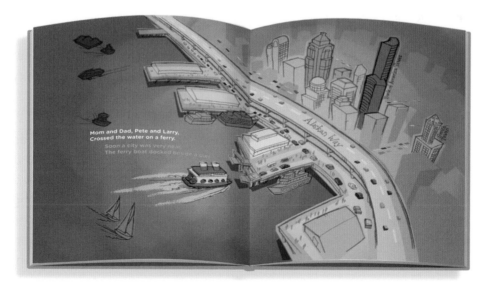

FIGURE 8.6 *Larry Gets Lost in Seattle* excerpt (© John Skewes)

Given the emphasis on this story, I folded some of the design aspects into my presentation. This included bold colors and some imagery from the *Larry Gets Lost* series (used with permission from the author). Figure 8.7 shows the title slide for my presentation (you may recognize it; a thumbnail was included in Chapter 6 as a conference presentation title slide).

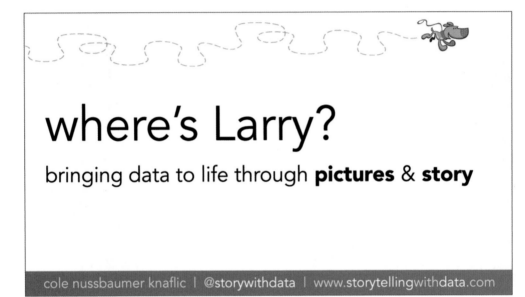

FIGURE 8.7 My presentation title slide, inspired by *Larry Gets Lost in Seattle*

It is also sometimes useful to incorporate images simply to break up content or give people something to look at while you're speaking. While this seems counter to my earlier advice, I'd suggest not solely using images in this manner. Look for opportunities where one of the other purposes we've discussed can be met as well.

Using images in virtual presentations

With the shift toward more virtual meetings and presentations, I've found myself incorporating images in more ways. When setting context, describing a scenario, or telling a story in a live situation, I sometimes use a blank slide to ensure attention is on me. I tend not to do this when presenting virtually. It can be misinterpreted as a technical glitch or an invitation to turn attention to competing priorities (the email inbox is only a click away!). Instead, I've found myself including an image to give my audience something to look at while they listen to me. In one scenario about bank branch satisfaction, I used a picture of a bank branch while I was setting the context. On another occasion, the topic was back-to-school shopping, where I displayed an image from the given retailer while I spoke.

When using images in this way, they should directly tie to your topic and be something that others can look at without having to give it much thought—you still want their primary attention devoted to you and what you're saying. The picture is merely something that will entertain their eyes while their ears are on you. We'll discuss ways to hold your audience's attention through *how you speak* in a virtual environment in Chapter 10.

Given these powers of pictures, when designing a communication, step back and think about whether, where, and how your content could benefit from the inclusion of an image. As we've discussed already in the context of words and graphs—be intentional about your motivations for incorporating pictures into your presentations and specific about the purpose each serves. This will help you use images effectively.

You've seen a few examples of varied types of images already. Let's talk about three categories of pictures and some related tips and strategies.

Photographs, illustrations, and diagrams

I'm going to be broad with my definition of images and include visual content common to slide presentations that we've not yet covered in the chapters on words (Chapter 6) and graphs (Chapter 7). This includes photographs, illustrations, and diagrams. I'll discuss the use of each of these types of images, sharing related design considerations and additional illustrative examples.

I'll repeat a caveat that I expressed previously: I am not a trained designer. I have a good eye and have learned over time through trial and error, trusting my instincts, and learning from each instance. What follows are my pragmatic tips based on my experience using various forms of imagery in materials communicated in meetings and presentations.

Photographs

Probably the most common form of images encountered in business and other professional presentations is photographs.

I recall helping my husband with a slide deck when he was working at a wearables technology company. The founder was hyper-focused on great design when it came to their products, which was a feeling that needed to flow through to the visual communications used within the company, too. Given this context, in scenarios where I may otherwise have opted for words or graphs as content, we used striking imagery from photo archives that the company maintained. To discuss introducing an annual employee survey in one Quarterly Business Review—rather than a bulleted slide detailing the specifics (which the founder cared little about)—we used an image of employees at an all-hands meeting, with the simple words, "Let's hear from the team."

This brings me to my first tip for using photographs in presentations: commit to the image. Don't let it seem like an afterthought, placed in the corner of a slide where you had some unused space. Let it take center stage. This generally means making the photo take up the entire slide. Let's look at an example from the energy company client I mentioned earlier in the chapter.

Figure 8.8 shows a slide from a deck I was helping revamp (modified slightly to preserve confidentiality).

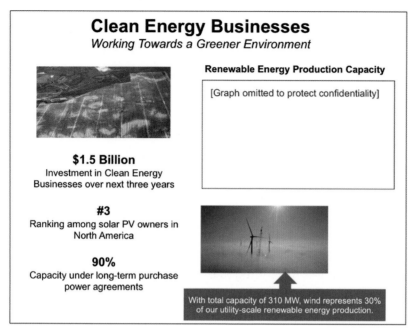

FIGURE 8.8 Original slide: suboptimal use of photographs

Note the callout near the bottom of the slide with the arrow pointing to the second photograph. Through discussion, I learned that this was one of the key points. Given this, I suggested that we convert the original slide into several, with each concentrating on a single primary message. The slide intended to do this for that final point is shown in Figure 8.9.

FIGURE 8.9 Commit to the image and pair with pithy text

In Figure 8.9, the photograph has been enlarged to cover the entire slide. When resizing photographs, take care not to stretch the image (changing the ratio between the original width and height will cause it to look distorted). Our eyes are quick to pick up on when this has been done, and it lends a feeling of unprofessionalism. Instead, you may have to crop one or more sides of the image to make the proportions work. Use high-resolution photographs that you can resize without looking fuzzy or grainy.

Where can I get photographs for my presentation?

There are a number of options for sourcing photographs. In some instances, it might make sense to take the photograph yourself, which is what I do when possible. This puts you in full control to make the picture exactly what you require without any concern over potential copyright issues.

Taking a photo to suit your situation won't always be possible. When it isn't, you may opt for stock photography. There are a variety of free and paid options. Here are a few that I have used:

- **iStock** by Getty Images (istockphoto.com) has a good library of paid photos and illustrations, with various pricing plans and subscriptions. Other popular pay-for-photo sites include **Shutterstock** (shutterstock.com), **Getty Images** (gettyimages.com), and **Adobe Stock** (stock.adobe.com).

- **Flickr Creative Commons** (flickr.com/creativecommons) offers various types of licenses (many of which only call for simple attribution).

- **Free Images** (freeimages.com), **pixabay** (pixabay.com), and **Unsplash** (unsplash.com) have free images for personal and commercial use.

These are a few of the many sites where you can search and access or purchase photographs. Always read the fine print so you are aware of any licensing or attribution requirements.

When it comes to orienting photographs and other imagery on your slides, one design tenet to be familiar with is the **Rule of Thirds**. This is a guideline that lends a well-composed feeling to your images (and can be more generally applied to slide design as well). Imagine dividing your image into thirds, both across length and height, leaving you with a grid of nine equal areas. The Rule of Thirds suggests placing the key subjects or graphic elements along the lines that divide the image into thirds or at the intersections of those lines. The general idea is that it gives the onlooker's eyes somewhere to move while viewing your photograph, image, or slide. This is in contrast to positioning key elements in the center.

Let's look at a photograph I've used before—one I took of my son, Dorian. I mentioned the scenario earlier in the chapter about two-year-old Dorian telling himself the story of *Larry Gets Lost in Seattle*. See Figure 8.10 for two versions of the photo that illustrates this.

FIGURE 8.10 Center focus compared to Rule of Thirds

Compare the left and right images in Figure 8.10. Do they feel different to you? Following the Rule of Thirds, we should favor the second version of the image, where Dorian is positioned at the left line in the 9-rectangle grid, rather than centered in the 4-rectangle grid. As a bonus, when it comes to using photographs in slides where we also want to overlay text, the latter version provides a bigger block of space in the upper right to do so.

I'll impart a final piece of advice on the topic of photographs, something I alluded to at the onset of this chapter. When integrating them into your presentation, avoid anything that is trite, unimaginative, or overused. Resist any urge to use pictures of money when you talk about sales, a bullseye for communicating targets, or a photo of the earth to discuss your global presence. These have been done before (many times!) and are not likely to add value or be memorable.

Instead, determine how you want people to feel and what you want them to understand or remember at given points during your presentation. Could a photograph help you accomplish these goals? This reflection alone will help you use photography purposefully.

Apply this sound advice to the next type of image we'll talk about, too: illustrations.

Illustrations

I use *illustration* to describe any type of visual content that is drawn. Drawn images will typically feel less polished than a photograph. I highlight this not as a negative quality but as an aspect that helps inform when and why you might opt to use an illustration in a presentation instead of a photograph. As we've been doing with each type of content we consider (words, graphs, photographs), when determining whether to include illustrations, start by being clear on your reason for doing so.

Illustrated images can take a variety of forms—refined or rough, realistic or abstract. Check out the illustrations in Figure 8.11.

FIGURE 8.11 Three drawings of a bird

What are a few adjectives you would use to describe each of the three birds in Figure 8.11?

Starting at the left, with the more realistic version of the heron, my list includes: stately, attentive, and statuesque. The middle bird strikes me as quick, bare, and bold. Finally, for the bird on the right, I would use descriptors like silly, lighthearted, and amusing.

Your lists of adjectives will look different than mine, and that's okay. The point is that different styles of illustrations (even when they are picturing basically the same thing) convey varying tones and evoke distinct sets of feelings. Understanding this will better equip you to choose an illustration style that will reinforce the general vibe you'd like to set.

I draw on paper—and, increasingly, an iPad

When a simple illustration will suit, I often tackle this myself and sketch it. I'm definitely not an artist, but I enjoy drawing. When I spend a little time, I can do it reasonably well. I'm most comfortable drawing on paper. To translate paper drawings to the electronic world, I'll either scan or take a picture of the image and then recolor or make other minor edits in PowerPoint so it will fully meet my needs. This definitely isn't the most technologically advanced technique, but it generally works for me!

Inspired by the enthusiasm expressed by some of my teammates who draw on their iPads (and their beautiful work), I've slowly started building my skills and experimenting there, too. I've tried a few different apps; my favorite is Procreate. I find it intuitive, and it has enough options to meet my objectives without feeling overwhelming. The herons in Figure 8.11 were drawn on my iPad using Procreate.

One place I used a number of illustrations was in my second book, *storytelling with data: let's practice!* While not a presentation per se, this is an example of the thought process behind using illustrations in visual communication. The book isn't one that's meant to simply be read; it is intended to be an immersive experience—I want people to roll up their sleeves and do some work. I knew early on when I was planning the content that I would want it to be illustrated for a number of reasons. First, I liked the idea of a large, potentially intimidating book contrasted with light and fun illustrations. My hope was that the images would make the book feel more accessible, too.

The hand-drawn look was intentional to visually reinforce the idea that approaching things in a less formal way is okay and invite readers to draw. The primary illustrated content includes sticky notes with hand-written text and chapter recaps to summarize key lessons in a visual manner. Figure 8.12 shows an example of the latter.

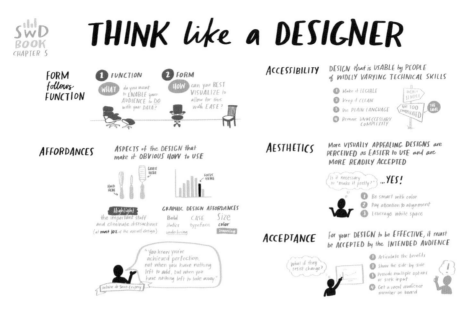

FIGURE 8.12 Chapter recap illustration from *storytelling with data: let's practice!*

Illustrated content can make sense in cases when you simply can't use a photograph. I'll bring to mind a previous example: communicating about a product that hasn't been created yet. A drawing helps people see and ensure they are envisioning the same thing rather than vastly different ideas. As another benefit of illustrations, if you are the one drawing or commissioning the work, you can specify details so that the resulting illustration is exactly what you want. It doesn't have to exist in reality in the way that's required with a photo.

Like photography, if you aren't skilled yourself, getting good illustrations will likely mean spending some money. A number of the stock photography sites listed earlier in this chapter have searchable illustrations as well. There may also be situations where it makes sense to hire a professional (that's what I did for this book and *storytelling with data: let's practice!*, which were illustrated by the talented Catherine Madden).

On the topic of illustrations, I recommend avoiding clip art (the pre-made illustrations that are available in your slide application) and comics. It's for the same reasons that I suggest avoiding trite photography—it does little good and can sometimes harm. There are probably reasonable exceptions on the comic front but proceed cautiously. They can undermine your credibility and the perceived professionalism and seriousness of what you are presenting.

Diagrams

Whereas photographs and illustrations evoke feelings and help introduce or reinforce ideas, when there's a process, concept, or relationship between elements that is helpful to see, opt for a diagram. Diagrams can take a variety of shapes and forms. Rather than review specific types of diagrams in this section, I'll outline some general tips.

To start, as I did with photographs and illustrations, I encourage you to think about what it is you want to communicate in your diagram. A great tool to assist your thought process is a blank piece of paper. This will allow you to test different shapes quickly to find a general form that works. Then determine whether any predefined templates exist in your slideware to use as a starting point or if you need to build your diagram from scratch.

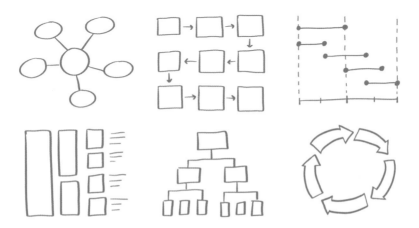

FIGURE 8.13 Diagram sketches

Another benefit of designing first on paper is that it makes it more difficult for clutter to work its way into your design. The same lessons that we covered in Chapters 6 and 7 for eliminating clutter and using sparing contrast to direct attention in text and graphs apply to diagrams as well. Some common clutter culprits to watch out for in diagrams are distracting borders or shapes and unnecessary or suboptimal uses of color.

Borders and connecting shapes like lines and arrows can often be pushed to the background. As we experienced when we de-emphasized elements of our graphs in Chapter 7, this makes it easier to create contrast to focus attention in what remains. If there is a node or section where you'd like others to look, make it visually distinct from the rest. For example, use color only there.

You can also use contrast in a live setting to help you talk through your diagram. In the same way we built graphs piece by piece in Chapter 7, it sometimes makes sense to reveal diagrams gradually as well. This ensures people don't jump ahead. Or, if it's helpful to see the shape of the overall diagram, use sparing color or other emphasis to progress through nodes or sections. This both acts as a guide to you as you're speaking as well as visual anchoring for your audience so they know exactly where to look in the diagram at any given time.

For example, Figure 8.14 shows two versions of the same simple diagram. The left-hand side has heavy borders and connecting arrows plus quite a lot of color. Compare this to the version on the right. Borders and even some background shading were eliminated. The arrows and remaining background shading were changed to gray—still present to set apart the discrete steps and help us understand the flow but not competing for attention. I assumed on the right that I'm discussing the diagram live and emphasizing a single node at a time as I progress through it, with current emphasis on the Sign In step that takes place on the Day of Event. Notice how much more flexibility exists for creating contrast and directing attention in the version on the right.

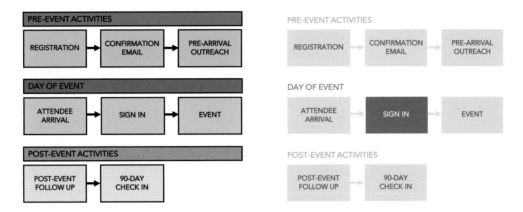

FIGURE 8.14 Two versions of the same diagram

A diagram used well will make something easier to understand, not feel more complicated. When creating a diagram, there's a delicate balance between choosing the right amount of information to show and draw attention to. This may mean that some of the specifics in your diagram become talking points and that you display a stripped down or simplified version in your presentation.

Expanding on this idea, one approach—which is particularly useful when there is important information to communicate at the high level and the specifics are also important—can be to show a simplified version of the entire diagram. Use this to set the context of the full picture for your audience. Then highlight a specific node or section and go into detail about that on subsequent slides. I might use the diagram on the right-hand side of Figure 8.14 to introduce the sign-in activity, then go to a slide or series of slides that explains what that entails.

Following this, you can then reorient people with the same simplified version of the high-level diagram before moving on to the detail in another section. This idea is similar to the navigation scheme we've looked at several times already for helping orient others in your presentation, where the diagram itself becomes your navigation scheme.

What about maps?

Is a map a picture, a data visualization, or a diagram? Maps can take on any of these roles, depending on how you use them, and sometimes serve multiple purposes simultaneously. Maps work well when there's something about the geospatial aspect that is important for people to know—for instance, if it's a lesser known geographical area and the specifics are critical. Another instance is when you are communicating data and there is a clear regional concentration (high or low) that would be otherwise difficult to ascertain.

For those who build—or would like to build—maps, a fantastic resource is the book *Cartography* by Kenneth Field (Esri, 2018). Listen to me chat with Kenneth in Episode 41 of the *storytelling with data* podcast (storytellingwithdata.com/podcast).

There are a number of tips and strategies that have come up over the course of this book in multiple places. I'll list a few of them: using a navigation scheme to orient yourself and your audience, decluttering and focusing attention, always being intentional about *why* you're using the content you're including. Many of the design aspects I've talked about specific to one area or type of content apply to others, too. I encourage you to think holistically about the content you create and how you can make it work best for you and for your audience.

Diagrams assist your explanation and increase others' understanding. Illustrations set and reinforce tone. Photographs help people relate to you and your topic. Pictures in general help your audience remember what you said. All of these things are pretty powerful. After our review, I hope you are thinking differently about when and how you'll use images in your presentations.

This wraps up the *create* section of the book. You'll recall that we began in Chapter 5 by bringing the low-tech plan that we created in the first section into our slideware, setting the design and structure of our presentation. Then we explored concepts and saw many examples of how to develop content: say it with words, show data in graphs, and illustrate with images.

If you're working on a project as you read and have been developing your content slides as we've progressed through the past few chapters, now is an excellent time to take a step back and look again at how it all fits together. This is often a good point at which to share your work with others and solicit feedback as well. There will be opportunities to continue to refine your materials now with this comprehensive view.

But don't spend *all* of your remaining time here. The materials you present are only one part of the equation. *You* are the other. Your role is a critically important one, which we'll delve into in the final section of the book.

Before we do that, let's return to the case study and determine whether and how to incorporate images into the presentation content.

Illustrate with images: TRIX case study

Could the materials I'm preparing for my client team at Nosh benefit from the inclusion of any images? To help make this determination, let's revisit the structure that we set in Chapter 6 and consider where there might be opportunities. You will recall that we've looked at this previously in slide sorter view. For easy reading, I'll list out the draft slide titles of my planned storyline:

- TRIX trail mix: most popular product
- Ah nuts! Macadamia price increase
- Decision: increase price or reduce cost?
- We tested packaging

- Taste test: assessed three mixes
- Participants prefer the original mix
- Apricots made Alternative A too soft
- Alternative B: people don't like hazelnuts
- Alternative B: people love coconut
- Decisions to weigh

In reading through this list, I don't see any obvious ways to incorporate photographs of my kids or my amateur sketches (kidding!); let's contemplate what other imagery might prove useful.

In Chapter 5, I showed a slide illustrating the winding path, shown again in Figure 8.15.

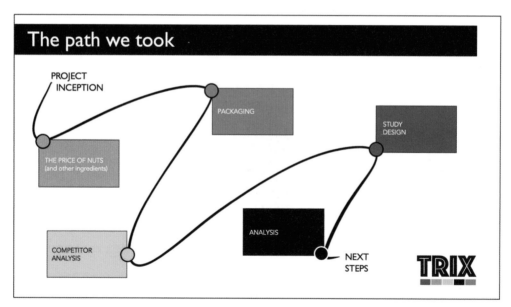

FIGURE 8.15 A diagram to show the winding path

This diagram will help me explain the general path we took to come up with our recommendations (and will also act as a navigation scheme for the information that I'll include as supplementary material in the appendix of my slide deck). I sketched it on paper first and am happy I did so. If I'd jumped straight into templated diagrams in my tool, it would have been easy to end up with a linear flow. By starting with paper, it encouraged me to think about what I wanted to show my audience: that it *wasn't* a straight path, and we took a number of twists and turns to get to the final step. Once I had the concept on paper, I made my own shapes in PowerPoint (I drew the curved line, and the rest are simple rectangles that I've formatted as desired).

As we've discussed, this is a high-stakes presentation about an important component of the client group's business. When it comes to incorporating other types of pictures, I have to be discerning in my use of images if I do include them.

As part of our testing, we compared the current packaging to a new version that incorporates a view window so consumers can see the trail mix. This seems like an obvious place to include photographs of the two types of packages. Doing so will visually reinforce the topic and ensure everyone is picturing the same thing when I refer to the view window that was preferred.

FIGURE 8.16 Photo of product packaging tested

We'll also be discussing trail mixes of various compositions. We can certainly do this verbally and describe what is in each or even list the ingredients on a slide. It could also work to show them directly so that people *see* them, providing everyone a visual cue.

This is an instance where I require specific photographs: close-ups of each of the three trail mixes tested where we clearly see the composition of each (and the differences in composition between the three). No stock photos are going to help with this! I am lucky to have a teammate, Alex, who has a keen eye for detail and some time to help me with this. I ask Alex to stage photos of the three mixes. See Figure 8.17.

FIGURE 8.17 Photos of the three trail mixes tested

These trail mix images look pretty fantastic! Alex is not a photographer, and she didn't use any fancy tools, but she *did* incorporate her ingenuity. Each trail mix was put in a small clear glass prep bowl to contain it and lend a circular shape. She placed the bowls on a white window sill, both for the neutral background and natural light. Then Alex photographed them (with her iPhone 8 camera), trying different angles and playing with the arrangement of the ingredients in the bowls. Because there was clear contrast between the nuts, the glass bowl, and the white window sill, she didn't do much after that to modify the images. Alex used PowerPoint's built-in functionality to remove the background (those who don't have PowerPoint might use remove.bg, a free online tool). In all, the process from arranging trail mix ingredients in a bowl to what you see in Figure 8.17 took about 30 minutes—and yielded custom and professional-looking photos to incorporate into my deck.

I plan to introduce the trail mix images one by one on the same slide so that my audience sees the ingredients as I describe the composition of each. In this manner, the photograph will help me both remember and reinforce for others the makeup of each mix. After that, I think there may be opportunities to integrate the images again on some of the data slides as I review with the Nosh team the results of our taste test. This will help keep everyone straight about the different mixes and relative preferences across the various dimensions for each.

I've started some solid content for my presentation deck. I'll finish fleshing it out and get feedback from my team. I also plan to share it with some friendly folks in my client group to get confirmation that this will be an effective approach for the broader audience. You'll get an opportunity to see the entire presentation a little later in the book.

As the date for my meeting with the client team draws near, I need to make sure I'm spending time developing not just my content but myself, too. Next, let's turn our attention to what I can do—and what *you* can do—to prepare to deliver a stellar presentation.

deliver

refine through practice

You've planned and created your content. But amazing content can fall flat if it isn't communicated well. In this chapter, we concentrate our attention on *you*—the presenter.

When you are the one talking through your analysis, project, or presentation, you play a critical role in that process. Consider presentations that you've sat through in the past. If you're like me, they run the gamut, from awful to awesome. Which end of that spectrum they fall closer to often depends primarily on one thing: the person communicating the information. Does the way they talk make me want to listen?

I once attended a conference where there was a short presentation about a rare bird in New Zealand (the kākāpō, which is in danger of becoming extinct). I didn't intentionally choose this session; it was a single-track event, and I happened to be sitting in a comfortable chair near friends I don't get to see often. I was surprised at how intriguing I found the topic. It did not engage me because I was interested in this particular subject matter, but because the presenter was clearly so passionate about it. That type of excitement is contagious. I could see how much he cared about the topic, and it actually made *me* care more than I otherwise would have. The speaker used some good visuals, too, but those were icing on the cake. *He* was the one who made it engaging.

A polished presenter is able to overcome mediocre materials. The opposite is not true. You may have fantastic content: great images, beautiful data visualizations, and thoughtfully designed slides—but if you can't get people's attention and talk in a way that will resonate, you run the risk of all of your hard work being for naught.

Don't let that happen! Here's the best part: we can all be great presenters.

This doesn't magically occur. It takes time and careful, active practice. All of this transpires behind the scenes, so it's easy to overlook. You don't observe the work that goes into developing a good presenter; you only witness the results when you see it done well. Have you ever watched a skillful presenter and thought to yourself: I wish I had that talent for public speaking; how lucky they are to feel comfortable and confident in front of an audience!

TED talks are a great case in point. An unassuming person walks onto the stage, looking effortlessly put together, and delivers a spectacular presentation of inspiring content. It sometimes seems like they aren't even trying!

If you rewind the tape, what you *don't* see are the months of expert planning and coaching that go into making those twenty minutes look so easy.

I certainly didn't start out as a confident public speaker, and it showed through my shaky hands, wavering voice, and abundance of filler words. My presentation skills are the result of deliberate preparation and a great deal of practice. Over time, I have cultivated this ability in myself and in my team. As a result, I am an absolute believer that we can all become increasingly effective and nuanced in the role that we play when we communicate.

In this chapter and the following, we'll study specific strategies and tactics to employ while you prepare yourself to present with poise. This chapter centers on how to practice presenting specific content you have developed. We'll examine concrete ways to do so that will help you both continue to refine your supporting slides and be well positioned to deliver them adeptly. In Chapter 10, we'll sharpen the focus on you and build your confidence as a presenter.

Let's begin with the simple practice of saying things out loud.

Practice out loud

My number one tip as you prepare to speak in any important scenario—whether seated around a table with colleagues, presenting virtually, or standing on a stage—is to spend time practicing aloud.

One important aspect that we pay more attention to when we practice audibly is our transitions. Specifically, I am referring to the shifts between slides, graphs, or topics. When you sit at your desk and advance through slides on your computer, it helps you become clear about what you want to say on each slide. However, it's easy to skip thinking about how you'll get from one to the next. When you talk through your content out loud, you are forced to articulate this step. You have to find the words that actively connect the pieces for yourself and for others. Doing this will both help you form thoughtful transitions and continue to improve your content so that it works well to support your spoken words. Good transitions take a presentation from feeling haphazard or disjointed to polished and smooth.

There are benefits to practicing out loud in a few different manners. When I'm preparing to give an important presentation, I'll practice my content aloud in slide sorter view, one slide at a time, and finally, without my slides. Let's discuss each of these approaches.

Practice out loud: slide sorter view

Recall that I suggested you talk through your story aloud way back in Chapter 4 when we were arranging ideas along the narrative arc. We brought that storyline into slideware in Chapter 5 and vetted the flow (at that point, with simple titles on empty slides) in slide sorter view. Now that you have your content fleshed out, this is a great time to look at it again from this perspective and talk through it.

This helps you test the general order, form smooth transitions, and start to commit the progression to memory. It can also highlight specific adjustments to make so your content better supports you. If something feels off or you're having a hard time figuring out how to move from one slide to another, this often indicates that changing the order or introducing additional connecting content will help. Doing this with a static view of your slides also allows you to identify whether and when animation (elements appearing, becoming transparent, or disappearing) on a given slide may prove useful, too. We'll look at a specific example of this in the case study at the end of this chapter.

Say it out loud

Speaking aloud helps us refine, practice, and identify better solutions—for our graphs, slides, and overarching presentations. I've long been an advocate of this simple and underutilized strategy. To hear more on this idea, check out Episode 6 of the *storytelling with data* podcast, entitled "say it out loud" (storytellingwithdata.com/podcast).

Practice out loud: one slide at a time

Once you're comfortable with the general flow, it is often useful to talk through your deck slide by slide. Whereas your review in slide sorter view is likely to stay at a higher level, this is where you will identify specific speaking points. You can test the appropriate level of detail to go into on each slide and get comfortable with the words you'll use and the general order you'll approach things. Doing this several times (particularly if there's a piece that's tripping you up) will allow you to test out different strategies and figure out what works best.

We'll come back to the practice of talking aloud through your slides a little later in this chapter when I encourage you to do a full dry run emulating the environment in which you'll ultimately present. For now, use your audible practice to clearly articulate your main points and make sure your content is set up to support you well. If there's something important that you're afraid of forgetting, build prompts directly into your slides. For example, add or animate a reminder word, phrase, or point of emphasis to bring it to your attention. Be aware of rough patches or anything that's tripping you up—either continue to practice until it feels smooth or modify your content. If you have the benefit of additional time, return to any problem areas after you've taken a break. With a fresh mind, you may have better success.

How much should I practice?

I am an advocate of practicing until you feel comfortable with your content and are able to talk through it eloquently. That's going to look a little different as the situation changes. In this chapter, I share the comprehensive varieties of practice that I personally combine for a high-stakes presentation. This doesn't mean that you have to follow each of these strategies every time you present. In some cases, a single run-through in slide sorter view might suffice; in others, you may practice one transition many times to make it smooth. Choose the method that will best suit your needs given your comfort with your topic, time constraints, and other factors. The more important the occasion, the more time I'd recommend devoting to practicing.

I've heard the notion that over-rehearsing is a bad thing, but I disagree. If you prepare to the point that you feel comfortable with your content, it leaves some brainpower free to pay attention to other things when you ultimately present. For example, you can watch facial expressions of those in the room and adjust your delivery in response or move about the physical space in intentional ways (which we'll discuss further in Chapter 12). The goal is to sound polished *without* sounding scripted.

When I'm getting clear on my main points for a given slide, I'll sometimes make use of speaker notes in my presentation software. To do this, add text in the pane below the slide in normal slide view (the same view where you edit slide content). I don't recommend writing out a full script, but adding a few words or short phrases to prompt your memory can be helpful (assuming you'll be able to see these notes when you present). You can also use speaker notes to reinforce key points or lend supporting details to your materials if someone else will be presenting them or if they will be shared with your audience.

Practice out loud: *without* your slides

I also advocate practicing out loud without your slides. I do this a lot. One benefit is that you can do it anywhere. I often take long walks around my neighborhood talking to myself, audibly reinforcing my content (fortunately, I don't usually run into too many neighbors when doing so!). This assists me in a couple of ways. First, it helps with the transitions that I mentioned before. Each time I move from one idea or concept to another, I expand the number of already-established pathways in my brain to pull from for smooth connections when I ultimately present. I hear how I sound and explore ways to use my voice (we'll discuss this in depth in Chapter 10).

Also, without my slides in front of me, I'm forced to anticipate and remember what's coming. Repetition is key here. The more often I do that, the easier the progression will be to recall. When I know what to expect, I can be clever in how I lead from what I'm saying currently into what I'm going to say next. As I do this aloud, I'm forming transitions and choosing my words while simultaneously thinking about what's coming—there's a lot going on in my brain! All of this effort spent ahead of time will ultimately make it easier for me to communicate in a composed and thoughtful way.

As an additional benefit to practicing without my slides, I sometimes forget the exact planned order of content and walk through something in a different manner that works better than what I originally designed. So this practice of talking aloud without slides illuminates improvements to make to my content, too.

Commit it to memory while you [...]

In the days leading up to presenting new content—this could be for a key-note address, a virtual event, or a training session—I practice any rough patches in my head as I brush my teeth. This is uninterrupted alone time where I work through different words and phrasing to come up with options. When I'm doing this, I'll think through the same part a few times because I find the repetition helpful. The intermittent nature of this ritual (I don't necessarily do it every time I brush: in some cases, it's once in the morning and again that night or on consecutive mornings) also helps me commit the flow to memory. Consider when during your day you do something routine that doesn't require active thought. Can you repurpose headspace during that time to hone your words and message?

I don't advocate memorizing—it's too risky. If you forget an important word or phrase that you want to say, it may throw everything off. But I am a fan of committing strategic points to memory. Something that is useful to nail down is the general progression of your material: what comes first, what comes after that, and so on. Practicing without slides helps you do this.

While I don't recommend memorizing, I *do* encourage you to plan how you will start and the way you will end.

Plan the beginning and end

The beginning and end of your presentation are important points. The way you start is the first impression you will make on others. It's in those initial few minutes that people decide whether they are going to continue to devote their attention to you or turn it to something else. Make those first moments especially count. Pique your audience's interest—both for your topic as well as for you and how you speak about your topic. At the other end of the spectrum is the way you wrap up your presentation: this is the final and lasting impression. Make it a positive one, too.

Start strong

Let's focus first on crafting the beginning. I plan the way I'll start any time I'm going to be discussing something new. I recently recorded a podcast where I interviewed a guest in person. In addition to audio, we also recorded video and streamed it to viewers watching live. With an audio-only podcast, I typically draft my introduction ahead of time, actually writing it out. Then I practice out loud a few times so it sounds natural by the time we record it.

Given the nature of this particular podcast, that technique wasn't going to work—I needed to connect with my guest and those watching, not read from a script. To achieve a strong start, I plotted the general flow. I would begin by introducing myself. I would give some context about my guest and why others would find him interesting. From there, I would delve into the story of how I got to know him and tell specific anecdotes to pique people's interest. Then I would jump into my first question. Those were the topics I wanted to hit and in that order.

I practiced aloud. The way I did it was a little different each time, and that was useful. I found distinct ways to get from points A to B to C to D, which gave me a lot of flexibility when I got to the eventual conversation—I knew I'd have various trajectories I could take. As another benefit of practicing out loud: in several instances, I'd realize I was talking down a path that I didn't want to follow. When practicing, it's easy to reign that back in and start again at a prior point. It's much better to learn from that process than to meander through my words while others are listening!

Knowing the points you're going to tackle at the beginning is also helpful if you're prone to nervousness when you speak in front of others. Having a clear plan on how you'll begin allows you to address those initial minutes with ease.

By the time you get through your introduction, your nerves will likely have calmed, allowing you to think better on your feet as you move through the rest of your content.

Plan the ending

It is equally important to be mindful about the close of your presentation. What feelings or ideas do you want to leave with your audience? Whether seeking to inspire your assemblage from on stage or sitting with colleagues around a meeting table and wanting them to remember your key point or act in light of the insights you've shared, the right ending can help facilitate it.

Make a powerful final statement

When I'm presenting, it's typically either on stage for a keynote-style presentation or at the front of a room full of people teaching a workshop. In both of these settings, I like to build to a crescendo of anticipation up to the end. Often, this means wrapping with a well-rehearsed illustrative example that reinforces key lessons to inspire attendees with what could be. Then I finish with a final message that encourages the audience to bring those same learnings into their own work. This closing statement will be intentional, planned ahead of time, and spoken with confidence. This also makes it clear that it is *the end*. Consider how you can make a powerful final statement and send people off inspired.

Make your ending match the occasion. At the conclusion of your topic in a business meeting, this might take the form of thanking your audience for their time, recapping next steps, or letting stakeholders know when the subsequent update will take place. If the final slide will be visible for a period of time (such as during discussion or Q&A), make smart use of the space by putting key takeaways or your main message on it as a visual reminder to yourself and your audience.

Knowing how you will close helps you wrap up gracefully. Even in a more casual situation, I recommend being thoughtful about planning the end. It's your opportunity to leave your audience with something salient and form a positive lasting impression.

Get feedback from others

You've practiced aloud in a few ways and planned how you'll start and finish: now is a great time to get input from someone else to direct your continued refinement. When seeking feedback on your content and delivery, be thoughtful both about whom you get feedback from and what type of input will be most useful. This will help you target your efforts.

Determine who to ask for feedback

Whose feedback will serve you best? One spectrum of potential reviewers to deliberate is supporter versus critic. If you're lacking confidence, getting early feedback from a **supporter** is a good place to start. This gives you a boost and helps set you on the right path. Asking a superfan is also a good course of action if you're short on time since someone on your side will likely be more willing to work within your constraints.

If you have more time and depending on the scenario, it occasionally makes sense to ask for input from a **critic**. This could be someone who is particularly tough on you or who you anticipate may be resistant to the message you want to get across. There are a couple benefits to this. First, by inviting feedback from someone who is not on board, you'll develop a better understanding of a different point of view. This can help to identify what is causing opposition so you are able to thoughtfully address it. Also, simply reaching out to a critic and asking for feedback is a vulnerable thing to do, which sends a strong message. If the person complies and offers guidance, act upon it. This exchange may have the added bonus of shifting them into the supporter category. Imagine you do this with someone who will be at the meeting where you'll present: they'll be rooting for you in a way they wouldn't have before you solicited their guidance.

Another aspect to consider when selecting the person to critique you is their level of familiarity with what you'll be communicating—will it be most helpful to talk to an expert or someone unfamiliar? On the **expert** side, someone with subject matter knowledge who can quickly process the content may have an easier time focusing on your delivery. They can also help you anticipate questions or let you know if you go off track or say anything overreaching, which is good to realize and address ahead of time. Ask an expert to take the counter-position—have them assume a different viewpoint or pose difficult questions. The more you practice foreseeing how things might take unexpected turns and prepare for them, the more proficient you'll be at dealing with any issues that arise during your final presentation.

When it comes to choosing **someone unfamiliar** with your topic, it may be useful to practice with a friend or family member who is distanced from what you will present. This can be helpful for figuring out if you're using inaccessible language or assessing the level of context you should set. Invite them to ask for clarification along the way, making it clear that you value their honest and direct feedback. The process of answering their questions forces you to articulate your rationale and land on different words and ways of explaining that you can subsequently roll into how you communicate.

Supporter input helps me refine my stories

When I need input, I often turn to my #1 fan—my husband, Randy. I know that he'll be candid and that he wants me to do well, so when he offers feedback, I listen. His observations often serve as a fresh perspective on whether I'm talking through concepts in an easy-to-understand way or if more simplification is necessary. He's also a masterful storyteller. I routinely seek his input on the stories I use to introduce content and illustrate or reinforce ideas. Who in your life can give you feedback to refine your presentations?

There are benefits to each of the aforementioned profiles. In critical situations or as you're simply looking to develop and hone your skills generally, it is often useful to get feedback from multiple people. Collecting various views also helps to validate opinions: one seemingly off-base comment may not warrant addressing, but if you're getting the same suggestion from multiple sources, it is worth listening to and adjusting accordingly.

Be specific about what feedback is needed

Also be clear on what type of feedback will be most useful for you from the given person. Do you want them to concentrate on the content and make sure the words you're using make sense? Or should they observe your delivery: how you're moving your body and the tone of your voice? Do you want them to raise questions and offer an assessment as you go or let you do your thing and wait until the end? Set expectations up front so the person giving you input will know what to watch for and feel comfortable voicing it.

Knowing what you want feedback on specifically helps you determine how to best run through content to get the desired input as well. For example, if you want to vet your general progression of content and get someone to review for errors or issues, start in slide sorter view. Share your screen in a virtual setting or have someone sit by you as you talk through your plan, clicking through individual slides in your presentation software. This method invites a fluid conversation, where you convey thoughts about your planned approach and get feedback along the way. On the other hand, if you seek input on your delivery, present your slides formally from start to finish. In that case, agree up front to discuss feedback at the end so it won't interrupt your flow.

When facing constraints that will have implications on whether and what adjustments are possible, disclose those, too. If your important meeting is tomorrow and you're simply interested in fine-tuning, that will warrant a different type and level of feedback than a presentation that is weeks away and allows you flexibility to make sweeping changes. The more explicit you are about what you need and the limitations you face with those who will provide feedback, the more actionable and useful an evaluation you will likely receive.

Do a dry run

If you solicited feedback from someone else, it's possible you framed it as a true trial run, delivering your content from start to finish as you intend to in your final presentation. If feedback was minimal and you're feeling good about your materials and delivery, you may not have to do another. However, if you didn't seek feedback, tackled it differently, or made modifications based on input—I'm an advocate of doing a separate dry run on your own. Use the learnings from this process to make final tweaks to your content, ensure you get the timing right, get comfortable with technology, and sound polished.

Emulate the presentation environment

To the extent possible, model the details of your mock session after your anticipated environment. If you'll be seated at a table, sit down and proceed through slides from your computer. Practice looking up from your screen like you will when others are there watching and listening. Will you be presenting from a stage or standing in front of a room? Get up and advance slides with a clicker. Look around the room as you talk, as you will in your final delivery. When preparing for a virtual presentation, focus on the camera while you speak.

Do as much as you can to make your practice presentation look and feel like the real thing.

Get comfortable with unfamiliar tech

If you'll be using any new technology, your dry run is a great time to become familiar with it. I touched on one example already. If you'll require a clicker to advance your slides, practice with one ahead of time (ideally, the same one, but if that's not possible, rehearsing with a surrogate is still worthwhile). If you know you'll use a handheld microphone, hold a placebo. Yes, it sounds silly (and will look funny, too!), but this allows you to work out important decisions ahead of time—if I have a clicker in one hand and a microphone in the other, what will I do if I want to take a sip of water?—so you feel more comfortable during your presentation.

This is especially the case for any technology that will impact your slide content or design. For instance, if you will present from a computer other than your own, anticipate challenges and prepare for them. As we discussed in Chapter 5, this may mean downloading special fonts on the presentation laptop or eliminating them altogether to avoid mishaps.

If you'll be in a virtual environment, practice with the technology you'll use to present (Zoom, Google Hangout, Microsoft Teams, Cisco WebEx, etc.). If possible, do this on your own or with a colleague *outside* of any official planning meetings. This gives you the flexibility to poke around without interruption, which will make it easier to take notes and commit to memory. Get comfortable sharing your screen, turning your video and audio on and off, and switching to other windows (e.g. chat, Q&A).

When I present virtually, I often use a switcher (my preferred device is the ATEM Mini Pro). This gadget allows me to pivot seamlessly between a livestream of me speaking and my slides, as well as picture-in-picture (where I have my slide as the primary visual, with a strategically placed camera feed of me within it or vice versa). If I plan to present this way, I design my slides with a placeholder where the picture-in-picture box will appear to ensure everything works well together with sufficient space and without any elements overlapping. Even though I use the switcher fairly regularly, I always find some kinks to work out when I incorporate it in my practice run.

You can even go so far as to wear the clothes and accessories that you will when you present. This may sound strange, but doing this helps you catch potential issues before they become real problems. If the shoes you plan to stand in for your hour-long presentation become uncomfortable after the first few minutes or the sharp new jacket you intend to wear makes you unbearably warm, you'll want to rethink them.

Time yourself

As you do your trial run, actively monitor the time and take notes. Check the clock when you begin. Try to maintain the pace you expect to keep during your final delivery. Jot down the times of key points or transitions as you mock-present your content. Note the time when you finish.

If you'll be inviting interaction, prompting discussion, or answering questions, make assumptions about or set parameters for how much additional time to allow. How does the timing of your trial run plus these estimated additions compare to the allotted time for your presentation? Do you need to make adjustments?

In the instance when you have a fixed amount of time to present—a 10-minute slot on the meeting agenda or a 45-minute keynote presentation—take specific steps to ensure you stay on track. Create a timing sheet so you know exactly how long to spend on each section. Have this available to refer to when you present so you know whether you should pick up the pace to remain on schedule or slow down to fill the allotted time (unless finishing early is a viable option).

You can also build **buffers** into your content. These are places where you can spend additional time if you find you are getting through your material faster than anticipated or move through swiftly if you are running behind. One type of buffer is break slides between sections (following the previously mentioned navigation scheme). Use these to recap what you've gone through and set up what comes next in a more expansive or condensed way, depending on how you're doing on time. Another candidate would be a dedicated point (or several over the course of your presentation) to invite audience interaction or input, such as Q&A. Again, this gives you the flexibility to spend more time if you have it or less if you are running behind.

Be precise with your words

The dry run is a great time to get specific about your word choice and phrasing, both to accurately make your intended points and to do so in ways that serve others. I attended a conference once where two speakers presented consecutively. I was impressed by one and offended by the other (so much so that I wrote down the notable quotes from the better presenter that I'll share with you here). It struck me that the primary difference came down to their respective word choices for framing.

The superb speaker accounted for audience diversity, honored experience, and established credibility:

"If you aren't familiar, I'll give you a quick tour; if you are, bear with me for a minute."

"You've seen this before, but I'm going to use it to…"

"I don't have evidence for this, but I suspect…"

This was in stark contrast to the subpar speaker, who introduced things I'd seen before as if they were brand new and then proceeded to discuss another concept that was totally unfamiliar to me as if it was commonly known. Did he mean to offend? Not likely, but it felt like he didn't bother to take his audience—me—into account, which made me less inclined to want to listen to him. Choose your words carefully, and use your dry run and other audible practice to form them.

Focus on *you* when you face time constraints

When we run up against a deadline, it's easy to think that time will be best spent perfecting our content. But in reality, you will often be better served by setting your materials aside, letting them remain as they are, and concentrating on you and your delivery of the content. Employ the strategies we've examined throughout this chapter. Practice out loud. Get to know your materials well, and in particular, how you'll transition between topics, sections, and slides. Plan a strong beginning and end. Get feedback ahead of time and integrate learnings. Do a dry run to prepare for how you'll present and keep things on schedule.

Don't you wish you attended more meetings and presentations where people did all of this?

In this chapter, we've explored a number of specific strategies that help us get to better know and be able to effectively talk through our materials. This thoughtful preparation in itself will build your self-assurance. *Everything* that we've covered up to this point will help you feel positively positioned as a presenter: getting to know your audience and crafting your message in a way that will work for them, developing story and building materials that will illustrate it effectively, and thoughtfully honing your content and delivery through practice.

Still, there is more that you can do to not only feel prepared but also demonstrate your ability to present with prowess. In the next chapter, we'll focus on techniques you can use as a presenter to feel and exude confidence.

Before we do that, let's revisit the case study we've been working on so I can share some of the specific tactics I employed to refine my content and delivery.

Refine through practice: TRIX case study

With my slide deck mostly done, I turn attention to myself as I prepare for the upcoming client meeting with Nosh. I've been deep in this project for so long that I know the details extremely well. That's good, but it can also be a little dangerous; this makes it easy to get caught up in the minutiae. I've built slide content that will hopefully stop me from doing this, but rehearsing what I intend to say is also critical.

I need to simply start talking in order to find my words and smoothly connect ideas and topics. I begin by putting my presentation deck in slide sorter view. Then I go through it—saying aloud the primary points I want to make on each slide and connecting it verbally to the next.

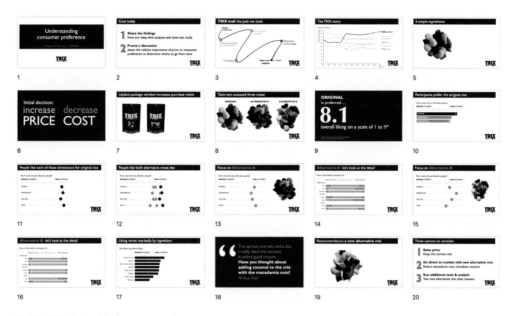

FIGURE 9.1 Slide sorter view

I realize a few things as I do this. First, there are a number of specifics I want to draw people's attention to in the story of TRIX trail mix over time (slide 4). Rather than a single static graph, this will be easier to do if I build it, using multiple views to highlight select data. This will facilitate things for me, since the slide progression itself will prompt me on the given points I want to illustrate. It will also help others, making it clear where they're meant to look as I'm speaking.

I identify a couple areas where additional slides will help me more smoothly transition between topics as well. On the "5 simple ingredients" slide (slide 5 in Figure 9.1), I found myself listing critical points about the importance of macadamia nuts and their recent price increase. I will draw more awareness to these topics by incorporating a separate slide for each. This will also allow me to reinforce my points since it means I'll be able to emphasize a single take-away with each slide title and then support it with the slide content.

I also need to add a slide to introduce the product package testing before I share the results of the test (the latter is shown on slide 7 within Figure 9.1). This seems obvious now, but it wasn't until I talked through my slides in this view that I realized it. I note a few other places to build in transitional content and progressions that will help me better explain my graphs and highlight important data points. After making these modifications, I exit slide sorter view and talk through my deck one slide at a time.

At this juncture, it becomes clear that I overengineered the animation on my line graph. I thought it would be cool to have the TRIX line appear year by year. But this is far too much clicking when I go through the slide! I'll still build the graph, but it will better support my words if I bring the data in as segments of the line (instead of individual data points). Similarly, rather than introduce each of the three competitor lines one at a time, I'll layer them all on simultaneously. This will reflect how I plan to talk through the content and my overarching storyline.

The top of Figure 9.2 shows my original progression. Each black circle represents a click to make the given element appear. The first click introduced the graph title and axes labels and titles. Then I built the dark blue TRIX line one year at a time. I layered on each competitor (gray lines) one by one and then the other TRIX products one at a time. In all, this amounted to 17 clicks!

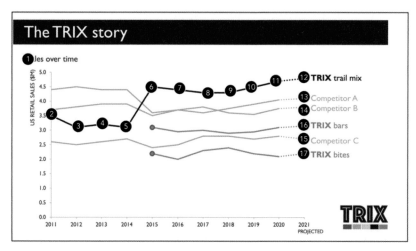

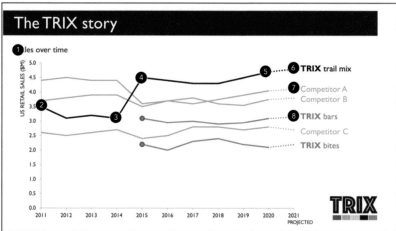

FIGURE 9.2 Scaling back from 17 to 8 clicks to build the graph progression

The bottom of Figure 9.2 shows my modified approach. I reduced the animation from 17 to 8 clicks and now have a progression that will both better guide and reinforce my talking points.

I talk through my slides on a few more occasions. I also look for opportunities to run through segments of content without my slides in front of me. I continue to make tweaks to my content and refine my delivery as I do so.

Part of what I plan through all this practice is how I'll start and end my presentation. I already have the perfect way to begin. I remind myself of that pithy and memorable phrase I formed in Chapter 6 for my presentation title: "The magic is in the macadamia nuts." I'll kick things off with this key message and launch from there into the story of TRIX, the issues faced, the tests we ran, what we learned, and our recommendation.

Thinking ahead to the ending, my goal is to drive an informed discussion among the client group. I've designed a slide with three clear options for consideration. I will use that to guide discussion and then repeat my title slide at the end, sending people off ready to act.

At this juncture, I reach out to some friendly folks at Nosh and schedule time to run them through my plans and get input. I start with Matt, Vanessa's chief of staff (you may recall that Vanessa is Head of Product for the product line that includes TRIX trail mix and is the one who commissioned this work). When we started this project, Matt had recently joined Nosh. Now that some time has passed, he has a better understanding of Vanessa's preferences and can help me make sure I address those. I'll also check with him to see if there are others it makes sense to meet with ahead of time.

I'll keep that conversation at a higher level and do my full dry run separately on my own, with an eye on the clock so that I get through my content in a reasonable amount of time.

It also occurs to me: we got early sign off on our general methodology from Abbey and Simon, the sensory analysts from Nosh's R&D team. Now would be a good time to sync with them again and run through the full analysis. This will be excellent practice for me in the event I have to get into any of these points during the main client meeting (in particular, if exacting divisional CFO Jack is in attendance). As an added benefit, having their support going into the final client meeting will help boost everyone else's confidence in our work.

Speaking of confidence, it's time to turn our attention there.

build your confidence

Let's kick off this chapter with a quick thought exercise. In a moment, I'm going to ask you to close your eyes. You'll take three deep breaths—in through your nose and out through your mouth. Then I want you to imagine that you have just given the most important presentation of your career, and it went fantastically well. Your audience was engaged. You changed their minds. They listened attentively, appreciated your perspective, and are now ready to act based on what you've shared. They applauded. People congratulated you afterwards on a job well done.

Go ahead: close your eyes, breathe, and envision the scene.

What does that success *feel* like? How does it show on your face and in your body? How does it express itself in your mind? Take a moment to identify several adjectives you would like others to use to describe you during that stellar presentation. When I do this activity, my list includes traits like comfortable, capable, self-assured, engaging, and poised. Keep your selected attributes in mind; we'll refer back to them soon.

Knowing your content is one thing, but commanding the attention of a room and creating the scenario you just imagined in reality is another. In this chapter, we'll explore strategies that will help you build your confidence to present powerfully. To start, I'll ask you to record yourself and assess your skills today. From there, we'll dive into ways to establish presence through how you move and speak. We'll discuss techniques to calm nerves and steps to take to feel prepared. All of this together will build your confidence—and your capability—to deliver a knockout presentation.

Record yourself: watch and listen

Recording oneself is the single most uncomfortable—yet mighty—way of improving how you present. When you watch and listen to yourself, you can honestly evaluate your current ability as a presenter and identify specific improvements to make. This is an imperative step toward looking like you know what you're doing when you're in front of people.

When I worked at Google and was preparing for my first training sessions on data visualization, I took part in a train-the-trainer program, together with other soon-to-be-teaching colleagues. At one point in this course, we were recorded while presenting. We were asked to select a presentation and use it to present approximately five minutes of content. The directive was to pick something we knew well so we'd focus less on what we were saying and more on the delivery. I felt confident about the slide I had prepped. My excitement was only slightly marred by a few nerves when I stepped in front of the camera.

After everyone had a turn, we viewed the recordings together, each person first making observations about themselves and then entertaining points of feedback from the group. When I watched my recording, there was one thing that stood out to me more than anything else: I was wearing shoes with heels, as I often do when I present, and was shifting awkwardly from front to back on my feet. This caused my entire body to sway. If someone had given me the feedback, "Try planting your feet while talking—it's distracting when you shift back and forth," it would have been easy for me to disregard. But seeing myself do it made me recognize a couple things. First, the resulting body sway was horribly distracting. I also realized with embarrassment that I had probably been doing that *every time I had been in front of an audience* up to that point! Once I became aware of my bad habit, I curbed it immediately.

The lesson: record yourself. You'll see things you're doing and hear things you're saying that you'll want to adjust. Let's talk about exactly how to do this.

Set yourself up and record

Start by determining what you will present. It doesn't have to be long—and shouldn't be, given the number of times I'm going to suggest you review it. Around five minutes of presenting is generally enough time to make a good assessment. Choose something that you know well and are able to comfortably talk through for that duration. You might pick a slide or two from a recent presentation, discuss your favorite pastime and why you like it, or introduce yourself (Chapter 11 explores the art of the introduction; if you don't have a topic handy to record, turn your attention there and then come back to this). Irrespective of the subject, approach it as though you are presenting it formally in a meeting or presentation setting. I recommend doing this once for practice and then a second time while recording.

Record both audio and video. When you do so, think ahead to how you'll ultimately present. If you're preparing for a virtual session or a meeting where you'll be seated at a table, record yourself seated while talking through your slides. If you'll be standing when you present, set up your camera so you can do this for the recording, too. Emulate the environment to see how you'll fare in the anticipated setting. Pretend the camera is your audience, and speak to it as you would to them.

Today's technology makes recording easy

It's funny to think back to the Google scenario. We used a camcorder on a tripod with a person at the helm to film. My performance was recorded onto a VHS tape that was subsequently put into a VCR connected to a television to view. Today, that process is much simpler: smart phones, computers with built-in cameras, and technology like Zoom make it fast and easy for anyone to record themself and watch it back. Take advantage of this ease and use it to improve the way you communicate!

After recording yourself, I suggest watching it several times, concentrating your assessment on different aspects of your presentation. I'll walk you through three rounds of review and what to look and listen for in each.

Review #1: overcome the awkwardness

If you've ever listened to your recorded voice played back before, you've perhaps experienced the reaction, "I don't sound like that!" It's true: you don't sound like that to yourself because you're used to hearing your voice from the perspective of the one speaking rather than the person listening. It's similarly uncomfortable to see yourself present for the first time and get hung up on something that comes across differently than you expected.

This first review is simply to recognize this common reaction and get over preconceived notions about how you look and sound. Let this initial assessment be about getting used to seeing and hearing yourself present and overcoming any awkwardness you feel when doing so. This will make it easier to more critically and helpfully evaluate the recording when you watch it again. With that reaction out of the way, you can pay close attention to the details and identify actionable improvements to make.

Review #2: watch yourself

Make your second viewing of the recording all about watching yourself. For this, I suggest muting the volume and focusing entirely on how you look and move. Take notes as you watch. What stands out to you? Look both for the details that are working well and also anything distracting or otherwise not ideal.

You'll likely have some obvious observations arise as you watch yourself. If you need a starting point, below are some specifics to pay attention to and related questions to consider.

- **Posture:** Are you standing or sitting up straight? Do you seem too loose or stiff?
- **Eyes:** Where are you looking? Are you blinking normally?
- **Facial expression:** Are you smiling, frowning, or making other notable faces?
- **Hands:** Where are they, and how are you using them?
- **Other body movement:** Are you doing anything too much or too little?

Take special note of whatever strikes you as awkward or comes across as uncomfortable or undesirable in other ways.

Recording to learn and get feedback as a new hire

In 2019, when data storytellers Mike Cisneros and Alex Velez joined the *storytelling with data* team (pre-pandemic, before virtual meetings were the norm), their top priority was to learn and get comfortable and confident delivering our popular half-day workshop. With each of us living in different cities and different time zones, we had to come up with creative ways to make it happen. Each week, they would read, study, and practice a given lesson from the workshop. At the end of the week, they'd record themselves talking through it and send the recording to me. This had dual benefits: they were able to watch the videos to critique and improve their own delivery, and I would also review, see progress, and offer input.

This strategy worked extremely well for onboarding new hires in our non-colocated environment. It also formed a great habit and ease for recording to refine. This is a practice that the rest of the team and I regularly employ. Given the shift toward virtual offices, video recording is a great way to learn and get feedback—both for new hires and for the rest of the team!

Review #3: listen to yourself

Now that you have a sense of how you look when you're presenting, it's time to pay attention to how you sound. Your voice is a powerful communication tool—one to which people generally don't pay sufficient attention. Turn off or minimize the video in this final review and listen to the audio. What do you notice?

Take notes like you did when you watched yourself. Below, I've outlined several considerations to be aware of in particular.

- **Filler words:** Are you saying anything unnecessary (um, like, etc.)?
- **Repeated words:** Are you overusing any specific words or phrases?
- **Pace of speech:** Are you speaking too quickly or slowly? Does the tempo vary?
- **Pauses:** Do you integrate any pauses? Do they seem like the right length?
- **Volume:** Are you too loud or soft? Does your volume fluctuate appropriately?
- **Pitch:** Does it range sufficiently, or do you sound monotone or singsongy?

Like you did when you watched yourself, pay attention both to the aspects of your speech that are working well and anything that stands out to you in a negative way.

Evaluate yourself: pull your observations together

You've watched and listened to yourself present. Reflect back on the adjectives I asked you to identify at the beginning of this chapter. What differences exist between who you'd like to be when you present and your current ways of doing so?

Don't be disappointed by any gaps you identify. Reframe how you think about them: these are opportunities! This is the fun part—you get to undertake specific actions to improve. I will reveal the tactics that my team and I employ to great effect. I am a strong believer that everyone can become increasingly adept when it comes to how they communicate with others. Now is your chance.

Watch and learn from others

One way to improve how you communicate is to learn from others: actively listen and watch others present. Pay close attention to mannerisms and delivery. What do they do well that you could emulate? What less-than-ideal behaviors do you observe that you'll want to steer clear of in your own delivery? How might you channel the techniques you see work well for others in a way that feels authentic to you?

To share your learnings from this process—and benefit from others' evaluations of various speakers—check out the SWD community exercise "learn from TED." Upon submitting your own solution, you'll be able to see those that peers have put forth (community.storytellingwithdata.com/exercises/learn-from-ted).

Look like someone people want to watch

When you present, I recommend trying to look like someone others are going to want to look at and pay attention to. Please don't misconstrue this to mean anything about physical beauty or attractiveness. I'm referring to the way you portray yourself through your body language: how you carry yourself and how you move. If you do this in a manner that looks comfortable and self-assured, it helps to put your audience at ease and have them perceive you as confident and capable, too.

Stand up, maintain good posture, move with intention, make eye contact, and do other proactive things to feel (and thus look) your best. Let's talk more about each of these.

Stand up

One thing I advocate whenever possible—and I think it's workable more often than people take advantage of—is to stand up when presenting during a meeting. This move alone can get your audience's attention and keep them engaged for longer because it's out of the norm. This seemingly minor modification makes an incredible difference. As I reflect back on my own path speaking in front of others, the simple change from seated to standing marked an interesting turning point in my own confidence and command as a presenter.

As part of the train-the-trainer program I mentioned earlier that I undertook while working at Google, one of the instructors, Niamh, attended my class to observe and offer feedback. I was delivering a two-hour training session on the topic of data visualization. We were in a room with a large conference table in the middle of it. My slides were projected onto a big screen at one end. I sat at the head of the table on the other side.

After the session, I got one of the best pieces of advice I've received in my career: stand up. Niamh said that during the training, she'd been constantly looking back and forth between me and the slides. The images on the slides were critical to illustrate the concepts I was teaching. But I—at the opposite end of the table—was so animated that she couldn't help but watch me. Given the current arrangement, the slides and I were competing against each other for attention. But the simple change of me standing up and moving to the front of the room meant we would work in concert.

Modify your position to shift the energy

Consider your physical positioning in the space as it relates to others. I've shared my advice to stand up; if everyone else is seated and you are standing, this gives you an air of authority over your audience that can be useful. When this is not desired, change it up. In a workshop where I've been standing to teach and want to pivot into casual discussion, I will pull up a chair and physically sit down. This action brings me level with participants, modifying the vibe of the situation. Alternatively, in a meeting where everyone is seated and you want to shift things in some way, standing up is a great way to garner attention. We'll explore this idea further and discuss some additional advantages standing up affords in Chapter 12.

Maintain good posture

Whether seated or standing, be aware of your posture.

Good posture maintains the natural curve of your spine. Benefits to maintaining good posture include less muscle strain, increased energy levels, better balance, easier coordination among body parts, expanded lung capacity, and improved self-confidence, to name a few. Maintaining good posture when presenting will help boost your stamina. It's also more pleasant for your audience to look at you when you exhibit the best posture that your body and environment allows.

If you are unable to stand while presenting, to achieve a proper seated position, start with your butt touching the back of your chair. Slouch forward and then draw yourself up, accentuating the curve of your back as far as possible. Release slightly, about ten degrees.

When standing, stand tall! Keep your head level and in line with your body (chin tucked slightly, not pushed forward). This means your ears will line up with the middle of your shoulders. Speaking of shoulders, they should be relaxed, down, and back—don't hunch forward. Pull in your abdomen. Place your feet shoulder-width apart, with knees slightly bent (don't lock them!) and your weight mostly on the balls of your feet. To test your standing posture, position yourself with your back to a wall, with your shoulders and butt touching it. The back of your head should lightly touch the wall.

Your body language says things, too

Establishing good posture is a great first step for the non-verbal communication that happens through your body language. When you stand up straight with your shoulders back, you exude confidence. There are numerous other signals people read from different postures, both good and bad. It is useful to understand these common interpretations because much of our body language happens subconsciously—until we become aware of and take steps to intentionally harness it.

On the negative side, putting your hands in your pockets can be interpreted as insecurity, shyness, or meekness. Crossing your arms in front of your body creates a barrier between you and others, often interpreted as a signal of disagreement, defensiveness, or anxiety. While leaning away typically indicates feelings of dislike or negativity, leaning in or toward others is a sign that you are interested and engaged.

We'll revisit and expand on some of these ideas as they relate to our audience in Chapter 12. In the same way they watch our body language as we present, there are important cues we can read from theirs in the meeting or presentation, too.

Now that we've got the sitting and standing down, let's shift to moving.

Move with intention

When you watched the recording of yourself presenting, you perhaps noticed movements you were making without realizing it. Movement itself isn't a bad thing—it helps the feeling and flow of a presentation—when it is done with intent. This is not the distracting rocking-back-and-forth motion that I described in my Google story; it's purposefully taking a step forward and throwing your hands in the air to signal something BIG (for example).

On the topic of hands, knowing what to do with them is sometimes a challenge. Did you notice anything about yours when you reviewed your recording? If not, you were probably using them well. Conversely, you may have noted an overuse of hand movement, or if you observed any stiffness to your delivery, it could be that you didn't use them enough.

When others are watching you, use **hand motion** to indicate when you'd like them to look at your slides by motioning toward the screen (this is particularly useful if you are standing in a different part of the room than where your slides are displayed, which we'll discuss momentarily). In a similar manner, you can use your hands to cue *who* to look at. If I'm going to pull Alicia into the conversation, I will gesture toward her, prompting others to look in her direction. I can also signal an invitation with my hands. When I ask my audience for input or to discuss, I open my arms out to them as I invite interaction and leave them there during the ensuing pause until the first person speaks up. Consider how to use hand motion to your advantage through intentional movements and when you will be better off allowing them to hang naturally so they don't distract.

No need to draw attention to your clicker

When using a clicker to advance slides, invest in one that has good range (I use the Logitech Spotlight Presentation Remote). This means you can stand anywhere in the room and progress through slides with ease. You do not have to physically hold it out, pointing it at your computer to advance the presentation. Instead, think of the clicker as an extension of your hand, letting it fall to your side or using it purposefully to get attention or reinforce your content.

You can also use your hands—and the rest of your body—to emphasize content by making **spatial associations**. I'll often use the following tactic when I'm referring to something *before* and then *after* a given change. Assuming I'm facing others from the front of the room, for *before*, I'll motion my hands and physically turn my body to my right. Those facing me will see this at their left, now associating the before state with left. Then, to describe *after*, I'll move my hands to my left (my audience's right) and direct my body in that direction. In this manner, I've created a physical association in the room (you can also envision how I might do this in a virtual setting with my hands front and center, moving them from right to left). Then, when I refer back to the before state verbally, I can indicate it physically by gesturing in that direction, helping reinforce it.

While I used *before* and *after* in the preceding explanation, this strategy can be applied generally to highlight a distinction between one state and another. Imagine how I could even extend this to a multi-state process from start to finish, where I begin on my right and physically take steps leftward as I verbalize the progression from one state to another until the end. Doing that across the front of a room creates spatial associations for my audience, which I can reference later to bring specific content or points of discussion back to my mind in potentially helpful ways.

When utilizing this technique, do it sparingly to avoid confusion. I mentioned this, but also be aware of how you are positioned relative to those watching you. In Western cultures, the natural flow for a process is from left to right; if I'm facing others, it makes sense for me to move from my right to my left to create an instinctive progression from the perspective of my audience.

Beyond using the physical space to associate with content and reinforce concepts, think about how you can best **move around the area** in which you present. Will it be helpful for others to see you and your slides simultaneously? If so, position yourself where this is possible. When presenting to a full room, you may walk from one side of the front of the room to the other, so that irrespective of where people are sitting, they feel equally addressed. In other cases, it might make sense to spend time walking to and presenting from different parts of the room. When I teach a workshop, I spend time teaching from the back of the room and from the sides of the room (when it doesn't compete with my projected materials) in addition to the front. If you aren't used to doing this, it feels uncomfortable at first. Like most things, continued practice can help you understand whether and when it will work and do it with increasing ease.

Make use of the space in virtual presentations

It probably won't make sense to walk around the room when you're presenting virtually, but you can still make use of the strategies we've discussed by modifying them for the virtual setting. Practice ahead of time while watching yourself through the camera. Take advantage of this to gain a thorough understanding of how much of your body others will see and how much space you have to each side and in front of you.

It is also useful to see yourself while you're presenting as long as you can do so in ways that don't distract you from looking primarily at the camera. For instance, when presenting virtually I have an external camera mounted directly above my computer screen. My camera has a built-in display that I position next to the lens, allowing me to see myself out of the corner of my eye while looking at the lens and presenting. This is helpful if I want to use my hands to emphasize something and make sure they are within the shot. The physical area in which I move is more constrained than in person, but I can still utilize it to my advantage.

Make eye contact

A simple way to engage your audience is to look them in the eyes. This is one aspect of presenting that is actually easier in a virtual environment because I am able to look my entire audience in the eyes (from their perspective) simultaneously when I focus directly on my camera. This same feat isn't possible in person if I'm presenting to more than a single individual! When presenting to multiple people or addressing a room, change where you are looking enough in order for everyone to feel included (and not ignored) but not so often or rapidly that it feels haphazard or jarring. This generally means making a statement or two with your attention directed toward one person or area in the room, then changing where you're looking. In a large room, you may simply face part of the room (without making specific eye contact or without holding it long enough for any individual to feel singled out). In a smaller setting, you will make eye contact with individuals.

If what I've just described ignites any feelings of discomfort, get comfortable by practicing. Stand up and address the room you're in now. This might mean making a statement to a chair, then a window, then a door. Also practice while watching yourself in the mirror. The goal is simply to look comfortable and natural. Also don't forget to blink!

What does your face say?

Think of your facial expression as a window into what you are thinking and how you are feeling. Are you happy to be there and passionate about your topic? Do you want to connect with and engage your audience? If so, smile! Or are you pensive, reflecting on a question someone just posed to you and requiring a moment to gather your thoughts? Look the part: you might bring a hand to your face, look up or to the side (which indicates thinking), or perhaps furrow your brow. Most of this will come naturally if you are genuinely engaged and interested in the subject and discussion.

If you're presenting on stage in a large group or have been diminished to a flat screen in the virtual environment, exaggerate your expressions a bit to ensure they are visible. This feels a little awkward at first, but it becomes easier with practice. Being animated in these scenarios where you've been reduced in size or dimension from the perspective of your audience will help ensure you don't come across as apathetic. Facial expression is especially important when presenting virtually since people typically see little else.

Do proactive things to feel your best

We've talked about a number of aspects you can pay attention to and practice that will help you establish good physical presence when you communicate. Beyond these specifics, think about what you can do generally that will make you feel good in your body and ready to present. Get enough sleep. Wear clothes that make you feel self-assured. Do things that will help you be the best version of yourself. When you feel confident, it is easier to get others to be confident in you, too.

Amp up your natural tendencies

Look closely at yourself and your innate ways, then actively fold the best parts of that into how you present. The next time you're chatting with a friend about something you're passionate about—sports, music, politics—take note of what you do. Be aware of how you position your body and your hands. Are you leaning in, or are your shoulders back? Does anything happen with the volume or pace of your speech? Ask a trusted friend to identify the mannerisms that make you shine. Think about how to integrate some of these characteristics into how you present when discussing other topics, too. Captivate others by exuding interest in your topic in a way that works for you (and engages them!).

Sound like someone people want to listen to

There is immense power in how you use your voice when presenting. How you speak makes the difference between keeping someone's attention and losing it. This is true in terms of what you say but also—and just as important—how you say it. Do you sound like someone people want to listen to?

Eliminate filler words

Start by identifying and removing any unnecessary repeated sounds, words, or phrases from your verbal communications. You likely noted some filler words when you listened to yourself present. These are the "ums," "ahs," and "you knows" that make us sound unprepared, uncertain, or lacking confidence. They distract, making it difficult to succinctly establish your point or clearly get your message across.

In addition to flagging the unnecessary sounds you make, work to understand in what instances you do so. This is key to curbing the bad habit. A common situation where filler words creep in is when you are thinking of a word that you want to use. To counter that, get comfortable with silence. Preceding your next word with "ummmmmmmmm…" comes across like you don't know what you're talking about, whereas pausing and then simply saying the appropriate word once your mind lands on it (even if it takes a couple seconds) sounds thoughtful and composed.

Read what you say to improve how you speak

Transcribing or reading the transcription of your verbal communication is an eye-opening experience that can help you quickly identify poor speaking habits. Revisit the recording I advised you to make earlier in the chapter. Listen again and write down what you say. Note the things that you're taking down repeatedly—these are likely superfluous sounds, words, or phrases.

If you don't have the patience for that, technology can help. The Descript Audio Editor will analyze audio against common filler words and give you a frequency count. My team and I learned about this through editing the *storytelling with data* podcast and started using it proactively with our workshop and presentation recordings to identify our verbal crutches and work to avoid them.

After eliminating unnecessary sounds, words, and phrases, you can continue to get more sophisticated when it comes to how you use your voice.

A strong voice starts with good breathing

You may be nervous, but you don't need to let a shaky voice divulge that to others! The first step to ensure vigor and volume in your voice is to make sure you are breathing well. We've discussed posture as it relates to how you sit and stand. Good carriage is key for your breathing—and thus your voice—too.

When you sit erect or stand tall, there is space for your lungs to expand. Breathe deeply: when your lungs have air, it enables you to have a loud and clear resonance. When you don't breathe frequently or deeply enough, it will lead to problems like a quivering voice.

Protect your voice!

Once, in the middle of a hectic business trip in Australia, I lost my voice entirely. It happened after several packed days of workshops and speaking appearances (including a pivotal one without a microphone where I had to project my voice, unaided, to a large audience). This was a wake up call to me on how critical my voice is to my work—and that I had better protect it. After diagnosing the issue as simply overuse with an otolaryngologist, I learned how to take better preemptive care: stay hydrated, avoid acidic foods, and always have a microphone available to reduce vocal strain when presenting.

Speaking without enough breath can also lead to something called **vocal fry**. This happens when insufficient air is pushed through the vocal chords—they can't rub together as they are meant to, which creates a raspy, creaky, or fried sound. If you notice that you sound different or run out of voice at the end of a long sentence, this is likely what's happening. To counter it, breathe deeply and use shorter sentences. Varying your vocal cadence also helps.

Vocal cadence: variety is key

Vocal cadence describes the rhythm or modulation of speech. I've also heard this described as the *texture* of voice. I like this term because it implies that there's something interesting and varied about it; if there's texture, it isn't flat or monotonous.

You possibly made observations related to these aspects of how you sound when you listened to the recording of yourself. After becoming aware of your natural cadence when presenting, think about why, when, and how you might alter it. Variety in pace, volume, and pitch make you sound more interesting and more interested in what you're saying.

Let's first consider the **pace** at which you speak. Increasing your speed is a way to express excitement about something. Alternatively, when reaching an important point, you could *slow down* to fully articulate and emphasize each word and allow time for the idea to sink in. Related to allowing time, pauses play a vital role in the rhythm of speech as well. You can pause as a way to get attention ahead of saying something crucial or after a statement to let the point you just made register fully. Pauses let you punctuate your spoken words. They also provide critical time for you to breathe deeply—something important for the next aspect we'll discuss.

You can also alter **volume** in interesting ways. At times, it might make sense to GET LOUD TO MAKE A POINT. Did it sound like I raised my voice just then? (Related note: be aware that text in all caps reads like you are yelling!) In other instances, I may speak *softly* or even whisper. Employed smartly, this can really get people's attention since they have to work harder to listen. This is a useful trick to get everyone to tune in before you say something important. (Use caution when employing this tactic, however; it's best to whisper only if you have a microphone amplifying it so everyone is still able to hear.)

Pitch is another component of your voice that you can vary. This is the relative lowness or highness. If you recall the vocal fry that I mentioned previously, this happens most commonly when speaking at the lower end of your vocal range; if you observe it happening, try adjusting your pitch to the middle of your range. Varying your pitch is what will keep you from sounding monotone. Use it to express excitement (higher pitch) or underscore the feelings you'd like to conjure in your audience. For example, when addressing something sad or serious, you may want to lower your pitch.

When finding your presenting voice and modifying your pace, volume, and pitch, be careful not to overdo it. The goal is to sound natural, authentic, and genuinely interested in what you are communicating.

Sound like you care

If you don't care what you're talking about—you've not found the passion or the interest—no one else is going to care about it, either. Not everything is naturally fascinating. But if you sound blasé about your topic, it will be difficult to elicit a positive response from others. Simply put, when we speak in a way that makes us appear and sound excited about our topic, we get our audience's attention in a totally different manner. Think back to the kākāpō anecdote I mentioned at the onset of Chapter 9: because the presenter was passionate about the topic at hand, I cared more than I otherwise would have. That is profound.

One way you can tap into aspects of this has to do with how you use your body when you communicate. Voice follows body. If my shoulders are hunched over and I'm looking at my feet—my voice sounds different. I don't exude confidence or feel confident. Try it. Assume the posture I've described. Look at the floor and say, "The kākāpō is critically endangered." Next, let's contrast this with some different body language. Stand up tall and put your shoulders back. Raise your hands in front of your body and use them for emphasis as you repeat the sentence: "The kākāpō is critically endangered." I sound totally different as a result of how I position my body; I'll bet you do, too. Consider how to do this when you present.

As a related aside: being aware of how you move and how you sound and having the wherewithal to adjust in the moment requires some free mindshare. This is one of the reasons I suggest that you spend so much time planning and practicing to get comfortable with your presentation content. If your whole brain is devoted to remembering what comes next, it's impossible to also think about how you look and sound. When you know your content well, it leaves space to pay attention to and play with these other aspects of how you communicate.

Before you present, there are a few final things I suggest doing to boost your confidence. Let's shift our conversation to these.

Actively prepare

One way to help get over any nerves you experience leading up to your important meeting or presentation is to take proactive steps to be fully prepared for what you will face when you present. This makes it easier to feel calm and collected.

Gather your equipment

Be equipped, and you will feel equipped! To achieve this, I'm an advocate of assembling a presenter pack. When you have your supplies packed and ready to go, you're less likely to forget something important. The specific contents will vary somewhat depending on your needs and will change over time as you learn what you must have and what you can safely omit. Figure 10.1 shows a presenter pack I assembled recently for the new hires on my team who will be traveling to facilitate workshops.

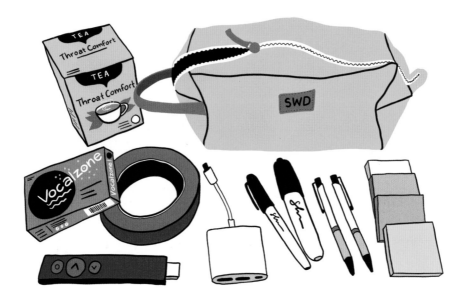

FIGURE 10.1 Presenter pack with select contents

My personal presenter pack typically includes:

- My favorite clicker to advance slides (with charging cable or back-up batteries)
- Laptop charger and HDMI adapter
- A thumb drive that I load my slide deck on ahead of time (just in case)
- Branded pens (to give to anyone who needs one)
- Sharpie markers (in the event I want to draw something for everyone to see)
- Voice and breath accoutrements (throat tea, lozenges, mints)
- Sticky notes (I never go anywhere without them)
- Blue Painter's Tape (useful for taping up signs, taping down cords, and more)
- Business cards and stickers (to remind people where to keep learning)
- A handy zipped case to hold it all

In addition to gathering my supplies, I'll also plan time to visit the space in which I'll present.

Visit the space

If it is possible, visit the room where you'll present ahead of time. This is an excellent way to identify potential problems and resolve them before they materialize. Also, the simple act of being in and familiarizing yourself with the space makes it less intimidating.

Plan dedicated time in the conference room if it's a meeting in your office, or schedule a tech check in advance of offsite presentations if possible. This gives you the opportunity to practice setting up your computer, running through your slides, and working out any related matters.

As part of this, you'll want to understand where and how both you and your audience will see your presentation. This will help you make final preparations in order for things to go smoothly. In some cases, you may have your laptop directly in front of you or otherwise in your line of sight with presenter mode enabled so you are able to see what slide comes next and your speaker notes. In other instances, you might have a confidence monitor at the foot of the stage you're standing on that shows the current slide so you can glance at it without turning your back to people. With this knowledge in hand, plan whether and how you'll move about the area.

This is also a great time to rehearse how you'll use your voice—and any technology you'll employ to amplify it. Get familiar with the microphone if you'll be using one. Learn how to turn it on and off and mute it. If it clips on your clothing, take note of how and whether to make adjustments to your planned attire.

More prepared means easier to roll with the unexpected

Years ago, I presented a keynote address at a large conference in Austria where I wasn't able to visit the venue or test technology ahead of time. Had I done so, I would have learned in advance that there were no good options for attaching the clip-on microphone to my dress and chosen something different to wear. No such luck. Moments before I walked on stage, a savvy audio-visual tech was able to fasten the battery pack in a less-than-ideal location at the back neckline of my dress (I could feel the low ponytail I'd arranged my hair in resting on it!).

If I hadn't felt well prepared in other ways—I knew my content and was confident in my abilities—this might have thrown off everything. However, given the thoroughness of the rest of my planning, it was a minor inconvenience during an otherwise ausgezeichnet (that's German for awesome) event.

Run through all of your slides. You don't have to talk through each of them at this point, but you should view them all because this can highlight any final changes to make to your content. Take on the perspective of your audience as you do this. Move around the space to see how it will display for those in different parts of the room. For example, if you find some text is too small to be legible from the back or a color doesn't come across well on the projector, modify it.

When preparing for a virtual meeting, have a planning call if you haven't already. Do so from the same spot in your home or office where you'll ultimately present. Determine how to set up the space and use the technology for a smooth session.

Now that you know what it looks like, visualize yourself in the space presenting with aplomb. It is also useful to foresee what may not go entirely as intended.

Anticipate where things could go wrong

When you foresee how something might go differently than planned, you can devise an appropriate course of action to deal with it. This will help you respond to the unexpected more eloquently when it comes up in your meeting or presentation—which almost always happens at some point.

Nothing ever goes exactly as planned. Recall the anecdote I shared when my voice gave out earlier. To deal with it, I canceled my involvement in the non-obligatory events in my schedule to preserve my voice. I reached out to the upcoming essential one—a client training—to give them a heads up and brainstorm solutions. Thankfully, a resourceful attendee volunteered to bring their own microphone and speakers for me to use. I adjusted the content for more group work to reduce the amount I'd be talking. My patient participants that day listened to me basically whisper the workshop.

Over the many hundreds of times I've spoken to a room of people, it seems like most everything has gone wrong at some point: a key constraint wasn't disclosed ahead of time, my flight got canceled and I had to drive four hours overnight to get to the event (I was seven months pregnant and got a speeding ticket in that instance!), the AV guy was late to work and no one else knew how to run the finicky projector, critical handouts for 100 attendees weren't printed ahead of time as planned, the audience resisted the change I'd been asked to communicate, the power went out. This is merely a sampling of issues I've faced that run the gamut! Interestingly, these undesirable situations often have a way of inspiring creative solutions that can be leveraged in the future. As you anticipate what could go wrong when you present, spend special time thinking about how to react gracefully (an idea we'll revisit in Chapter 12). It may improve not only the given presentation but also others to come.

A stoic approach to put things in perspective

One sometimes useful angle to take when thinking about your upcoming meeting or presentation and feeling nervous or anxious is to anticipate the worst that could happen. We tend to exaggerate the stakes in our minds and put undue pressure on ourselves. Unless you're dealing with true life-and-death topics, a single failed communication—while not ideal—is a far cry from the end of the world.

Remind yourself of this reality by imagining things going awry. What is the absolute worst thing that is likely to happen as a result of this? Often, that worst thing isn't really so awful. Also, once you've thought about how bad things can get, you'll get increased satisfaction when they go better than that. This reframing helps reduce your stress, leaving you better able to perform and appreciate what you've done.

It is often helpful to involve others in the exercise of anticipating problems. You can even make a game out of it with colleagues, brainstorming possible issues and how to resolve them. Think of it like disaster training. What technology dilemmas could arise—for example, what if you can't get your slides to project or your clicker runs out of batteries in the middle of your delivery? What back-up plans should you put in place? What people problems may you encounter? Perhaps a critical supporter has a last-minute conflict and can't attend, a stakeholder gets unruly, or you face resistance you didn't expect. Brainstorm questions and practice answering them and redirecting conversations if this is warranted. Anticipating the breadth of scenarios you might face ahead of time will help you respond elegantly to whatever arises.

You've done it: you've built your confidence. It's nearly go time! Before we get there, we have a couple final things to consider—including a quick look at the case study we've been working through.

Build your confidence: TRIX case study

To continue to prepare for the upcoming client meeting, I record myself talking through a short section of slides from my planned presentation. I've recorded myself a number of times before, so I am able to quickly identify changes to make. I look relatively good when it comes to my posture and how I'm moving, but I note several opportunities to tighten my words.

My goal is to sound prepared and polished without coming across as scripted or overly rehearsed. I need to inspire confidence—both to help guide my immediate client group to a smart decision and, more generally, to help us book Nosh as an ongoing client.

My list of refinements includes:

- **Don't use my hands as much.** I have to tone this down slightly so my hands don't distract from what I'm saying, particularly when I make a key point.

- **Don't start sentences with "So...."** I seem to be using this pointless word when I move from one slide to the next. I'll practice talking aloud through my content to identify better ways to transition.

- **Eliminate "sort of" from my vocabulary.** This unnecessary phrase found its way into my seven-minute video 11 times! It makes me sound wishy-washy in instances where I should be direct and confident. Striking it entirely will be super beneficial.

- **Reduce my use of "right?" to end sentences.** I seem to be doing this to be conversational and get affirmation while presenting, but it's annoying and unnecessary.

I write the words "So...," "sort of," and "right?" on a sticky note, draw a red X through them, and stick it on my computer monitor where I will see it regularly in the days leading up to my presentation. I alert my closest colleagues to flag these words and phrases and aim to strike any uses from my general daily conversations as well.

When I met recently with Matt at Nosh to review my plan for the presentation, we convened in the room where the final meeting will take place. I used that as an opportunity to practice presenting from my laptop and ran through my slides to confirm they look good. I also got a sense of the room and decided to stand when I present. This way, I can spend some time at the front with the slides and move around the room as makes sense during the meeting.

While at Nosh, I also checked in with sensory analysts Abbey and Simon and gathered some questions they had and some they expect others will raise during the meeting. I do some additional brainstorming with my team about what could go wrong and other queries that are likely to come up. I also ask them to role-play to practice answering and feel comfortable directing the conversation.

I assemble my presenter pack with my supplies. I am ready to present.

Before I get to my presentation, however, let's tackle one more chapter that is devoted entirely to *you*.

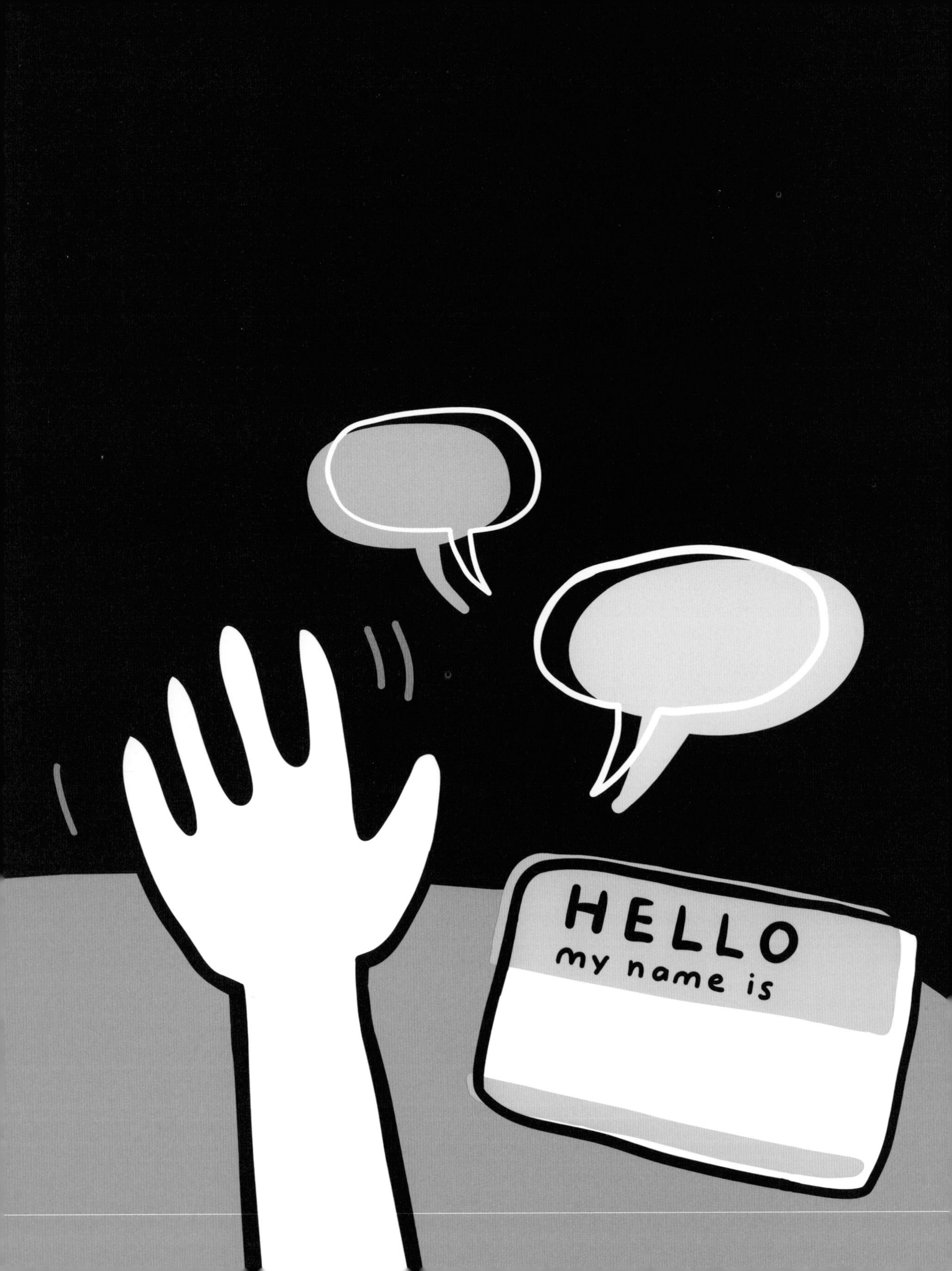
HELLO
my name is

introduce
yourself

You have surely introduced yourself before—perhaps during a job interview, when meeting the associate of a friend, at a networking event, or during the first few moments of a presentation.

But have you ever paused and given much thought to how you do so?

"Hi, my name is Cole, and I tell stories with data." I have said those words, standing in front of unfamiliar faces in venues all over the world, literally thousands of times over the past decade. I've done that despite being an introvert and definitely not considering myself to be a naturally stand-in-front-of-people-and-speak-comfortably kind of person. This didn't happen by accident; it evolved through careful planning and practice. Over the years, I've had the opportunity to help my team and clients craft their introductions as well. It is that same approach that I will share with you here.

It may strike you as odd to encounter an entire chapter devoted to this topic and to come across it so late in the process of planning, creating, and delivering your presentation. This is intentional. The way you introduce yourself—whether formally on a stage or in daily life—can have a profound impact on the way that others perceive you. It's an opportunity to form a personal connection and establish rapport. Building on the last chapter, being able to talk *about yourself* eloquently will increase your confidence, too.

The targeted process of composing your introduction that I outline in the following pages will give you the opportunity to tap into a number of the strategies we've examined throughout this book. You'll need to actually undertake the activities as I lay them out in this chapter, so grab a pen and paper (and some sticky notes if you have them handy) and get ready to do some work. Even if you don't have an important meeting or presentation on the horizon, you can still actively apply lessons and hone skills that will help you when you do. Bonus: the output of this process will be a compelling introduction that will serve you well—in your presentations and beyond!

Plan the story of *you*—starting with *them*

In the same way that we discussed it in the context of presentation design, spending ample time up front planning your introduction is key. Rarely—in a business setting, at least—will you tell your full life story. Which parts of your background, the specific combination of experiences, and level of detail you share should be driven by each scenario and what you hope to accomplish. While you'll be able to pull from the work you do here for similar occasions, when the situation in which you need to introduce yourself changes appreciably, you'll want to revisit this process.

Before you spend time thinking about yourself, let's start by acknowledging those who will be on the receiving side of your introduction: your audience.

I'll pose many of the same questions I asked you to think about in Chapter 1 early in the planning process. Who is your audience? What motivates them? What drives them and the things they do—or don't do? What do they care about? What is at stake for them? You may find it helpful to review and complete the Big Idea worksheet from Chapter 2. If you're crafting your intro with*out* a specific scenario and audience in mind, think generally about what you believe the people you'll be introducing yourself to will care about or be inspired by.

Identify key impressions

Contemplate the impressions you would like to make when you introduce yourself. How do you want others to perceive you? If someone were to describe you after you tell them about yourself, how would they do so—what words would they use? In thinking about this, don't focus on the reaction to what you say. Instead, target the perceptions that will be formed about *you*. Reflect on the qualities you want to ensure come across, the characteristics you want to demonstrate, and the feelings you want to evoke. You may recall that I asked you to do something similar at the onset of Chapter 10. In this instance, we're going to explore your desired attributes—and how to actively portray them—much more deeply.

Spend five minutes completing the following sentence in various ways: I would like to be described as _____. This will yield a list of adjectives, perhaps descriptors like confident, smart, or passionate. Five minutes is a long time for this simple exercise, and that is by design. It's to push you past the initial few words that come to mind and encourage you to think critically about the breadth of potential impressions that you would like to create among those to whom you introduce yourself. Consulting a thesaurus as part of this may be helpful.

Once you've made your list—and if it doesn't have at least ten adjectives, I suggest that you spend an additional minute or two—it's time to prioritize. From the adjectives you've assembled, identify the key impressions you absolutely must make on your audience. Aim for 3–5 attributes that are distinct from one another (if you have several similar ideas, group them together into a single category and pick the word or combination of words that best describes it). Hold onto this shortened list of key perceptions you'd like to create; it's going to assist what we do next.

Demonstrate through action

How can you create the impression you desire? Through the stories you tell. Let's take a simple example. Don't describe yourself as honest. Instead, tell the story about the time you, as a child, saw a $5 bill fall from the pocket of a man walking down the street and acted quickly to reunite the lost money with its rightful owner. Your introduction is an opportunity to paint a picture of yourself through your artfully conveyed experiences.

Compile the pieces

It's time to brainstorm specific experiences that will demonstrate the impressions you've prioritized. Consider your current and any previous work, roles, projects, interests, education, and history. What anecdotes, stories, or other points of evidence could you share that would help get one or more of these ideas across? Are there other ways to illustrate them?

I'm a fan of sticky notes for times like this (alternatively, blank paper cut into small squares will also work). When I undertake this process, I start by writing an individual sticky note for each of the attributes I want to get across. Then I find myself some space: I fully clear off my desk or sit at an empty table. I've even been known to undertake this activity on the floor of my office. I position each impression sticky note so it has some empty area around it. Then I start brainstorming. I write one idea per new sticky note (typically in another color) of things to potentially include in my introduction that will help demonstrate the given ideas. This might be a mix of experiences, projects, roles, situations, anecdotes, and stories. I put each sticky close to the key impression that it best highlights (in some cases, a given experience illustrates more than one attribute, so I'll position it between categories or make a note to indicate this).

Figure 11.1 shows what this general approach looks like. I'll walk you through this process in the case study at the end of this chapter.

FIGURE 11.1 Example introduction brainstorming

Don't edit at this point; generate ideas freely. The first things that come to mind are often simple facts: jobs you've held or projects you've worked on, for example. This is a fine place to start, but I encourage you to also move beyond the contents of your resume. What has happened over the course of your life and career that will give others real insight into who you are? Determine how you can complete this thought to share an experience or tell a story starting with, "I recall a time when...." This might include:

- **Success stories:** What examples could demonstrate a job well done?
- **Turning points:** Did something happen that changed your perspective?
- **Hardships or failures:** Have you dealt with something that went really wrong?
- **Enlightening situations:** Is there a time you had an unexpected learning?
- **Challenges overcome:** Can you demonstrate your problem-solving acumen?

If you're feeling stuck, there are a few things I suggest. Talk to someone who knows you well about the impressions you want to make. Discussing it with another person may jog your memory or prompt good ideas. If you're having trouble brainstorming ideas related to your key attributes, release yourself from that constraint. Think about defining moments in your career or life. What do they say about you—do the traits they highlight align with any of the impressions you've prioritized? If not, does that indicate you've missed something important that should be added?

Don't worry about order or how it all fits together; we'll do that momentarily. By the way, if this reminds you of the storyboarding activity that we covered in Chapter 3, it should, because it's rooted in the same process. Just like we did then, once you've spent some time brainstorming, it's time to edit and arrange your ideas into a story.

Form your story

Position the output of your brainstorming process so you are able to see all of the ideas. (This is why I gravitate toward sticky notes for activities like this: they are easy to move around.) How could the various pieces you've plotted fit together? Begin to arrange.

Consider how you want to structure the overall story of *you*.

Do you have a single powerful story that you want to tell in detail that will demonstrate the various attributes you've prioritized? Or will it make more sense to touch upon several different elements and work to weave them together into a cohesive narrative? There isn't a right answer here; it's going to depend on your scenario and personal preference.

Determine how you'll start and end. Identify the hook or point of tension that will help you get and maintain attention. Figure out where and how it will fit with the rest of the pieces. Start a discard pile and eliminate ideas you've generated that don't fit with your planned narrative. You may have identified seven different experiences that illustrate your three prioritized impressions.

However, trying to discuss every single one of them might create a disjointed account. Determine which reasonably fit together and eliminate those that don't. Have additional sticky notes available to add greater detail when necessary and connect ideas to ensure things flow smoothly.

Introduce your company or product following these steps

This process of crafting your personal introduction could easily be used to introduce a different topic to an unfamiliar audience, too: your industry, company, or product, for example.

To recap, here are the general steps:

1. **Know your audience:** identify who they are and what they care about
2. **Identify key impressions:** prioritize the attributes you want to communicate
3. **Compile the pieces:** brainstorm what points of evidence will demonstrate them
4. **Form the story:** pull the most important pieces together into a cohesive narrative
5. **Make it great:** practice aloud, get feedback, and apply various constraints

As another twist, consider how these steps might assist your preparation for a job interview. Take time to consider your interviewers, identify key impressions, and compile the pieces. In that instance, you don't necessarily need to form it into a story. Thoughtfully weave the experiences and anecdotes you've brainstormed into your responses to interview questions posed.

When else could you make use of this activity?

Let this be a fluid and iterative process. It's not likely that you'll look at your ideas, arrange them once, and be done. You may find yourself moving things around, rearranging and assessing, adding or taking away, then rearranging some more. As you weigh which path will work best, try talking through your ideas out loud. You'll find that some combinations lend themselves more easily to this and can use that knowledge to continue to refine.

At the end of this step, you will have a rough plan of attack for your introduction. Your next goal will be to polish it.

Practice to make it great

Now that you have your general story mapped out, it's time to apply the various strategies outlined in Chapters 9 and 10. This practice will help you refine your introduction. It's also a great opportunity to improve your delivery methods in general by communicating about a topic you know quite well—yourself!

First, **practice out loud**. Start talking, using the general story you created to get the words right. If helpful, you can write it out. Rather than memorize a script, I suggest getting clear about the primary points you want to make. Then practice aloud a number of times to identify the words, phrases, and connectors that will allow you to get your ideas across and move from one to the other. As part of this, determine the specific words you'll use to start and finish. Remember that these are important elements to hit particularly well.

Seek input from others once you feel happy about how your introduction sounds. Explain your goals and ask them to imagine the perspective of your audience. If there is specific feedback you'd like about your content or delivery, share that context up front. Give your introduction as if the person evaluating you is your intended audience. Following that, have a conversation about what worked well and where you might make changes. Try not to interrupt or be defensive: listen and ask questions. Adjust based on feedback or repeat with others if helpful.

Record yourself. Watch and listen. Make observations and take note of improvements to make. Now is when you get to play with the nuances of your delivery. How will you use your body and hands? When might you alter your pace, volume, or pitch to help get your ideas and personality across? Look for low-risk situations in which to test it out (like when meeting someone new socially), and continue to modify and improve content and delivery as needed.

Hi, my name is...

To listen about the art of the introduction, check out the *storytelling with data* podcast Episode #38, "hi, my name is...". I discuss a variation of the activities outlined here, as well as stories about and recordings of introductions from individuals on the *storytelling with data* team (storytellingwithdata.com/podcast).

When you have your robust introduction fully fleshed out and practiced, it is useful to put various time constraints on it. How would you introduce yourself if you had only two minutes? What about 30 seconds? A single sentence? Practice these versions, too. Then you'll be ready to face basically any scenario in which you need to introduce yourself.

While I've outlined things as a smooth progression, you should iterate as necessary. This may mean returning to earlier steps or pulling in a prior piece later in the process. The goal is to crush your introduction and leave others with a great impression. Use the combination of tips and strategies that will enable you to do that.

You've planned, created, and practiced your content. You can speak about yourself eloquently. All that's left now is to actually give your presentation!

Before we do that, let's direct our attention to the case study we've been working our way through and look at an application of the lessons learned in this penultimate chapter.

Introduce yourself: TRIX case study

My client group already knows me. Still, given the high-stakes nature of this project, I'm going to go through the full exercise of crafting my introduction. I may learn things from the process that I'll want to weave into the presentation. You never know, there may be a new face in the room when I present. With a thorough intro ready, I can pull from it and introduce myself quickly in the minutes before the meeting formally begins. Better safe than sorry. (And if things really go poorly, I will make use of it when I interview for a new job—kidding!)

I start by evaluating my audience and what impressions I'd like to create. The client team at Nosh I'll be presenting to is a mixed group. Vanessa, the Head of Product, is the person I most need to wow. She's going to have to be confident about the information I present and my abilities in general—both for the immediate decisions concerning TRIX and for determining whether to continue to work with us. I must also make a good impression on Jack, the divisional CFO; Riley, the VP of Marketing for the TRIX brand; and Charlie, who manages customer satisfaction. They will want to know that I've taken the time to understand their business and competing priorities and that I am guiding them in a prudent direction.

After taking this context into account and spending five minutes noting the various impressions I'd like to make, I compile the following list: *credible, confident, poised, articulate, trustworthy, thoughtful, smart, discerning, thorough, helpful, positive, excited, capable, experienced, considerate, supportive, collaborative, perceptive, intelligent, inquisitive, responsible, astute, professional, understanding,* and *empathetic.*

Next, I cull my list down to a few key impressions. In reviewing it, I note that there are a number of similar sentiments that can be grouped together (credible and trustworthy, or smart, intelligent, and astute, for example). It also occurs to me that I am able to demonstrate some of these attributes simply through how I speak and carry myself over the course of the presentation. Confident, poised, articulate—I don't need anecdotes or experiences to illustrate these. I will show them directly through how I present. This reduces my list in ways that are helpful.

To prioritize the key impressions from what remains, I bring our ultimate goal front and center: we want to win Nosh's business for an ongoing partnership. Given this, I decide that I want most to be seen as:

- **Collaborative:** I'm helpful, inclusive, and work well with others.
- **Discerning:** I show good judgment, make smart decisions, and recommend good paths.
- **Capable:** I am experienced, ask smart questions, and identify cogent solutions.

What points of reference will help me demonstrate these attributes? I grab my sticky notes and start jotting down ideas.

As I brainstorm, I find that a number of my ideas apply to multiple attributes. Given this, I arrange the attributes (written on blue stickies) into a triangular shape to make it easier to spatially orient the experiences that relate to multiple attributes. I also realize that there are aspects of my work on the TRIX project directly that I can pull in to demonstrate some of the ideas. These will give a good sense of how we will work together going forward (in a way that is collaborative and makes use of my discerning judgment) based on how we've done so during the current project. Fifteen minutes later, I've created the following.

FIGURE 11.2 My introduction brainstorm

My brainstorming session also leads to an idea that didn't tie directly to any of the key attributes I identified but seems useful. It occurs to me: I can remember the first time I encountered a whole macadamia nut in TRIX trail mix. That's pretty powerful! I was at work. I had taken a break and grabbed a snack from the micro-kitchen. Back at my desk, absentmindedly munching, that first whole macadamia nut brought me fully into the present moment. If I can do it genuinely and without it being corny, this feels like something worth more fully exploring and perhaps using in some way. For now, I put the sticky that references the anecdote in an empty corner of the large paper on which I had arranged the output of my brainstorming process. Then I step back to consider it all.

How do I weave these ideas together? It's time to start rearranging sticky notes. I set the blue attribute stickies to the side—their job is done. Now, I want to make sure those impressions come across through how I tell my story. I spend a few minutes unsticking, resticking, and writing additional notes, arranging everything into a gentle rise and fall mirroring the narrative arc (it comes together quickly once I take everything into account). In Figure 11.3, the yellow stickies are taken directly from my initial brainstorm; the orange ones are those I added during this formative step.

FIGURE 11.3 My introduction story

I'm going to start with my anecdote about the macadamia nut. Then I'll fast forward to today and my role on the TRIX project. If I were at a different point with the group—possibly meeting them for the first time—I would have used a past project to illustrate the ideas I want to get across. However, given that I can demonstrate them through the work we've done *on this project*, that seems like a better focus: much more relevant and convincing.

I'll introduce tension into my story by framing what an ineffective consulting-client relationship looks like, drawing on my firsthand experience during the initial years of my career. That was an awful time (and a lot of learning); I'll be able to paint a clear picture. I'll shift from there into what external consulting looks like when it is done thoughtfully, what I've learned, and the experience I've built in the years I've been at my current company. Then I'll pivot into how I've already included this insight in my work with the Nosh team and what I've done to fully understand and appreciate the brand and its history. I think there's an opportunity to refer to some of the special findings that I'll cover more deeply in the presentation to pique interest (and highlight my team's special superpower to glean actionable insights from research and data). I'll conclude by acknowledging how amazing it's been to be driving this project and highlight my strong hope for a continued partnership with Nosh.

With my general storyline established, it's time to start talking. I practice mock introducing myself aloud a few times, using the storyboard in Figure 11.3 as my guide. Once I feel good about it, I do a dry run with my colleague, Alex, and solicit her input. Alex knows the project (you may remember her as my skilled photographer) and me well, so she will be in a good position to assess and offer valuable input.

When it comes to the structure of my story, Alex suggests introducing the interesting questions we answered about TRIX earlier and using them to lead into how I've worked with the Nosh team and built my understanding of the TRIX brand. This could be compelling; I commit to try it. She also calls me out on one of my known filler words: "So...." When I record myself delivering my intro, I keep this in mind. To my delight, I find upon viewing that not only did I not integrate any unnecessary words, but I used my hands more effectively than when I recorded previously.

Even though I probably won't use this full introduction at the onset of my presentation with the Nosh team, this exercise has been extremely valuable. It brought attention to important experiences and aspects of the way I've worked on this project that I will want to integrate into my broader presentation. I now have those instances top of mind, and I've practiced the words to fluently speak about them. I know I'll be able to work some of these ideas into conversation as part of our discussion or in response to questions. As a result of this activity, my overall presentation is going to be stronger.

Also, if there's a new face in the room, I have my quick intro ready: "Hi, I'm Cole. I like to describe my team's superpower as our ability to glean action-able insights from robust research to help brands like TRIX thrive."

Imagine *you* have just been brought into this project. How would you intro-duce yourself?

(Don't spend too much time—the meeting is about to start!)

have a
stellar session

The date is quickly approaching: your important meeting or presentation is imminent!

This is a great point to reflect back on the various steps we've taken to get here. It all started with the planning: understanding your audience, carefully crafting your message, compiling the pieces, and then weaving it all together into a story. You created your content: first setting the style and structure of your presentation, and then filling in the specifics—thoughtfully designing slides with words, graphs, and images. As part of your preparations to deliver, you refined your content and spoken words through practice, built your confidence, and learned the art of the introduction.

We have invested a great deal of energy readying you for this. And now, *you are ready*. I have a few final tips to share: strategies to use in the days leading up to your session and in the moments before, during, and after. But more than anything, I encourage you to be fully present and enjoy yourself. You've put in a tremendous amount of effort. Now is when all of that hard work pays off.

It is time to engage people and inspire the action that you seek.

Final prep: the days leading up to your session

When you first started thinking about this project, it's possible you were facing months or weeks before your final presentation. Perhaps you've been working on it a little at a time over a long period, or maybe you've been in crunch mode trying to get everything quickly finished. Irrespective of how much time you've spent: you'll reach the point where only days (or hours!) remain between you and your session.

Envision success

Reflect on your primary goals for your meeting or presentation: what precisely do you hope to achieve? Think about success from a couple of perspectives. First, consider what you hope *for your audience*. How do you want them to feel, what do you expect to have happen, and what action should they take?

Recognize that even if people respond differently than you wish, that won't necessarily indicate that you were unsuccessful. Perhaps your audience will decide—in light of what you share or because of the insightful discussion you prompt—that another course of action is warranted. This would still be a great outcome.

Also think about success in terms of *yourself*. What do you want to experience before, during, and after your session? Given all that you've learned as you've practiced and prepared, are there things you hope to actively do or avoid?

Write down a few goals that you would like to accomplish. I'll ask you to refer back to this after you present. Your personal expectations in particular are worth recording: how you measure and judge your own success presenting in meetings, standing on stage, and in other presentation settings will change over time. Devote a journal to document your journey to storyteller, and observe your progress firsthand as you become increasingly effective.

Now that you've spent some time in self-reflection, let's figure out how to involve others.

Don't go at it alone

You may be the one responsible for some or all of the presentation, but that doesn't mean you have to do it on your own. Consider where and how you might get support from others. This can take a variety of forms; I'll list a few below.

- **Plant a friendly face in the audience.** Have a friend or your spouse attend your keynote address and sit where you are able to see them. Invite your manager to be present at your important meeting. In a virtual setting, ask a supportive colleague to join and organize your screen so they are in clear view. It's amazing what positive reinforcement a slight nod or smile from a friendly face lends while presenting.

- **Identify or develop a supporter.** Meet with select stakeholders individually ahead of time. Then you'll know who is in your court during the session. Alternatively, if someone is not supportive, meeting with them can help you better understand any resistance and work to resolve it ahead of time. In a conference setting, accomplish this through interactions with participants before your session begins.

- **Enlist a co-presenter or helper.** Line someone up to assist with the actual presentation or meeting. This could be a moderator for Q&A, an official co-presenter who will cover parts of the planned content, or someone you prep to weigh in or be ready to ask or address certain questions or discussion topics. In a virtual setting, particularly if participants can interact in various ways, it is often useful to recruit a colleague to help manage chat or lend a voice to the questions that get posed there.

- **Line someone up to give you feedback.** Identify someone who will be in attendance to offer their input afterwards (this can be someone you've also selected to play one of the previous roles described). Let them know your specific goals ahead of time. The simple act of asking for their assessment will have them rooting for you during your presentation.

Virtual setting: post a motivating picture

Sometimes even when you have supporters in the virtual environment, it's impossible to tell because either the faces on your screen are too small or you can't see your audience at all. As a substitute, post a picture of someone you'd like to make proud in your line of sight to offer encouragement in absentia: your child, parent, partner, or friend. This can both help remind you that you are speaking to people (not a computer screen) and help you feel encouraged while you do.

Before closing your eyes on the eve of your event...

Setting yourself up for success starts much earlier than twenty-four hours before an important session. That said, there are things you can do on that final day—especially during the evening—directly prior to your presentation that will have a positive impact.

Do everything in your power to ensure good, restorative rest. I recommend eating an early dinner and avoiding sugar, caffeine, and alcohol. Eating two to three hours before bedtime can drastically improve your sleep. When we eat late, it means that the muscles that digest and metabolize our food have to keep working when they could be resting. This has a negative impact on your ability to fall asleep and prevents you from getting the deep sleep you require to feel refreshed the next day.

Use some of the time between dinner and bedtime to review your materials. Before an important presentation, my routine is to have my slides be the last thing I look at before going to sleep. I advance through them on my laptop to make sure I'm clear on order and flow. I'll review my notes to myself as well: reminders on filler words to avoid, how I plan to move, and anything else I want to have top of mind for my session. I like to think (and there's some research to back it up) that this practice helps important points move from my short-term memory to my long-term memory overnight.

This is not the time to be working on your content! I recognize that sometimes it's unavoidable: you had a less-than-ideal amount of time to get it all done and simply have to finish the deck. Even in that instance (and especially in the one where your materials are already sufficient): spend as little additional time as possible. The hours that separate you from your meeting or presentation should be focused on *you*—ensuring you'll have the energy to present power-fully—not continued tweaks or minor improvements to your slides.

Get to bed early. Also set your alarm to ensure you have ample time before your session, because there are a few things I'll suggest you do during the minutes before your presentation as well. Speaking of time, plan to wear a watch tomorrow—you're going to need it!

Wear a watch

It will be important to monitor the time leading up to and during your session. Unless you're certain there will be an easily visible clock, I highly recommend wearing a watch. A quick glance at your wrist is an unob-trusive way to check the time. Don't rely on your phone for this—you don't want to inadvertently give the impression that the possibility of an incoming text or email is more important than your audience!

Take a deep breath: it's about to start!

On the day of your session, I have a single piece of advice: arrive early. The flex time this provides can be used in a number of ways to help ensure things go well.

Arrive early

If you are able to get into the room where you'll present ahead of time, do it. Set up your equipment and assess whether there are other things to be done. I've been known to rearrange furniture—pulling a podium out of the way or situating tables or chairs to better facilitate discussion.

While I don't prefer to use a podium, I do want somewhere to set my water, coffee or tea, and notebook, so I'll work out the best place to do that. On that note, I'll also make sure I have said beverages (personally, I opt for coffee in the morning, tea in the afternoon, and always have water on hand). In a meeting room, I'll simply bring them with me and place them somewhere I can access. When presenting formally from a stage, sometimes you have the option to stash them in a podium. At an event with multiple speakers, often organizers will have bottled water available on stage.

Eat before you present—but not too much!

To keep your energy up, I recommend eating something light an hour or two before your important meeting or presentation. As was the case with spacing your dinner before sleep, it's important to allow some time between your pre-session meal and the session itself so you can direct all of your faculties to your presentation.

Depending on the length, you may need to eat during your session as well. This won't be necessary in shorter presentations (I'd avoid it to preserve professionalism). During longer sessions—for instance, a half-day offsite or a full-day training—you should eat to maintain stamina. But not too much! Eating a large or heavy meal makes you feel sluggish. I also find that even after a small lunch during the all-day workshops that I teach, I have trouble fully catching my breath. This is the result of some of my body's attention being put toward digestion. To counter this, I've reworked post-lunch content to start with a group discussion, giving my body a little extra time before I have to be fully on again.

Walk all the way around the room to gain perspective and plot where to stand and how to move about the space if you didn't have the opportunity ahead of time. In an ideal world, you will have already run through your slides in the given venue. If that *didn't* happen and it's possible now, quickly take advantage of it (if attendees are already present, I'd suggest skipping it to avoid inadvertently starting a premature discussion).

If there is a mobile whiteboard or flipchart that you plan to draw on, move it to where you want it. When I intend to present mainly from the front of the room (and if people are generally facing frontward), I tend to opt for side-of-the-room placement if the physical space allows for it. I'll position it in the back or where I can best minimize the number of people who have to turn to see it if the audience is seated around one large table. These arrangements give me a reason and reminder to move to different parts of the room as I present or guide discussion. Use this also as an opportunity to test markers and eliminate any that might fail you when you go to emphasize a point or draw an example.

Ideally, all of this last-minute prep happens before others arrive. Once attendees begin filing into the room, chat with them. This is a great opportunity. If you already know individuals, the interaction with friendly faces can help calm nerves or give you fodder to draw on if it makes sense during the session. Introduce yourself to those with whom you aren't familiar. Work to remember or write down names if that makes sense given your scenario (acknowledging individuals by name is an excellent way to establish rapport during the session). Use the informal time to build support and create advocates by connecting with the individuals who will comprise your audience.

Seed what you need

If there's something you will expect from an attendee, use the time before the session begins to give them a heads up. This might include if you want someone to volunteer a specific answer in response to a question, express immediate support for a position you raise, be prepared to address a certain topic, or participate in other ways. The ahead-of-time prep helps you avoid an awkward pause or unexpected response.

Take a quiet moment

Before things officially start, take a quiet moment for yourself. In a formal presentation setting, you may already have a dedicated area for this: backstage or in a green room. If not, locate a private space. I've been known to wander and find an empty conference room or office for this. If all else fails, there's always the restroom. Use this time to ground yourself.

What this looks like exactly will vary from person to person. I encourage you to establish your own routine that works for you. If you're not sure what that entails, here are some ideas.

- **Assume a power pose.** Put both hands on your hips with your shoulders back and smile. Or if you have ample space, put your arms out behind you like you're Superwoman (or Superman) flying through the air. Yes, this sounds super silly. Yes, I've totally done it in the bathroom stall before going on stage at an important event.

- **Breathe deeply.** Take a long, deep breath in through your nose with your shoulders relaxed. Exhale slowly through your mouth, pursing your lips slightly (so it's audible) but with your jaw relaxed. Repeat several times.

- **Put things into perspective.** Look at a photo of your family, pet, or something else that brings you joy. Use it to remind yourself that this single event likely won't make or break you and that there are more important things in life.

Get ready to have some fun—it's showtime!

Have a knockout meeting or presentation

You know your stuff incredibly well. Many of the specifics of what you'll say and do live were explored deeply through the practice you undertook in Chapters 9, 10, and 11. Your job while presenting is to let all of that go—you don't have to actively think about it, because it's still in your mind and muscle memory. Simply concentrate on doing your best, connecting with people, and responding with grace to whatever comes your way.

Be in the moment

Work to stay fully present. This means fighting any urge to rush immediately into your content. Take a moment to actively notice where you are and who is around you. Breathe deeply. Smile.

You know how you're going to start because you planned and practiced it. As you progress through your content, continue to observe. This may mean pausing to invite input, interaction, or discussion or to make a quick note about something you don't want to forget if appropriate.

Nerves got the better of you? Pause and reset

I promised you that your planned start would carry you beyond your nerves. However, if this doesn't happen, all is not lost. In the situation where you find you're going too fast, having a hard time breathing, and your voice is quivering: stop. Pause. Take a drink of water. Breathe deeply to reset. Yes, it's a little awkward to do this in front of others, but it's much better to take this moment and recover from it to deliver a great presentation than to continue in a stressed-out state. The latter makes everyone uncomfortable. The former shows you're human and can even endear you to those in attendance, who may develop a heightened sense of your poise (once you regain it).

If you have a set amount of time on the meeting agenda or designated start and ends, you'll also need to keep an eye on the clock. In some scenarios, you may rely on the timing sheet you developed during your dry run. Use it to assess where you are in your content and understand whether it means making adjustments in the moment. In other cases, you're simply going to have to be aware of how long different segments are taking and move things along appropriately. Stick to your predetermined or planned time; this shows that you respect your audience.

Aren't you glad you wore that watch I suggested?

While you keep an eye on the clock, you'll also want to pay attention to others in the room. Observing reactions is a great way to gauge how things are going. Responding thoughtfully to what you see is a fantastic way to ensure things go well.

Watch and adjust

When presenting, make sure you are talking to the people in the room—not your slides. Make eye contact. When you know your content well, you can more easily observe audience cues and take action.

When you look at others in the room as you're presenting, what do you see?

Smiles and nods are positive signals that likely indicate what you're saying and how you're saying it are landing well. But what about when brows are furrowed and lips are pursed? Sometimes, people simply look that way when they are absorbing information—but it may also be a sign that they are confused about or in disagreement with something you've said. In some instances, it might make sense to pause and dig into that. Do it directly ("Chris, I think I see con-fusion on your face: what questions do you have?") or generally ("I think I'm observing disagreement in the room. Who can help me understand it?").

Blinded by the light

There are times—presenting formally from a stage, lights bearing down and in your face—that you can't see your audience at all. This is a chal-lenge. In some instances, it's possible to still view those seated near the front. Use them as your visual cues to assess how things are going, but continue to look out into the audience or others will feel ignored. If you can't see anyone at all, it's similar to presenting virtually. When this hap-pens, I'm a proponent of imagining others are smiling, nodding, and lov-ing what you do. You don't have signals to tell you otherwise, so you may as well use this opportunity to boost your confidence while presenting!

When you are actively watching others in the room, sometimes you can catch a specific moment when attitudes change: a general relaxing of demeanors (a good thing) or a stiffening (not usually such a good thing but still a useful signal). Consider how to use this information. With less positive responses, should you do anything to address them, do something differently to keep from making it worse, or simply continue to push forward in hopes that you'll bring them around? On the brighter side, if hearts have just warmed or credibility was gained, is that enough to carry you through, or will you lean into the actions or words that helped you make it happen?

Speaking of leaning: that's another way to read your audience. As we noted in Chapter 10, leaning in signals interest (unless a hand is aggressively on the table or a finger is out—these typically indicate that the person wants to say something!). Leaning back is a sign of confidence, though read this one carefully, since it can also signal feelings of dislike or negativity (this is a subconscious response; we are naturally inclined to try to distance ourselves from things that are unpleasant) or indifference.

Another sign of indifference—or, taking things a step further, *disinterest*—is when an audience member visibly turns their attention to something else. When someone starts rifling through papers in front of them, opens their laptop and begins to type, or picks up their phone and starts scrolling: you've lost them. Their actions speak loudly. When you observe this happening, you have to decide whether you're going to do anything about it. This obviously depends on the situation and who the person is. Your course of action (or lack thereof) will be different if it is a couple of people in a big presentation compared to a key stakeholder who you need to have engaged.

This is one of the reasons I suggested you stand while presenting. It affords you some effective tricks. To address the disengaged stakeholder, walking to near where they are seated and continuing to talk from there can sometimes lead to a laptop being shut or phone being set down. It's uncomfortable for an individual to be focused on something else when they know that you—the speaker—are close and that all eyes are looking in that direction.

Podium pet peeves

While I generally like to teach by framing things positively—proactive things you can do to improve or be more effective—sharing what doesn't work well also lends insight. You want to connect with your audience. Don't let potential irritations impair your ability to do so. With that in mind, here are some of my personal presenter pet peeves.

Please *don't*...

- **Start with "Can you hear me?"** Work this out ahead of time.

- **Now that we've established the microphone is working...use it poorly.** Your audience doesn't want to listen to your p's popping, but they do want to hear you clearly. When using a handheld mic, this generally means holding it close to, but not touching, your mouth. Test and adjust hands-free microphones before you start to ensure they don't rub noisily against clothing or hair.

- **Stand behind the podium.** Don't let a physical barrier come between you and others! Step out from behind the podium (or rearrange the furniture ahead of time to remove obstacles in your way). Don't let anything block your face. Ensure people have a clear line of sight so they can connect with you.

- **Dishonor your audience.** This can take a variety of forms: making an obscure reference that only a portion of attendees will know or relate to or telling them something generally known as if it were novel are a couple examples. Watch for things you say or do that could be interpreted by your audience to signal that you don't understand them.

- **Call attention to technical difficulties.** Either it wasn't obvious, in which case you've now pointed it out to them, or it was blatant and they were already aware. There's no reason to emphasize the issue.

- **Read your notes.** You cannot connect with others when you do this! It's also a credibility killer because it gives the impression that you aren't comfortable with your content. It's fine to refer to a note now and then (for example, to remind yourself of a specific reference or read a quote), but in general, avoid reading from notes or slides.

- **Make self-deprecating comments.** Your audience would like to be confident in you. If you aren't self-assured, that makes it difficult for them.

- **End with "That's it" or "That's what I have for you."** As we discussed in Chapter 9, plan a powerful close, reinforcing salient points and leaving people inspired and ready to act.

There are additional actions you can take (particularly if the disengagement you've observed is with more than a tiny fraction of those in attendance). Use your voice—or lack of voice. If you've been talking, talking, talking…

Simply…stop.

The shift from constant chatter to silence is attention garnering. The other means of audible contrast that we discussed in Chapter 10 can also be used: slow down, speed up, make a point LOUDLY to get people to tune in. Use your hands in a grand gesture. Run into the audience!

Connect with people

Well, okay, probably don't run into the audience. Though I have actually done something similar before—I *stepped off* of the stage into the crowd during a large conference presentation. It wasn't to get others to engage; they were already paying attention. I had been building to a crescendo and wanted to impart this pivotal moment in the same physical space with everyone. This broke the invisible barrier in an interesting way. And it meant I could really see faces, make eye contact, and connect.

I brought my audience into my presentation by going to them. Another way to relate is to bring them (figuratively) to you: invite interaction. This can take many different forms and will vary widely depending on your situation. It might be handled via questions addressed in the moment or discussion that happens over the course of your meeting. Encourage people to shout out short responses in a large group or have a microphone runner who helps amplify voices and ideas. You can integrate interactive polls or invite attendees to share thoughts via chat in your virtual presentation. Look for ways to include your audience—they will be more engaged and attentive. In the event that decisions are being made, they will be more bought in, too.

If someone raises a topic or poses a question that you know you are going to want to redirect to someone else who is present, acknowledge it: "That's a great question, Sarah! Brian, I'm going to turn to you momentarily so you can let us know your thoughts. Before I do that, I'll tell you my immediate reaction." This is especially effective in a virtual setting, where it's possible that Brian got distracted by his email. Calling him out by name and warning him that you're turning things over to him soon gets his attention back and provides him a moment to collect his thoughts.

I've framed this instance as having a more intimate setting, where you know the individuals. A variation of this works in other scenarios as well. Imagine a workshop setting where someone poses a question that I want to use to invite additional interaction. I could respond with something like, "Great point. I'd like to hear some experiences from the group. First, I'll share one that comes to my mind...." This gives people the time both to think about whether they have something to contribute and to gather their courage to speak up. Or if I want to give *myself* some time to think, I can flip this around: "That's an excellent question. Before I lend my thoughts, I'm going to open it up to the room—what do others think?"

Addressing questions

I've mentioned one strategy I sometimes use when facing questions. I've also been known to respond to off-the-wall questions with a redirect. "That's an interesting thought. Another question people commonly have about this topic is...." That won't always be appropriate, but it is another trick to have up your sleeve as you try to maintain order when fielding queries. For more tips and strategies related to handling Q&A sessions and eloquently responding to questions in general, check out the *storytelling with data* podcast Episode 46, "questions about questions" (storytellingwithdata.com/podcast).

Respond gracefully to the unexpected

I've seen Murphy's Law play out time after time in my own meetings, workshops, and presentations: if anything can go wrong, it will. While this may seem like a pessimistic observation, I don't view it that way. I appreciate the unexpected things that arise—these are instances that help keep me in the moment, on my toes, and learning.

While you might be totally flustered on the inside while trying to figure out how to handle the situation, magic is created when you project calmness—in spite of the troubles—to others. Further, if you *look* composed, it helps you start to feel that way, too. Take a deep breath, then consider a feasible course of action. Here are some tactics I've used over time:

- **Smile, recognize it, and move on.** I once fully tripped on a cord while on stage. In one moment, I was walking and talking; in the following, I was flat on the floor, handheld microphone bouncing loudly across the stage. What to do?! I took a moment to try to regain my composure (impossible on the inside, but I deliberately put on a brave face), stood up, took the microphone from the nice man who grabbed it for me, and paused. I took a deep breath, smiled at my audience, and said sarcastically, "You've just witnessed my impeccable grace." Then I resumed my presentation from where I left off. (This is the primary reason I now have blue tape in my presenter pack—my heels won't catch on cords that are properly taped down!)

- **Solicit help.** Midway through an important meeting, my computer crashed and refused to come back to life. Fortunately, one of my colleagues was also in attendance. I borrowed his computer and asked him to take control of the room by facilitating an impromptu discussion while I downloaded my slides (which were luckily saved to the cloud) until I was ready to resume.

- **Change your plans.** On an occasion that I touched upon previously, I was about to start a workshop but was having trouble getting the projector to work. Several others tried to help without success. The AV guy—who was apparently the only one who knew how to run it—wasn't available, so it was clear I would have to begin the session without my slides. This highlights another great reason to arrive early. In the minutes before start time, I was able to reorganize my content, starting with a topic that didn't rely heavily on slides and drawing on the whiteboard when visual aid was crucial. When tech support finally arrived, we took a break and got the slides up and running for the rest of the session.

- **Improvise.** In another instance, I was preparing to facilitate an interactive off-site session for a group of 100. The multi-page handouts I had emailed ahead of time to be printed for the day that contained our hands-on exercises had been forgotten at the office 60 miles away. I sent one of the organizers to the nearby copy and print store with the handouts on a thumb drive, another to locate blank paper to pass out to attendees, and then set to work creating additional slides to direct the hands-on activities until the hard copies arrived.

- **Provide another solution.** In a virtual training session, we once encountered tech issues that prevented some participants from joining until halfway through the hour. To make up for it, we offered them a spot in a future session and also provided video content that covered the concepts that were missed.

- **Reschedule.** There are times when the session simply can't go on as planned. We can't control or fix everything. A critical stakeholder can't attend, the video conferencing application has an outage, the power goes out. In these extreme cases, rescheduling may be the best option.

When things do go awry, don't dwell on it. Also try not to let it impact the rest of your session.

The unexpected comes in many flavors. I've shared some anecdotes of things gone wrong, but there are also instances where the scenario simply isn't what you anticipated. For example, you're planning to start your keynote presentation by introducing yourself, then the person who you thought was simply going to say your name and hand you the microphone gives a full rundown of your background before doing so. Ideally, you'll know ahead of time whether to expect this. Otherwise, you need to think on your feet and decide how to respond. You might skip your intro altogether and jump straight into content. Or make the succession of events appear purposeful with an additive statement: "That was a great overview. I do want to tell you a little more about myself, but I'm going to do it in a different way…" (and then launch into the story of you as you intended).

As another case of things going a little differently than planned, I was once getting ready to deliver a keynote session. Directly before I went on stage, the organizer asked everyone to get out their phone to take a picture of a QR code that was projected on the screen and complete a brief survey. *Aargh!* The *last* thing I wanted to do was begin my presentation while everyone was distracted on their phone. I had to determine quickly how to get their attention back. I walked out onto the stage and stood dead center, silent. I looked out at the audience, smiling, for what was probably an awkward amount of time. But it worked. Phones were put away and eyes were directed to me. When I launched in with my powerful planned start, I had their full attention.

These situations—and others like them—can cause some discomfort. You may experience bad feelings simply reading about them or thinking about the various aspects of your own presentations that could take unexpected turns. I like to think of this as *productive discomfort*. If you can get comfortable being a little uncomfortable, you will be able to respond to any scenario that arises (or at least the majority of them!) with eloquence.

Embrace the unexpected. It's when some of your most transformational presentation moments will happen.

Time to reflect—and refine for next time!

You did it: you were present in the moment, you watched your audience and adjusted, you connected with people, and you responded elegantly to the unexpected. You are finished giving your presentation!

The hard work is complete, but you are not done. There isn't an end point to being a skilled presenter. Every presentation is another opportunity to try something new, learn, and improve.

After your session is over, take a few moments to reflect. Did the things you hoped would take place happen? Look back at the goals you outlined for yourself ahead of time. Were you successful? What learnings or refinements will you pull forward into forthcoming presentations? Connect with the person you identified to give you feedback. See whether and how this changes your perception and goals. Set your plan for your next presentation. And then do it all again!

As you think about the future, let's take one final look back—to the case study we've been working our way through.

Have a stellar session: TRIX case study

You've accompanied me along quite a journey as I planned, created, and prepared to deliver my presentation to the client team at Nosh. As I write these words, that final presentation is already behind me. Months of analysis, followed by weeks of preparation—all that work culminated in a single critical hour that felt like it flew by in an instant.

How did the meeting go? I'll let you judge for yourself. Watch it at storytellingwithyou.com/finale. You can also view my slide deck on the following pages.

My final words to you (for now) as you plan, create, and deliver: strive to continually refine and improve. Here's to your next presentation. Make it a stellar one!

the complete TRIX slide deck

As you should expect by now, the following slides are not meant to stand on their own. They were crafted to support my verbal presentation. Given this static view and to avoid repetition, I've omitted some of the intermediate animation and slides (I also did not include the appendix).

See the full progression—together with my delivery as intended—at storytellingwithyou.com/finale.

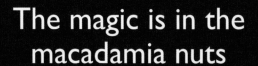

FIGURE A.1

FIGURE A.2

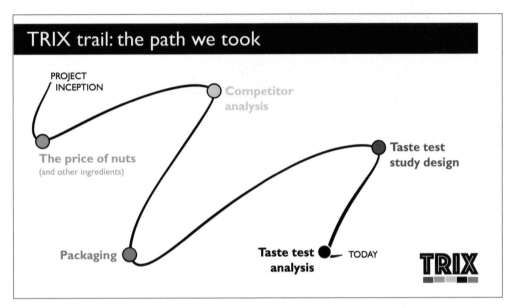

FIGURE A.3

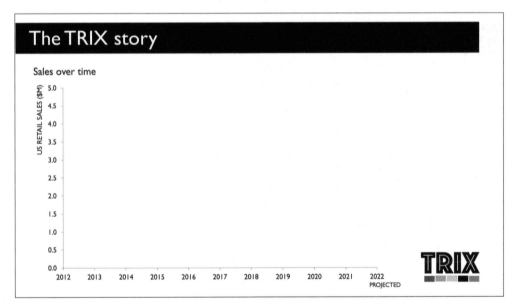

FIGURE A.4

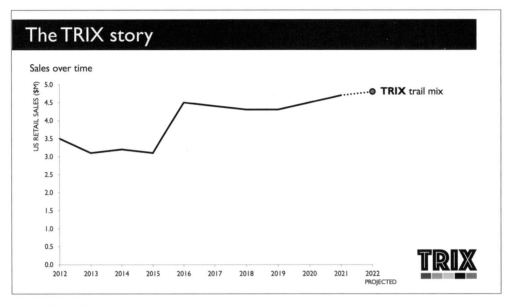

FIGURE A.5

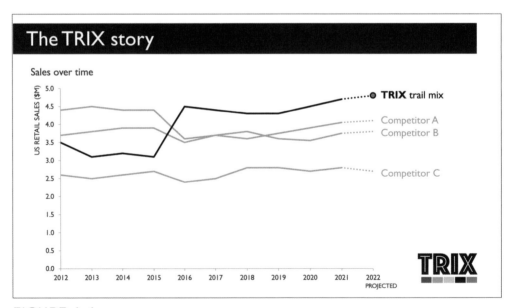

FIGURE A.6

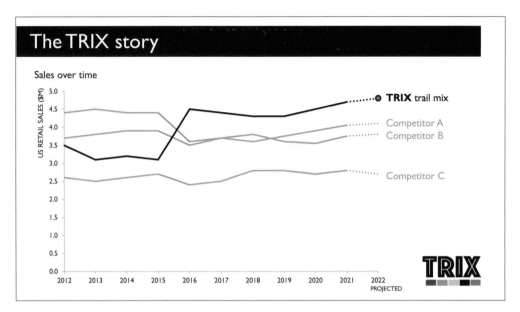

FIGURE A.7

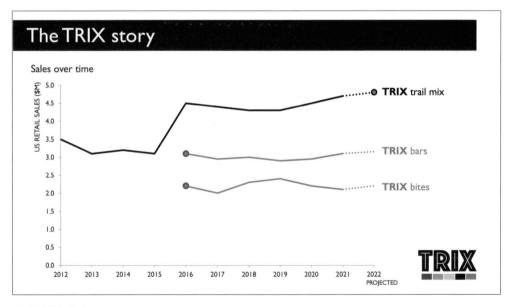

FIGURE A.8

FIGURE A.9

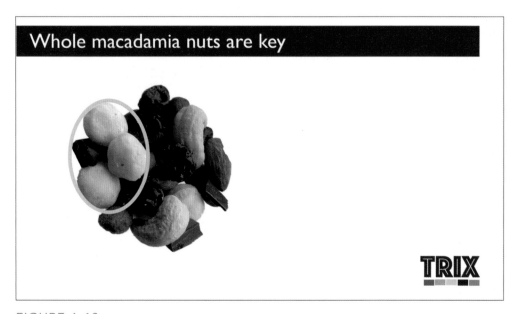

FIGURE A.10

Ah, nuts!

37%

macadamia nut price increase

FIGURE A.11

Initial decision:

increase   decrease

PRICE   COST

FIGURE A.12

We tested packaging

FIGURE A.13

Update package: window increases purchase intent

FIGURE A.14

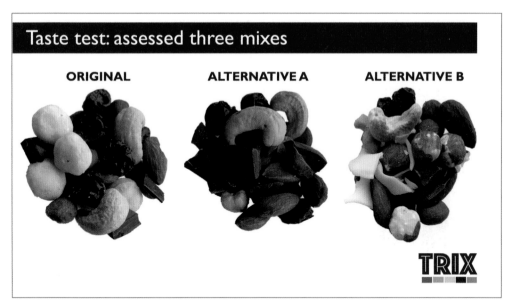

FIGURE A.15

FIGURE A.16

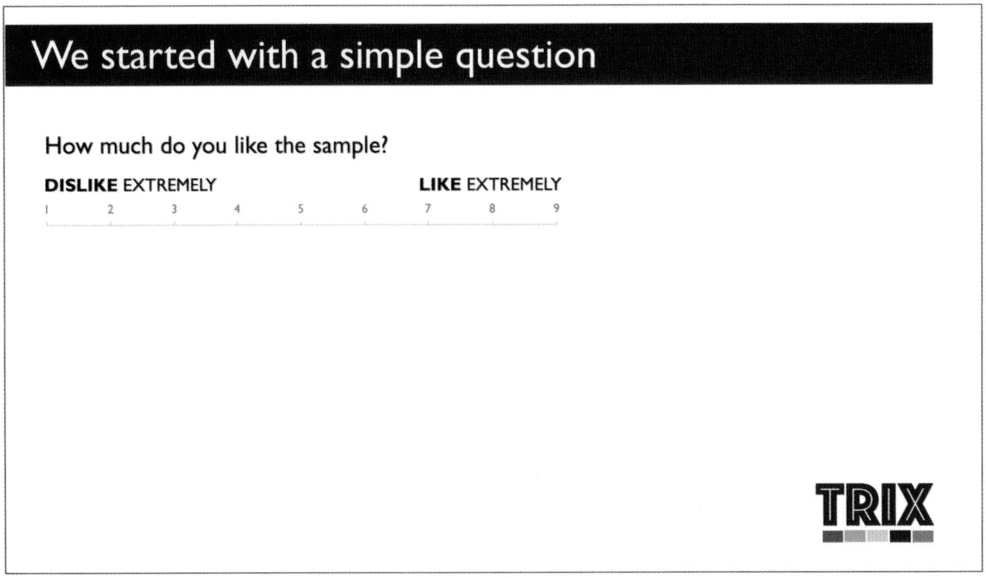

FIGURE A.17

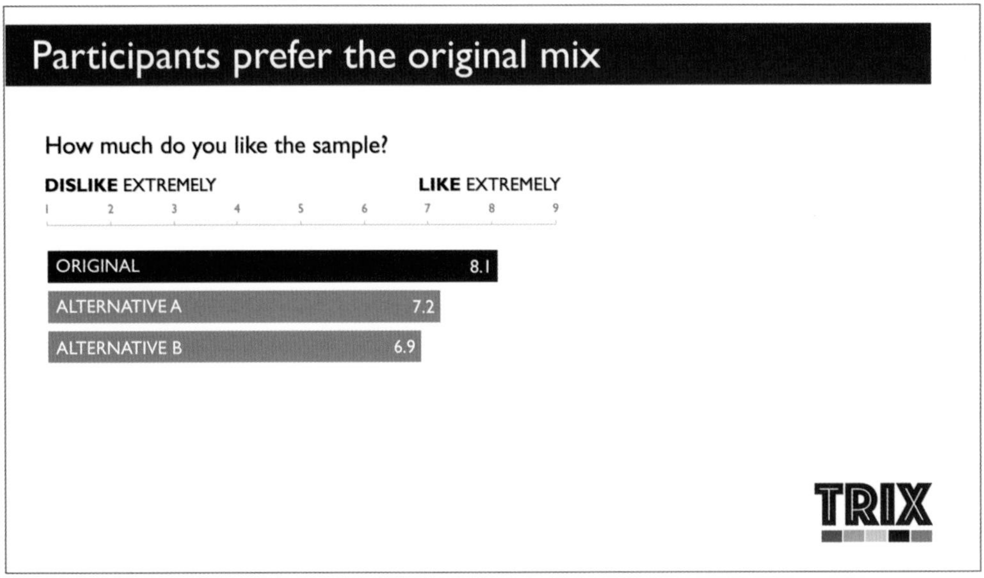

FIGURE A.18

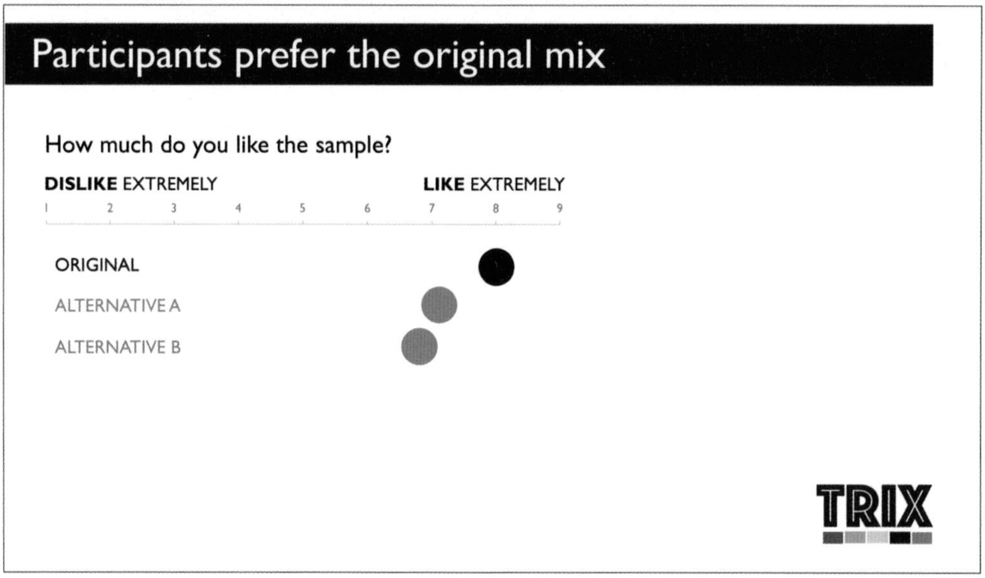

FIGURE A.19

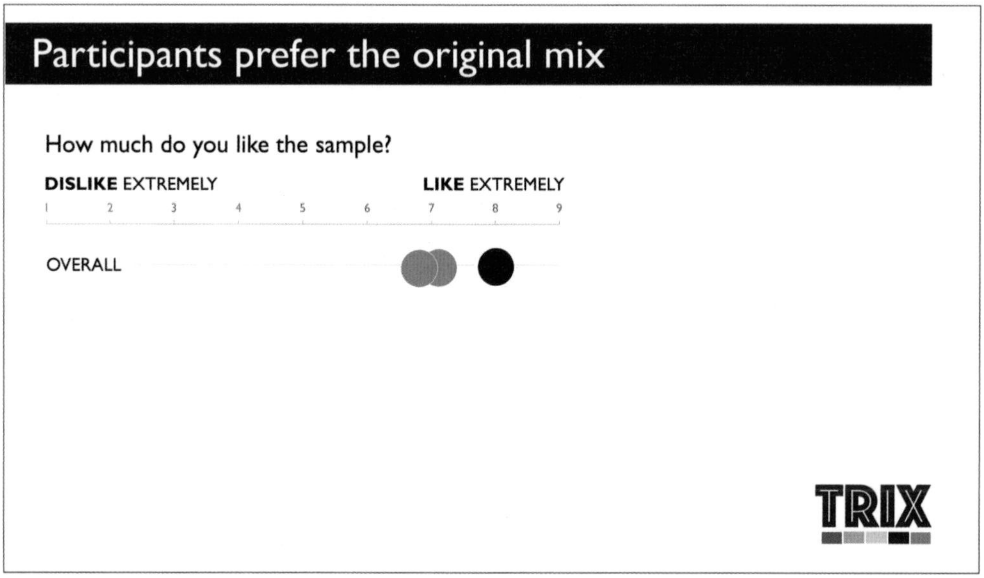

FIGURE A.20

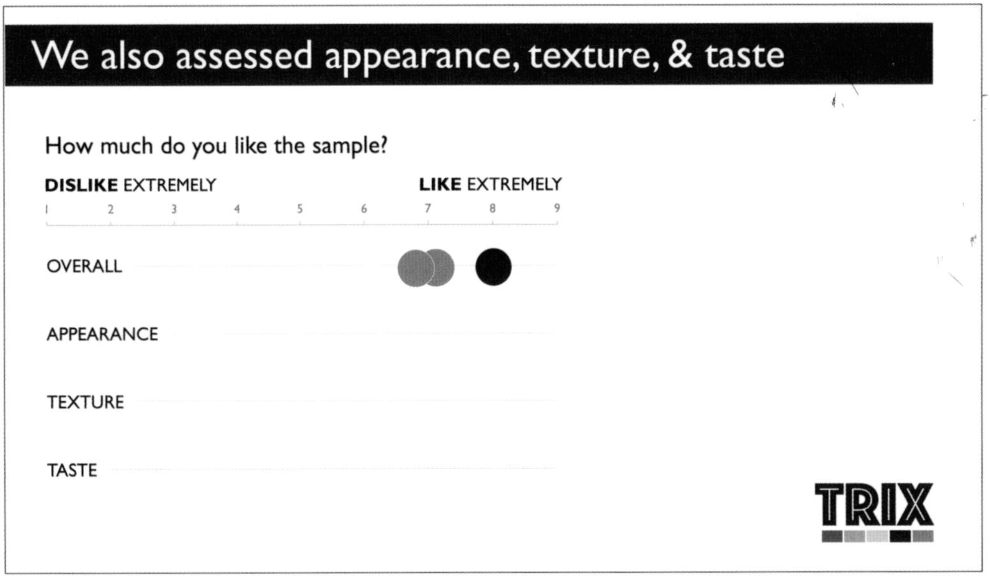

FIGURE A.21

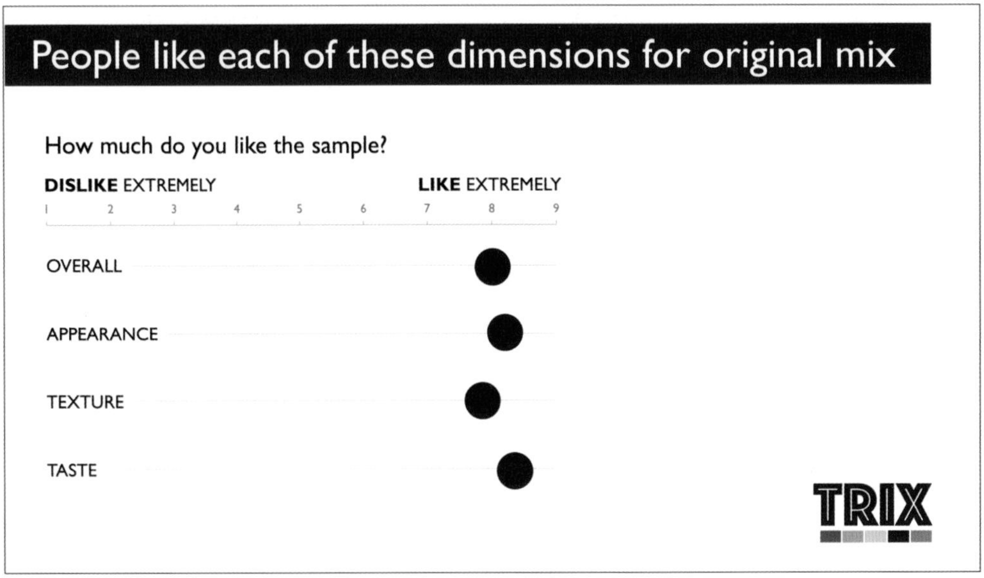

FIGURE A.22

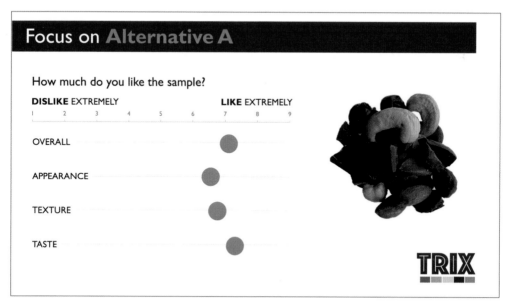

FIGURE A.23

FIGURE A.24

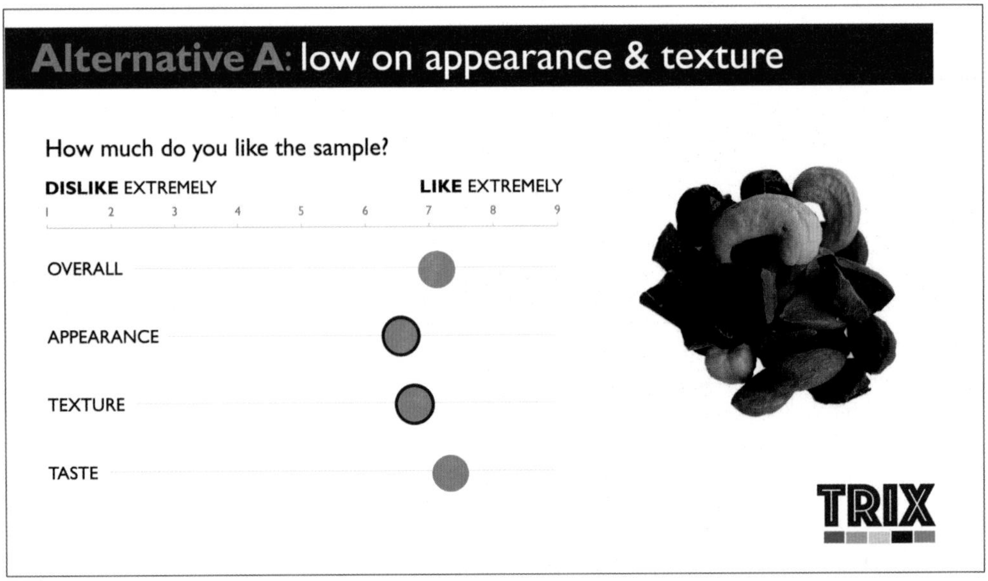

FIGURE A.25

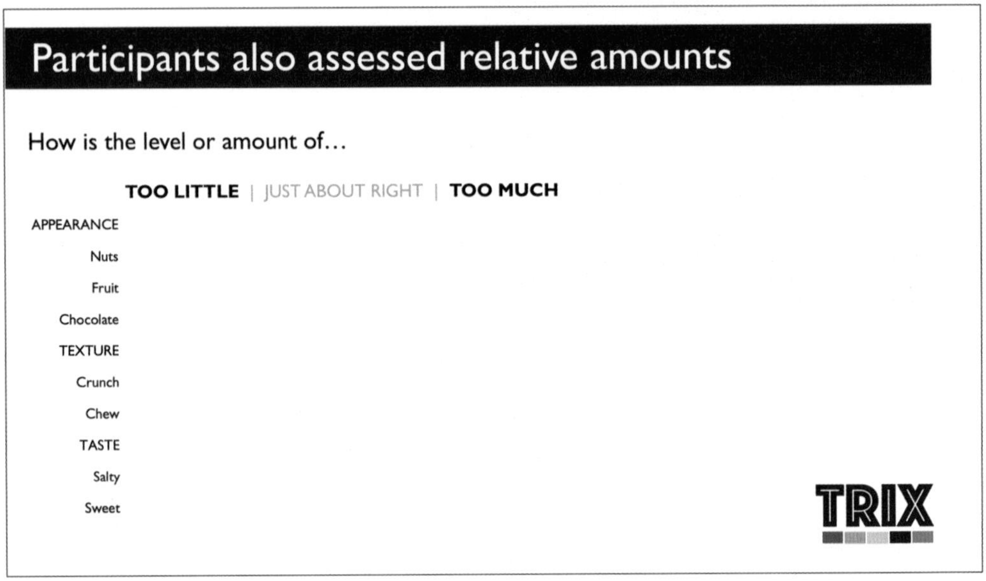

FIGURE A.26

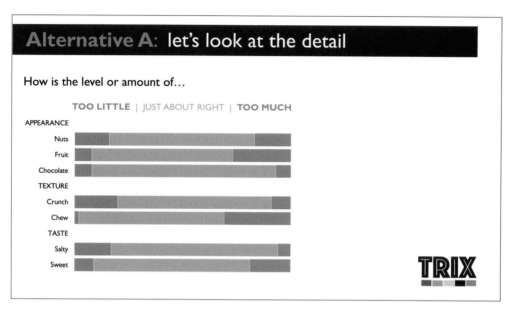

FIGURE A.27

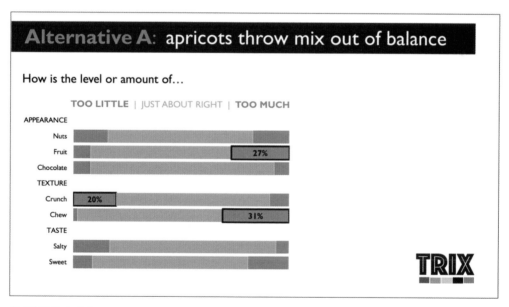

FIGURE A.28

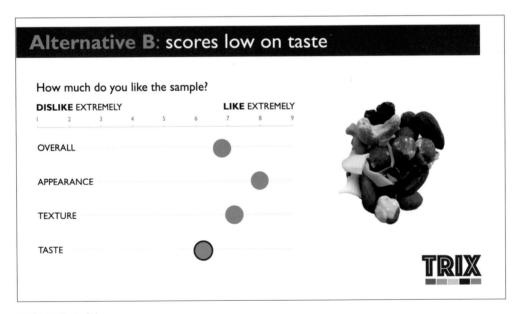

FIGURE A.29

FIGURE A.30

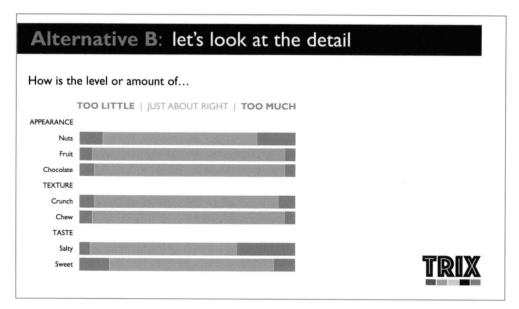

FIGURE A.31

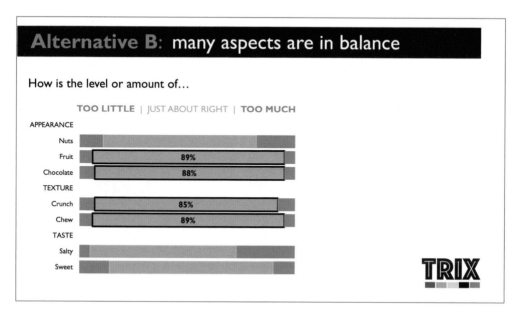

FIGURE A.32

Alternative B: too salty
How is the level or amount of...
TOO LITTLE | JUST ABOUT RIGHT | TOO MUCH
APPEARANCE
Nuts
Fruit
Chocolate
TEXTURE
Crunch
Chew
TASTE
Salty
27%
Sweet
TRIX

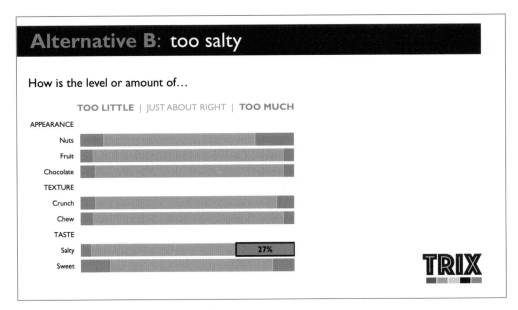

FIGURE A.33

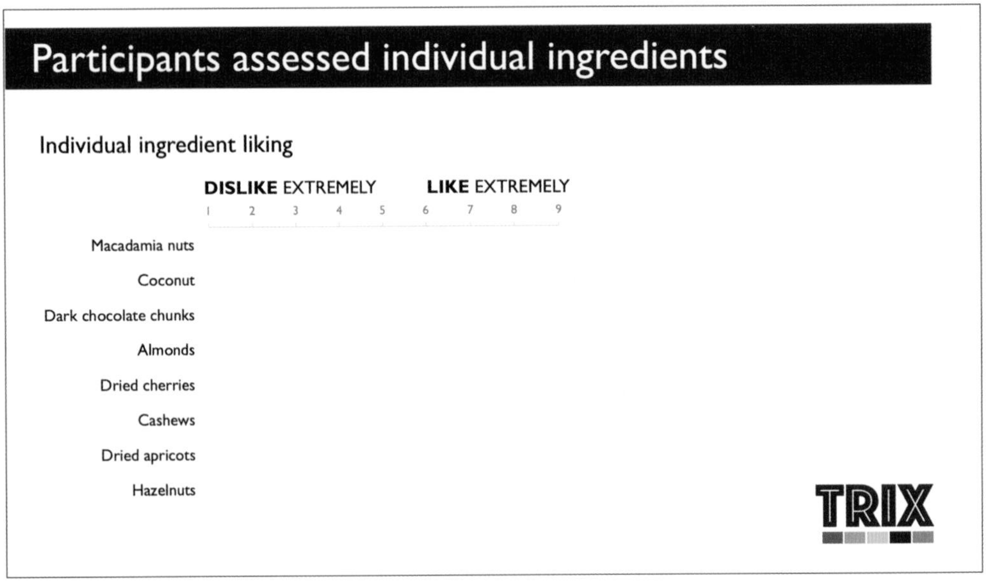

Participants assessed individual ingredients
Individual ingredient liking
DISLIKE EXTREMELY
LIKE EXTREMELY
1 2 3 4 5 6 7 8 9
Macadamia nuts
Coconut
Dark chocolate chunks
Almonds
Dried cherries
Cashews
Dried apricots
Hazelnuts
TRIX

FIGURE A.34

FIGURE A.35

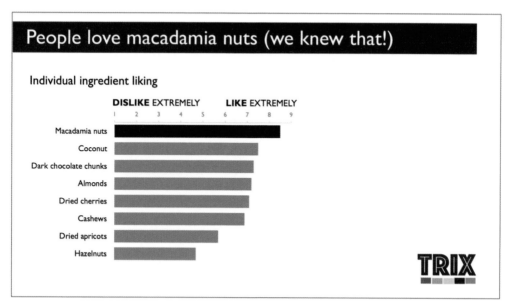

FIGURE A.36

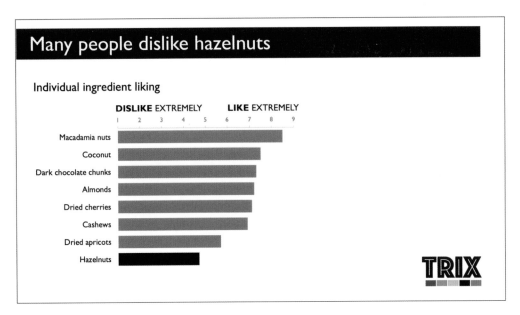

FIGURE A.37

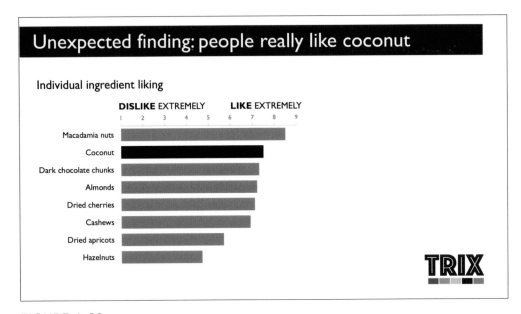

FIGURE A.38

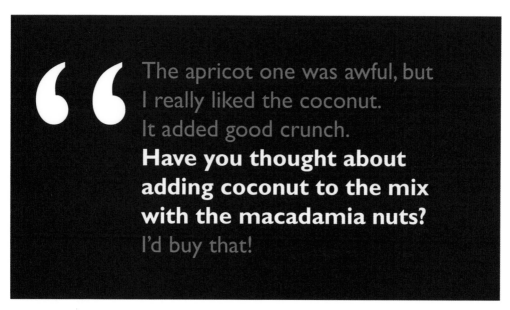

FIGURE A.39

FIGURE A.40

Three options to consider

1 Raise price
Keep the current mix

2 Go direct to market with new alternative mix
Reduce macadamia nuts, introduce coconut

3 Run additional tests & analysis
Test new alternative mix, then reassess

FIGURE A.41

The magic is in the macadamia nuts

Strategic Client Services | October 2022

FIGURE A.42

index

A

actions to take
    ending in a narrative arc with, 81
    identifying for your audience, 26, 78
    recommending as part of your point of view, 29
    stating in the Big Idea, 29, 36
    stating in the closing slides, 143
Adobe, color palettes from, 96
Adobe Stock, 201
Ajani, K., 169
animation, on slides, 169, 171, 175, 222, 223, 238–239
appearance during presentations, self-recording of, 247
area charts, 157
Arial font, 98, 99
Aristotle, 70, 73
assumptions about your audience, 16
ATEM Mini Pro, 233
audience, 3–22
    brainstorming and considering various perspectives of, 51–52
    citing the competition to motivate, 6

collecting data about, 15
complexity of communicating to others and, 3
connecting with, during your presentation, 302–303
considering a list of people and groups in, 4
different types of people with varying requirements in, 4
drawing and brainstorming to understand, 14
focusing attention of on graph details, 167–170
forming a story for, 75
framing what is at stake for, in the Big Idea, 29, 33–34
having a clear single-person audience, 5–6
having a mixed audience, 6–12
identifying and pressure testing assumptions about, 16
identifying tension known to, in composing a story, 78–79
identifying the action for your audience to take, 26
images for helping to understand content by, 188–190